DETROIT MUSCLE

CHARLES MORRIS

Factory Lightweights and Purpose-Built Muscle Cars

CarTech®

CarTech®, Inc.
838 Lake Street South
Forest Lake, MN 55025
Phone: 651-277-1200 or 800-551-4754
Fax: 651-277-1203
www.cartechbooks.com

© 2017 by Charles Morris

Edit by Bob Wilson
Layout by Connie DeFlorin

ISBN 978-1-61325-301-4
Item No. CT579

Library of Congress Cataloging-in-Publication Data Available

Written, edited, and designed in the U.S.A.
Printed in China
10 9 8 7 6 5 4 3 2 1

Front Flap: This emblem, when affixed to a 1960s-era Pontiac, indicated that the car had received the special touches available from Ace Wilson's Royal Pontiac. Various levels of Bobcat kits were available, from performance tuning to internal engine modifications. (Photo Courtesy Ken Skistimas)

Endpapers: The sloping roofline of the Starliner provided improved aerodynamics and, along with the increase in engine displacement/horsepower, allowed Ford to become more competitive in stock car racing during the 1961 season. (Photo Courtesy Zach Straits)

Title Page: American Motors collaborated with Hurst in the development and construction of 50 specially equipped AMX-based cars for competition in NHRA Super/Stock. With touches by racing legends such as H. L. Shahan and Howard Maselles, the Super Stock AMX package made an immediate impression in drag racing. (Photo Courtesy Doug Boyce)

Table of Contents: Strickler and Jenkins were the recipients of one of the 50 factory lightweight Impalas powered by the Z-11 427 engine in 1963. Strickler took this car to victory in the AFX class and Little Eliminator category at the NHRA Nations. (Photo Courtesy Bob Wenzelburger)

Back Cover Photos
Top: Some of the most successful Pontiac drag cars of the 1960s hailed from Ace Wilson's Royal Pontiac dealership and were handled by GM ad man Jim Wangers. (Photo Courtesy Bob Knudson)

Bottom Left: The big news from Chevrolet in 1965 came in the form of an all-new big-block engine. A particularly great performance version of the mid-size Chevelle, designated Z-16, was a true performer with 375 hp, heavier chassis design, and better suspension and brakes.

Bottom Middle: These completed 2012 Cobra Jet Mustangs are covered in plastic to protect them from dust and dirt prior to delivery. The 2012 version of the Cobra Jet was available in three patriotic colors: red, white, and blue. (Photo Courtesy Evan Smith)

Bottom Right: The "427" emblems on the hood scoop of this Corvette informed the world that the car meant business. The bulge in the hood looked good and provided needed clearance for the big-block V-8.

DISTRIBUTION BY:

Europe
PGUK
63 Hatton Garden
London EC1N 8LE, England
Phone: 020 7061 1980 • Fax: 020 7242 3725
www.pguk.co.uk

Australia
Renniks Publications Ltd.
3/37-39 Green Street
Banksmeadow, NSW 2109, Australia
Phone: 2 9695 7055 • Fax: 2 9695 7355
www.renniks.com

TABLE OF CONTENTS

ACKNOWLEDGMENTS

Thanks to my friends Nick Smith, Don Snyder, Bill Bartels, and Kayo Erwin for allowing me access to their fabulous car collections. To Bob Smith and Andrew Hinkley for their vast knowledge of 135 Cobra Jets and Yenko cars, respectively. And to all those who have so generously shared their photos.

PREFACE

The 1950s and 1960s in America was a great time to grow up and an even greater time to be a car enthusiast. I proudly proclaim myself to be a member of the generation that developed a lifelong passion for the American automobile very early on, and for whom little made the heart beat faster than to gaze upon the latest model from our favorite car line or hear the thumping sound of a V-8 engine. I devoured auto magazines, seized every opportunity to attend auto races, counted race drivers among my heroes, and planned my future around a career in the automotive field. Observing the advances in performance and innovative styling achieved by Detroit's automakers during those two decades, it was impossible to believe that it could ever come to an end. But end it did.

Within a few short years, in the early 1970s, government meddling in the name of safety and clean air, coupled with price gouging by oil companies and the insurance industry, created an environment where automakers were forced into developing stop-gap measures to meet government standards that the available technology of the time could not support. The result was automobiles rolling out of Detroit that ran poorly, performed poorly, and suffered from poor quality control, and it appeared, for all intents and purposes, that styling was little more than an afterthought.

These dark years for the auto industry, and to those who viewed the automobile as more than just a means of conveyance, lasted well into the 1980s. It was then that, in my opinion, two things happened: (1) The technology caught up with the demands of knee-jerk government legislation, and (2) U.S. automobile manufacturers came to the conclusion that performance sells cars and that the public longed for vehicles made in the United States that were second to none in the world.

Thus the millennium was greeted by an auto industry dramatically changed for the better. Retro styling breathed new life into models that had been around for decades and, perhaps most important, advances in technology resulted in the production of cars with fewer emissions, fuel mileage only previously dreamed of, and world-class performance in acceleration, top speed, and the entire driving experience. For those of us with perhaps a little more than one foot anchored in the past, the exhaust note of a thumping V-8 engine was back with a vengeance.

INTRODUCTION

By the 1950s, Detroit automakers already understood that performance sold cars, even though it was nearly a decade before the advent of production cars equipped with lightweight components and specifically built for drag racing competition. This was an era when stock car racing actually involved stock cars: real production models barely removed from those the average person drove to and from work each day and to church on Sunday. The Big Three automakers, Ford, General Motors, and Chrysler, along with other brands that have long since faded into obscurity, showcased the power, handling, and durability of their products in organized stock car racing competitions, where it was hoped that victory would result in showroom sales. After all, if a particular brand of car could withstand the rigors of competition on the racetrack, would that not equate to a car that would last many years under normal driving conditions by John Q. Public?

The sport of drag racing, while in its infancy in the 1950s, was growing in popularity and becoming an outlet for youth to test their mechanical skills and driving prowess in contests of timed acceleration while behind the wheel of their favorite brand of vehicle. And the formation of brand loyalty, which often lasts a lifetime among auto enthusiasts, could many times be directly related to which auto company garnered the most checkered flags on the stock car racing circuits.

From the time of its introduction in 1932 and well into the early 1950s, the engine of choice among many professional racers and young "hot rodders" alike was the legendary Ford flathead V-8. America's first mass-produced and affordable V-8 was compact, lightweight, and powerful for its time. The flathead was plentiful and lent itself well to performance-enhancing modifications. And it was the demand to squeeze more power from the popular Ford V-8 that can well be credited with making the production of aftermarket performance parts (more popularly known as speed equipment) the multimillion dollar industry it is today.

Names such as Edelbrock, Offenhauser, Weiand, Clay Smith, Navarro, and others became synonymous with putting your flathead Ford V-8 out in front of the competition. As years passed and other, more sophisticated engine designs for production cars rolled out of Detroit, the performance aftermarket parts industry grew, flourished, and in some cases became a surrogate for the auto maker's engineers, who eagerly adopted already developed, tested, and competition-proven speed parts for their repertoire of optional equipment.

The performance trend in Detroit continued until its pinnacle in mid-1957, when two factors entered into play. The Automobile Manufacturers Association (AMA), of which George Romney of American Motors was the president, passed a mandate stating that their members would no longer promote or actively support auto racing. This was done in the name of highway safety, apparently drawing some connection between high-performance automobiles, factory-supported racing in sanctioned events, and traffic accidents.

The second factor was an economic recession, which impacted the nation and the auto industry in 1958. While some car makers (American Motors, Ford, and the Oldsmobile and Buick Divisions of General Motors) were strict adherents to the AMA ban on performance, Chrysler Corporation, Chevrolet, and Pontiac turned a blind eye to the mandate and continued to develop and market high-performance parts under the auspices of optional "Police Packages."

Chrysler even went so far as to promote its multiple-carbureted Ram Induction intake system as a safety enhancement because it shortened the passing distance between cars at highway speeds. Nonetheless, the overt practice of advertising performance and selling cars based on speedway victories pretty much had come to a screeching halt in Detroit before the end of the 1957 model year. Factory-built high-performance cars did not fully return until the early 1960s, when a renewed youth market emerged and cooler heads within the auto industry recognized the fact that winning races on Sunday had a direct correlation to showroom sales on Monday.

This gave rise to what became known as The Horsepower War and drag racing, by now wildly popular among the youth of America, became the prominent battleground for the auto manufacturers bent on gaining the lion's share of the youth performance market.

Publisher's Note: In reporting history, the images required to tell the tale will vary greatly in quality, especially by modern photographic standards. While some images in this volume are not up to those digital standards, we have included them, as we feel they are an important element in telling the story.

CHAPTER 1

THE MANUFACTURERS: A PROLOGUE TO AN INCREDIBLE ERA

The United States was a country full of new ideas and technological innovation in the 1950s. It was a decade when bigger was considered better, and that theme carried over into automobiles. Gasoline was inexpensive, automotive styling was opulent, and horsepower had become king.

The first run of Corvettes in 1953 was available in white only, but the introduction of the 1954 models provided a choice of colors. The drivetrain remained the same, and it wasn't until 1955 that the Corvette gained a reputation as a performance car. (Photo Courtesy CarTech Archive)

Chevrolet

OUT WITH THE STOVEBOLT AND IN WITH THE SMALL-BLOCK.

GM's Chevrolet division took a big leap forward in 1953 when it introduced a vehicle that became known as America's sports car, the Corvette. From a performance standpoint, the fiberglass-bodied two-seater wasn't exactly a world-beater. The only effort to pump up the anemic 235-ci inline overhead valve (OHV) 6-cylinder (affectionately named the Stovebolt Six) that powered the Corvette was the addition of three side-draft single-barrel carburetors.

Throw in the fact that the only transmission available was the 2-speed Powerglide automatic and it was easy to see that the Corvette needed help in the "go" department. That help came in 1955 in the form of new Chief Engineer Ed Cole and his design for Chevy's first modern V-8. In just 15 weeks, Cole and his team designed an engine that enthusiasts now know as the small-block; it quickly became the darling of the automotive press and hot rodders for generations.

In its first configuration, the small-block Chevy V-8, which the company called Turbo Fire, had a bore of 3.75 inches and a 3.00-inch stroke. Connect-ing rods with a 5.7-inch center length and rocker arms that were independent of shafts for less weight made an engine that revved quicker than most of the competition. With a compression ratio of 8.0:1, the 265 delivered 162 hp at 4,400 rpm and 257 ft-lbs of torque at 2,200 rpm when equipped with a 2-barrel carburetor, and 180 hp at 4,600 rpm and 260 ft-lbs of torque at 2,800 rpm when topped with a Rochester WCFB 4-barrel carburetor.

Chevrolet put the new engine to the test on the National Association for Stock Car Auto Racing (NASCAR) circuit with the winning combination of Smokey Yunick preparing the cars and Herb Thomas driving. While the fledgling Chevy race teams scored only two NASCAR victories for 1955, one of them was at the legendary Southern 500 in Darlington, South Carolina, and it took little time for GM's marketing firm to make the most of Herb Thomas's win in his new Chevrolet. The Corvette also received the new small-block V-8 in 1955, and although just 700 cars were sold, the engine upgrade and the addition of a standard transmission are credited in many circles with saving America's sports car.

General Motors wasted no time squeezing more power out of the 265 for 1956 with the addition of the Power Pack option, consisting of improved cylinder heads for 9.25:1 compression, a higher lift camshaft, and either single- or dual 4-barrel carburetion. When fitted with the single carburetor, the 265 delivered 205 hp at 4,600 rpm with 268 ft-lbs of torque at 3,000 rpm. The dual 4-barrel induction boosted the power output to 225 hp at 5,200 rpm with 270 ft-lbs of torque at 3,600 rpm.

The 265 power pack also powered the Corvette, which was all new for 1956, and based upon sales numbers of 3,467 units, the performance potential

In 1953, Chevrolet introduced America's first fiberglass-bodied, production line–built, two-seat sports car, the Corvette. Since Chevrolet had yet to produce its first modern V-8 engine, power for the Corvette came from the old reliable Blue Flame "stove-bolt" inline OHV 6-cylinder engine that powered passenger cars. The only concession to performance came from a special intake manifold mounting three side-draft carburetors. Further hampering the Corvette's performance numbers was the fact that the only available transmission was the 2-speed Powerglide automatic.

The interior of the 1953 Corvette was pure sports car. Devoid of most creature comforts, such as roll-up side windows, it was equipped with a proper array of gauges for monitoring engine functions. One departure that true sports car fans disliked was the anemic shift lever attached to an automatic transmission. (Photo Courtesy CarTech Archive)

The 1955 Chevy models received all-new styling that was an instant success. The company had finally shed its stodgy image and the youth of America had begun to take notice. (Photo Courtesy CarTech Archive)

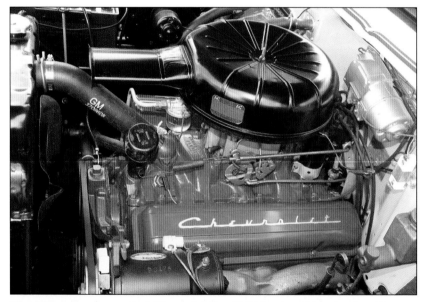

The biggest news out of Chevrolet for 1955 had nothing to do with styling; it was the company's first mass-produced, OHV V-8 engine. This powerplant, universally known as the small-block Chevy V-8, was lightweight, compact, and powerful. Initially introduced at 265 ci, it soon grew to 283, and later 327, 350, and 400 ci, as it evolved. The engineers at Chevrolet showed their performance mindset by offering a version of the 265 called the Power Pack, which featured improved cylinder heads and a Rochester 4-barrel carburetor.

The clean lines of the 1955 Chevy, along with the new 265-ci small-block V-8, made it one of the most popular cars with hot rodders for decades. (Photo Courtesy CarTech Archive)

of a 2,980-pound, 225-hp, two-seat sports car that could scoot from a standing start to 60 mph in 7.3 seconds, and cover the quarter-mile in 15.8, had really begun to catch on with the American public.

And for the truly discerning high-performance driver, Chevrolet made an even more aggressive solid lifter camshaft available through the dealer parts network. The Duntov Cam, as it came to be known, bumped the power output of the 265 to an impressive 240 hp. Zora Arkus-Duntov and Ed Cole were tasked with preparing a 1956 Corvette to run in the Daytona Beach Speed Trials in February 1956.

Arkus-Duntov rolled out a single-seat test car, powered by a 240-hp 265 and backed by a ZF 4-speed transmission. What made the engine

The combination of a light body, an engine that lent itself well to modification, and a plentiful supply of inexpensive aftermarket performance parts made the Tri-Five (1955, 1956 and 1957) Chevys a favorite among drag racers. They could be found competing in classes ranging from Stock to A/Gas well into the late 1960s. Gassers such as this one were the funny cars of their time. (Photo Courtesy Doug Boyce)

The Chevy passenger car line underwent minor styling changes for 1956. One of the models continued was the Nomad, a two-door sporty station wagon that, in spite of being designed to carry the family and luggage, became a big hit with the hot rod set when equipped with the small-block V-8 engine. Many racing teams also chose the Nomad as a support vehicle. (Photo Courtesy CarTech Archive)

In the mid- to late 1960s, the early Chevy models were still very prevalent in drag racing, where by this time they were running in the lower stock classes. A Junior Stock Eliminator bracket was established, and thanks to a very liberal interpretation of the rules, many combinations of early Chevy body style, engine, and transmission were considered legal by the NHRA. The 1956 Chevy sedan delivery run by Jessel Performance was one such car and proved to be a winning combination. (Photo Courtesy Doug Boyce)

To this day the most popular Tri-Five Chevy model year was 1957, with the sporty Bel Air hardtop convertible (a version with no B-pillar so that when all the windows were rolled down, the interior was more open to the outside) in both two- and four-door versions. (Photo Courtesy CarTech Archive)

particularly unique was the experimental Rochester fuel-injection unit that was being tested. After reworking the cylinder heads and increasing the ratio to 10.3:1, the engine produced 255 hp, which was good enough to propel the Corvette to a two-way average run of 147.3 mph on the Beach.

When it came to performance, the 3,390-pound 1956 Bel Air coupe was no match for a similarly equipped Corvette, but it was still more than a match for most offerings from competing manufacturers. The 0–60 on the 225-hp version, when equipped with the 3-speed manual transmission, was 8.8 seconds, while the quarter-mile came up in 16.8.

Chevrolet really became serious in NASCAR for 1956. While factory team drivers Herb Thomas and Paul Goldsmith combined for just three wins in the hardtop series, Chevys scored 18 victories in the new and very popular convertible series, with driver Bob Welborn bringing home the championship for Chevrolet that year.

Much like their rivals at Ford, the folks at Chevrolet went all out in the performance department in 1957. They started things by enlarging the small-block V-8 to 283 ci, thanks to an increase in cylinder bore to 3.87 inches. The base version of the 283 delivered 185 hp, and things just got better from there. With a 4-barrel carburetor, the horses jumped to 220 and the addition of a dual 4-barrel induction system bumped it up to 245. Add a solid lifter camshaft and the two 4-equipped 283s pumped out 270 ponies.

Perhaps the best of all, and one of the first American V-8s to produce

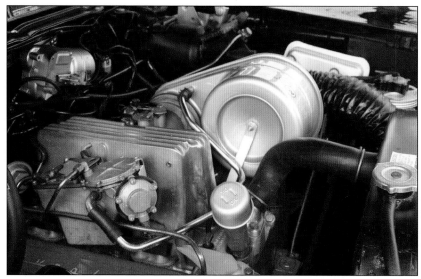

Once again Chevy's great styling took a back seat to engine options. Now at 283 ci, the potent small-block V-8 was available with higher compression, solid lifter camshafts, and either a dual 4-barrel carburetor version that produced 270 hp or the all-new Rochester fuel-injected engine that punched out one horsepower per cubic inch at 283. Both of these engines were also optionally available in the Corvette, making it one of America's hottest performance cars.

one horsepower per cubic inch of displacement, was the 283 when optioned with the Ram Jet fuel-injection system. Designed by GM engineers, including Zora Arkus-Duntov, the Rochester fuel-injection unit was mounted on a specially cast two-piece aluminum intake manifold. In concert with a 10.5:1 compression ratio and a Duntov-designed solid lifter camshaft, the high-winding small-block developed 283 hp at 6,200 rpm and 290 ft-lbs of torque at 4,400 rpm. When mated to a 2,880-pound Corvette, backed with the all-new 4-speed transmission, a performance-minded buyer could travel from 0–60 mph in a shade over 6 seconds.

Chevrolet wasted no time in showcasing the new performance models as they rolled onto the beach for the Daytona Speed Weeks with numerous cars, many prepared by top mechanic Smokey Yunick and driven by some of the biggest names in racing. At the top of the heap was the SR-2 Corvette, a wild, tail-finned, hand-built car designed by Chevrolet design engineer Jerry Earl and powered by a Yunick-built fuel-injected 283 that had been bored and stroked to 336 ci. The car weighed 2,300 pounds, thanks to doors that weighed a mere 10 pounds each and a 20-pound hood. Intended to compete in sports car competitions, as well as straight-line acceleration events, the SR-2 featured duct-cooled brakes and a 48-gallon fuel tank.

In the hands of top stock car driver Buck Baker, the SR-2 blistered the beach in the Flying Mile Modified class at 152.85 mph, taking home first-place honors. Baker came back to claim the Standing Mile Modified class with a run of 93.04 mph, while Paul Goldsmith, Johnny Beauchamp, and Betty Skelton drove Corvettes to the top three spots in the Standing Mile Production class. Goldsmith also took home honors with his Corvette

Like the other Tri-Five Chevys, the 1957 was a favorite among drag racers, and they continued to soldier on in the lower Stock, Gas, and Modified Production classes for many years. This 1957 two-door sedan model was a favorite because it was lighter than the hardtop. The wide range of engine and transmission combinations allowed by the NHRA almost guaranteed that a Tri-Five Chevy would be a perfect fit for a chosen Junior Stock Eliminator class. This particular 1957 is shown later in its racing career when it was classified as an M/Stocker. (Photo Courtesy Doug Boyce)

The entire GM line underwent a radical restyle for the 1958 model year and Chevrolet was no exception. Whether it was the national recession that hit America that year or a case of too much too soon after the very popular 1957 models, the 1958 was not the sales success that its predecessor had been. Along with the restyle, Chevrolet gained a new sport model called Impala for 1958. The Impala had a distinct roofline that it shared with the Pontiac Bonneville in 1958. (Photo Courtesy CarTech Archive)

A new engine series was introduced to power the larger, heavier Chevy line for 1958. A unique big-block V-8 with combustion chambers in the cylinder block as opposed to the heads, the 348 Turbo-Thrust, initially designed as a truck engine, displaced 348 ci. As proof that Chevrolet had merely winked at the AMA ban on performance, the 348 was optionally available in a version with a solid lifter camshaft, 11.1:1 compression, and three Rochester 2-barrel carburetors. Producing 315 hp, the high-performance 348 was listed as a "Law Enforcement" option. The 348 was not available in the Corvette, which remained powered by the 283-ci small-block. (Photo Courtesy CarTech Archive)

in the Flying Mile Production class, recording a 131.94-mph run. A full-size 1957 Chevy won the Flying Mile, single carburetor, Stock class at 118.46 mph, and Yunick-prepared Chevys won both the Class 4 and Class 5 categories, with Goldsmith wheeling a fuel-injected model to the Class 5 win while eclipsing the previous record by more than 4 mph. Chevrolets went on to take home the top 34 positions in Class 5.

At least some of the 1957 Chevys that competed at the Speed Week in Daytona were cars that were specially prepared by Southern Engineering Development Corporation (SEDCO).

General Motors had hired Vince Piggins, the man behind Hudson's successes in stock car racing, to prepare a series of vehicles for competition in NASCAR using Nalley Chevrolet, an Atlanta dealership, as corporate cover. The cars that later became known as Black Widows (because of the SEDCO team colors of black and white) were based on 150 model utility sedans (no backseat and fixed rear-quarter glass), the lightest model available. Detroit-built cars were shipped by rail to SEDCO, rather than sourcing cars from the Atlanta assembly plant due to the latter having stronger frames.

A minimum of six cars, some say there were two mule cars and an additional ten, were modified by the installation of dual shock absorbers, six-lug wheels, heavy-duty brakes, radiator, roll bar, special front seat, and a 20-gallon fuel tank, which was in violation of NASCAR rules. To skirt

this rule, and cover the fact that SEDCO had removed the spare tire well from the trunk of the cars to accommodate the tank, General Motors had the subcontractor that produced the trunk mat provide pieces without the cutout for the spare tire well to fool the NASCAR inspectors.

The fuel-injected 283 engines could not be modified as per the rules; however, after careful blue printing and the installation of free-flowing Fenton exhaust manifolds, the engines were capable of delivering 27 additional horsepower (310) over the factory rating. The cars were also equipped with heavy-duty 3-speed manual transmissions and ultimately delivered into the hands of top factory drivers such as Buck Baker, who won 10 of 40 NASCAR stock car races that year to take home the series championship.

In April 1957, Chevrolet had provided 411 select dealers with the stock car competition guide, which provided the GM part numbers of all pieces used in the Black Widow cars, along with detailed instructions on how to modify a car for competition. Some of the cars, alternately referred to as Duntov cars or black and whites, also found their way into the hands of factory-connected drag racers and they, along with the supercharged Fords and other multiple carbureted models rolling out of Detroit, caused the National Hot Rod Association (NHRA) to mandate a new class, designated as Super/Stock to accommodate these factory hot rods.

Chevrolet styling took a turn toward the wild in 1959 with huge horizontal wings and cat's-eye taillights dominating the look. The Impala was once again the sportiest model. Similar to the 1958 model, the 1959 Chevy's lovers and detractors were pretty evenly divided, and new car sales were down once again. (Photo Courtesy CarTech Archive)

The biggest displacement, highest horsepower engine for Chevrolet in the 1959 model year was once again the 348 Turbo-Thrust; the thinly veiled law-enforcement version of the engine remained available.

In June 1957 when the AMA ban was instituted, General Motors announced the end of all factory support for racing and sold the remaining special parts inventory to top drivers Baker, Speedy Thompson, and Jack Smith. Interestingly enough, with the NASCAR ban on fuel injection, superchargers, and multiple carburetors, Chevrolet made available single-carburetor induction systems for those racers who continued in competition. Chevrolet continued back-door support of top racers, as did other auto manufacturers.

Oddly, in 1958 with an economic recession looming and the AMA ban on factory participation in racing in its first full year, the designers and engineers at Chevrolet not only introduced a radically restyled car but also developed a new engine series to power it. While it was called a truck engine, the new 348-ci big-block V-8 was available across the Chevrolet product line (except for the Corvette) and was a unique engine series. The combustion chambers were in the cylinders, calling for a wedge-shaped dome on the pistons, and the cylinder heads taking on the shape of the letter W.

With a 4.12-inch bore and 3.25-inch stroke, 9.5:1 compression, and a 4-barrel carburetor, the 348 developed 250 hp at 4,000 rpm and 355 ft-lbs of torque at 2,800 rpm. It is interesting to note that a company that was not in the business of building performance offered several optional versions of the 348 that piqued the interest of the hot rod set and very often found their way into the hands of enterprising drag racers.

RPO 579E: THE AIR BOX CORVETTES

Chevrolet showed just how serious it was about winning in all forms of motorsports in 1957 when it built 43 specially equipped Corvettes for the highly competitive sports car racing circuit. Although available to individuals through dealerships, the Air Box Corvettes were true factory race cars.

Devoid of any creature comfort options such as radio or heater, the cars were beefed up and highly modified with heavy-duty suspension components, brakes, quicker ratio steering boxes, wider wheels. The item that gave them their nickname, the fiberglass ductwork on the driver-side inner fender channeled cooler outside air into the fuel-injected engine to add even more horsepower to the already potent 283.

Proof that Corvettes optioned in this fashion were not for the faint of heart and surely intended for the serious racer was the price tag of $7,026.30. As of the mid-1960s, at least one Air Box Corvette was still actively competing on the SCCA circuit, and today the remaining cars are highly sought after by collectors.

Another optional engine for the full-size Chevy line in 1959 that was largely overlooked, due to the "bigger is better" atmosphere that prevailed in the late 1950s, was the fuel-injected 283-ci Corvette V-8. When backed with a 4-speed transmission, this combination was more than a match for most 348 cars due to its lighter weight and high-RPM capabilities.

and performance came at a price, however, as the option cost was an additional $484.20 over the base 283. It should also be noted that the top-performing 290-hp Corvette engine was also available in the full-size line, although it appears not to have been as popular as the 348, perhaps due to the price.

Chevrolet styling became even more radical for 1959, with a love-it or hate-it look that featured large horizontal fins and cat's-eye taillights. Still available were the 315-hp 348 big-block, as well as the 290-hp fuel-injected small-block.

It is very interesting to note how many 1959 Chevys appeared on the NASCAR circuit that year with local dealer sponsorship. An indication that either the factory was attempting to maintain an image of compliance with the AMA ban or there were numerous independent dealers who still believed that winning races sold cars. All told, Chevrolet won 18 races on the NASCAR circuit in 1959, and while three of these races were won by independents still running 1957 models, it appeared that the new cars performed pretty well with their "Law Enforcement" engines.

Perhaps the most interesting 1959 Chevys were the 40 cars specially ordered and prepared at the direction of Zora Arkus-Duntov. Chosen was the lightest available body style (21), the Biscayne two-door sedan, which had a normal curb weight of 3,535 pounds. Arkus-Duntov took things a step further for these special cars as the order also called for them to be the 3-P utility sedan. This option eliminated the backseat and also had fixed rear-quarter window glass, bringing the curb weight to 3,480 pounds. Arkus-Duntov equipped these cars not with the heavy 348 big-block but the lighter, high-winding 290-hp, fuel-injected, 283, backed by the 4-speed transmission.

While no records could be found of the intended purpose or disposition of these cars, it is doubtful that they were built for police use. Could these limited production Biscaynes be the first example of a coming trend in Detroit, where cars that appeared as regular showroom models were stripped of all necessary weight and packed with high-performance engines to win drag races? Aside from some cosmetics, the Corvette remained pretty much unchanged for 1959 with the 290-hp 283 still sitting atop the heap in the performance department. *Road & Track* tested a fuel-injected 1959 Corvette and was able to better previous 0–60 times, getting down to 6.6 seconds and blistering the quarter-mile in 14.5 seconds at 96 mph, a very impressive performance.

A 280-hp version of the 348 mounted three Rochester 2-barrel carburetors atop an otherwise unchanged engine, while the 300-hp option featured a solid lifter camshaft and 4-barrel induction. At the top of the heap was the 315-hp, Super Turbo Thrust model, which sported 11.1:1 compression, an aggressive-grind solid lifter camshaft, and triple carburetors.

In January 1958, *Sports Car Illustrated* road tested a new Chevy Bel Air equipped with the 315-hp "Law Enforcement" 348-ci engine, backed up with a 4-speed manual transmission and 4.11 differential gears. From the performance numbers recorded on the 3,520-pound Bel Air, there were few cars on the road that could outrun the law enforcement agency equipped with this model, as the car accelerated from 0 to 60 mph in 7.3 seconds and recorded a quarter-mile elapsed time of 15.3 seconds at 96 mph.

Corvette also received a redesign in 1958, though not quite as radical as the full-size models. Chevrolet's sports car retained its 283-ci powerplant but picked up some power over the previous year with four performance options offered. The top two engine options were the 270-hp version, which sported 10.5:1 compression, a solid lifer camshaft, and a dual 4-barrel induction system. At the top of the heap was the fuel-injected version that delivered 290 hp at 6,200 rpm, which was potent enough to propel a 4-speed car from 0 to 60 mph in 6.9 seconds. All this power

Pontiac

LATE TO THE PARTY, BUT THE SUPER DUTY GROUP SOON MADE HER THE BELLE OF THE BALL.

Pontiac received its first OHV V-8 engine in 1955, along with all-new styling from the previous year. The new engine, called the Strato Streak, displaced 287 ci based on 3.75-inch bore and 3.25-inch stroke. In base form with a 2-barrel carburetor, the horsepower rating was 180, and when equipped with the optional 4-barrel Power Pack induction, the number jumped to 200. No world-beater even by 1955 standards, the 3,568-pound Pontiac could manage only 12.7 seconds from 0 to 60 mph. The engine's bore size was enlarged to 3.93 inches in 1956, making the displacement 316 ci. The base version now had an advertised 205 hp, while the addition of a 4-barrel carburetor bumped the number to 227.

Some hope was found for Pontiac fans in a little-known high-performance version of the 316, which produced 285 hp at 5,100 rpm and 330 ft-lbs of torque at 2,600 rpm, thanks to an increase in compression to 10.0:1, a hotter camshaft, and a dual 4-barrel induction system.

Although Pontiac didn't get much attention on the racetrack or from the automotive press with the new performance option, it did set some records. Legendary driver Ab Jenkins, at the wheel of Pontiac's lightest model, a Chieftain Sedan packing the optional 285-hp engine, set a speed and endurance record by covering 2,841 miles in 24 hours, with an average speed of 118.375 mph. During the course of this run, Jenkins had achieved a top speed of 126.65 mph on one 10-mile leg.

The Pontiac Motor Division was in trouble as 1957 loomed, and to correct matters, Semon "Bunkie" Knudson was hired to take command. Knudson ordered a complete restyle of the Pontiac line, being quoted as saying, "You can sell an old man a young man's car, but you can't sell a young man an old man's car." The Pontiac V-8 engine received an increase in stroke to 3.56 inches, bringing the displacement to 347 ci.

Perhaps the best news for Pontiac in the performance department was Knudson's creation of the Super Duty Group, a carefully selected team of engineers that brought a new approach to getting the most performance out of an engine. The standard 347-ci V-8 for 1957 had an advertised horsepower of 252. Add a 4-barrel carburetor and the rating jumped to 270 horses. This allowed the new Pontiac to go from 0 to 60 mph 5 seconds quicker than the 1955 model. Also an option was a 290-hp version that gulped fuel through three 2-barrel carburetors, the famous Pontiac Tri-Power setup.

As if this weren't enough, Pontiac showed just how serious it was about claiming a portion of the performance market by offering the NASCAR-certified version of the 347, which had a solid lifter camshaft and could move the big Pontiac from 0 to 60 in less than 8 seconds.

Thanks to the hiring of Semon E. "Bunkie" Knudson to run things at Pontiac, the line received a styling upgrade, a new model called the Bonneville, and the company's first high-performance engine options in 1957. Knudson gave the model line a facelift and a big performance shot in the arm. At 347 ci the Pontiac V-8 was in the same engine family introduced in 1955 at 287 ci. Now available with a trio of Rochester 2-barrel carburetors and an optional camshaft that allowed for 290 hp, Pontiacs began setting records and winning races. Another option was the same type of Rochester fuel injection used by Chevrolet that year. Available only in the Bonneville model, the fuel-injected 347 produced 310 hp, and in spite of the Bonneville's additional bulk it out-performed all other Pontiac models that year. (Photo Courtesy CarTech Archive)

Any time the words camshaft and Pontiac are mentioned in the same sentence, the name Malcolm "Mac" McKellar should be included. Mac, who held the title Assistant Motor Engineer, was one of Knudson's Super Duty Group. He was a wizard when it came to camshafts, and his designs gave Pontiac engines plenty of punch. So highly regarded was McKellar that Pontiac began labeling the high-performance camshafts with his name; for example, McKellar #10 (for the specific grind number).

Pontiac didn't merely label one of the engines "NASCAR certified," they took it racing. At the Daytona Beach Speed Trials, Indy racer John Zink posted the fastest run ever by an American production sedan in the Flying Mile with a 141.2 blast. And Cotton Owens wheeled his Ray Nichels–prepared Pontiac to a win in the prestigious 160-mile NASCAR Grand National and Beach race.

Pontiac also announced a new model, a version of the Rochester fuel-injection unit for 1957. The new model was called Bonneville after the racing venue where records were set. In 1957, it was available only in a convertible and the only model available with fuel injection. Although the

Along with the rest of the GM line, Pontiac received all-new styling for 1958. Most noticeable was the lack of tailfins and the new-that-year quad headlamps and taillamps. The Bonneville was once again the top-of-the-line model with additional trim and a special roofline that set it apart from other models. (Photo Courtesy Steve Savage)

Pontiac's engine had grown to 370 ci for 1958 and the optional fuel injection was available on the Bonneville for the last time. The big news was the two Super Duty engines available that year, both of which were chock full of the strongest and best parts that Pontiac's engineers could develop, including some sourced from the aftermarket. The single 4-barrel NASCAR Super Duty 370 produced 290 hp, while the tri-carburetor version, designed for use in racing series that had not banned multiple carburetion, produced 315 hp. Both proved to be potent competitors. (Photos Courtesy Steve Savage)

The 1958 Bonneville received an interior makeover with the addition of first-time leather bucket-style seats. And, of course, the tons of chrome that by this time was common for all high-end car models in the GM line. (Photo Courtesy Steve Savage)

Although the heavier Pontiacs didn't do as well in competition during the 1958 season, factory driver Paul Goldsmith won the Daytona Beach race, for the second-straight Pontiac victory there. A drag racer from the American heartland named Arnie Beswick made the switch to Pontiac that year, beginning a long and successful association with the brand that helped make him famous.

In 1959, Pontiac introduced the newly redesigned Wide Track, which was longer, lower, and wider than its predecessor. Along with the dimensions of the body, the engine grew in size also. An increase in stroke brought the displacement to 389 ci. The optional 420-A Tempest V-8 featured the first Super Duty cylinder block with four-bolt main bearing caps and stuffed full of high-performance goodies such as a forged-steel crankshaft and connecting rods, a McKellar camshaft, and 10.5:1 compression. Two versions of the engine were offered: a 330-hp, single 4-barrel and the Tri-Power model with 345 hp.

One tactic used by other manufacturers in an effort to skirt the AMA ban was to list high-performance engines as "Police" options. Well, apparently Pontiac was having none of that, as while there was a Police engine option listed, it featured none of the go-fast parts from the Super Duty Group.

Pontiac had other firsts in 1959. A 4-speed transmission was offered for the first time and a top NASCAR driver named Glen "Fireball" Roberts came on board to drive a Pontiac. Roberts went on to make Pontiac the brand to beat on the NASCAR circuit. The Super Duty Group was just getting warmed up.

Buick

AN EARLY PLAYER IN THE PERFORMANCE GAME.

In 1953, Buick abandoned the antiquated OHV inline 8-cylinder engine and, along with all-new styling, introduced what became known as the Nailhead V-8 engine series. The term nailhead came from the vertical position of the valves in the cylinder heads, their relatively small diameter heads, and long, thin stems.

While small intake and exhaust valves are not normally associated with high-performance engines, Buick compensated by using a higher lift, longer duration camshaft, which, in concert with small intake and exhaust ports, a tall cylinder block deck (allowing for longer connecting rods), a big bore (4.00 inches), and short stroke (3.20 inches), resulted in an engine that made tons of torque. Two versions of the nailhead were available, the larger of which was 322 ci in displacement. With an 8.5:1 compression ratio, it delivered a respectable 188 hp when equipped with a single 4-barrel carburetor.

Mated with the smaller and lighter Special model in 1956, the 322 nailhead received some notice from the hot rod set. Most notably was a young television actor turned drag racer from California named Tommy Ivo. "T.V.

fuel-injected 347 had a higher compression ratio at 10.25:1, it was only rated at 310 hp at 4,800 rpm and 400 ft-lbs of torque at 3,400 rpm.

The Bonneville convertible was also heavier than the other Pontiac models that year, weighing more than 4,000 pounds. It still recorded a 0–60 time 1/2 second quicker than a lighter model equipped with the 290-hp engine.

In 1958, Pontiac suffered from the economic recession but that didn't stop Knudson from ordering another restyle and some important engineering changes. The new Pontiac models featured a coil-spring rear suspension for the first time, and the engine grew in displacement to 370 ci. Still available were the three carburetor and fuel-injection options (fuel injection on the Bonneville model only) and the Tri-Power engine made 300 hp.

Also making a return, in spite of the fact that Pontiac was supposedly under a racing ban from the AMA, were two versions the NASCAR-certified engine, now referred to as the Super Duty. This version was available with a single 4-barrel carburetor (NASCAR had banned multiple carburetion, fuel injection, and super chargers in mid-1957) that produced 315 hp and a Tri-Power model (for competition in other racing series) that was rated at 330 hp.

The Buick V-8 had grown dramatically in displacement and horse-power by 1956, producing 255 hp from 322 ci. California drag racers "T.V. Tommy" Ivo's (nicknamed as a result of his many television appearances) and Gas Ronda's success with Buick power gained the attention of other young men who had the means to buy such an expensive model.

Like the Olds Rocket 88, the Buick "nailhead" V-8, so named due to its small valves and unique vertical design cylinder heads, responded well to performance modifications and became a popular engine for use in upgrading older vehicles and drag cars. This nailhead has been fitted with two 4-barrel carburetors and powers a 1932 Ford coupe, one of the most popular hot rods to this day.

Tommy," as he came to be known, strolled into his local Buick dealer at the tender age of 16 shopping for a new car. By Ivo's account, he was not exactly taken seriously by the sales staff, but it didn't take long before his bankroll more than made up for his youthful appearance, and T.V. Tommy was off to the local dragstrip in his new Buick. The success he enjoyed on the track with his Buick led Ivo to create some of the most innovative drag cars of the mid-1950s, all powered by nailhead Buick engines, including a four-engine, four-wheel-drive monster.

Following Ivo's example, many young hot rodders chose Buick power for their racers, and the nailhead became a popular swap in early Fords for a number of years. Future Ford factory driver Gas Ronda was one of those who chose Buick when an acquaintance who owned a Buick dealership convinced the young drag racer that a new Buick would be more successful on the dragstrip than the Hudson Hornet he was currently racing. Ronda continued his winning ways with nailhead power for almost two years.

Buick also claimed two victories on the NASCAR stock car circuit in 1955 and 1956. However, in 1957, GM's Buick Division was one of those that abided by the AMA ban, and it wasn't long before Buick faded back into being known as a manufacturer of cars for the older set.

In the mid-1960s, Buick cashed in on the muscle car craze by fielding a series of vehicles that directly competed with GM cousins, the Pontiac GTO and Olds 442. By the end of the decade, the company had developed a car that many describe as the ultimate gentleman's muscle car, the Buick GS Stage 1.

Oldsmobile

ENTER THE ROCKET 88: AMERICA'S FIRST MASS-PRODUCED OHV V-8.

One of America's oldest car companies, Oldsmobile, was founded in 1900 by Ransom E. Olds. The brand soon became part of General Motors as a member of its mid-price line and remained so until the parent company dissolved the Oldsmobile Division in 2004.

The Rocket 88 was so potent they wrote songs about it: "Make a date with a Rocket 88."

The commonly accepted definition of a muscle car is when a manufacturer installs the largest displacement engine in its line into the smallest, lightest model that will accept it. That being said, many like to think that the 1964 Pontiac GTO was the original muscle car in America. Going by definition, it appeared that Oldsmobile trumped its cousins at Pontiac by more than a decade when it installed its top-of-the-line 303-ci OHV V-8 in the newest and lightest model, the Futuramic B-Body platform known as the Olds 88.

Riding on a 119-inch wheelbase and tipping the scales at a svelte (for an Oldsmobile of that era) 3,542 pounds, the new 1949 model was packed full of America's first mass-produced OHV V-8 engine. At 303 ci, the revolutionary new powerplant used a 3.75-inch bore and 3.43-inch stroke, had a compression ratio of 7.25:1, and was fed by a 2-barrel carburetor. Horsepower was rated at 135 at 3,600 rpm with torque numbers of 283 ft-lbs.

The emblem used on Oldsmobiles of the 1950s featured a globe representing a world-class car known for quality, style, and performance. The Rocket logo on an Olds valvecover meant power. Sadly, General Motors dropped the Oldsmobile Division from the line in 2004.

While other Olds models carried more weight than the Club Coupe in the early 1950s, it had styling that could not be denied and still packed that Rocket 88 and Hydra-Matic transmission.

Backed by GM's Hydramatic automatic transmission, the Rocket could achieve 60 mph from a standing start in 13 seconds, far eclipsing anything either Ford or Chevrolet had to offer, and topped out at 100 mph.

Motor Trend described the new Olds Rocket 88 as the first production car it tested to exceed 90 mph. It didn't take long for the new Oldsmobiles to catch the eye of racers who were on the lookout for the latest performance models. In its first year of production, the Olds 88 won six races out of 49 on the NASCAR stock car circuit.

Oldsmobile had an even better year in 1950, not only taking home 10 victories out of 19 NASCAR races, but a Rocket 88 driven by Hershel McGriff won its class at the Carrera Pan Americana, the grueling Mexican Road Race.

By 1952, the 303-ci Rocket V-8 had gained a 4-barrel carburetor and an increase in horsepower to 160. That year the Rocket took home wins in nearly half of the NASCAR series races, with a record of 20 out of 41.

In 1953, the compression ratio was increased to 8.0:1, which bumped the horsepower to 165, but by that point Oldsmobile's star had already begun to fade on the stock car circuit due to overwhelming factory support for teams running the superior-handling Hudson Hornet. But the Rocket 88 was far from done, as the potent engine found itself a popular swap for stock powerplants in early Ford models. It also became the motivation behind some of the quickest and fastest Gassers and Rails popping up on America's dragstrips, where they remained popular for many years.

From the standpoint of performance in a production car, little was heard from the Oldsmobile camp again until 1957, a year when it seemed that every auto manufacturer had high performance on the mind. Although

Oldsmobile was second only to Cadillac when it came to luxury in the GM line, and this 1955 88 Convertible is a prime example. Loaded with power options and, of course, the powerful Rocket 88 V-8, Oldsmobile had much to offer in the 1950s. (Photo Courtesy Greg Cook)

Oldsmobile interiors were filled with miles of chrome, deeply cushioned leather seats, a huge steering wheel, and in this case, an optional spotlight controlled by the handle to the left of the wheel. (Photo Courtesy Greg Cook)

The pinnacle of Oldsmobile power in this era came in 1957 with the introduction of the J-2 Golden Rocket option. By this time the Olds V-8 had grown to 371 ci. This $314 option consisted of thinner head gaskets that raised the compression ratio to 10.0:1 and three Rochester 2-barrel carburetors mounted on a cast-iron intake manifold with a special air cleaner. The J-2 option boosted the 371's horsepower to 300 with 425 ft-lbs of torque. A special camshaft, available through the dealer parts network, bumped horsepower an additional dozen.

The Olds Rocket V-8 lent itself well to aftermarket horsepower-enhancing modifications and as a result it was a favorite of hot rodders, who used it to power everything from old Ford coupes to all-out drag cars. This Rocket has been fitted with six 2-barrel carburetors on a log manifold and other aftermarket speed parts.

it had grown in girth, the 1957 Olds weighed a crushing 4,170 pounds, the Rocket powerplant had grown in size to 371 ci by virtue of a 4.0-inch bore and 3.7-inch stroke. The top-of-the-line performance option for the year was the J-2 Golden Rocket, which mounted three Rochester 2-barrel carburetors atop a cast-iron intake manifold and punched out an impressive 312 hp at 4,600 rpm and stump-pulling torque numbers of 415 ft-lbs at 2,800 rpm, thanks to the extra induction and thinner head gaskets, which bumped compression to 10.0:1.

And 1957 was the last year that Oldsmobile was seen on the stock car circuit, as Lee Petty claimed 4 victories and 15 top-5 finishes on the NASCAR stock car circuit with his J-2 Rocket Olds. Fred Lorenzen, a young driver who went on to great fame in NASCAR, scored two top-5 finishes in the United States Auto Club (USAC) stock car series in his native Midwest in a 1957 Olds.

Along with the AMA ban of 1957 came a mandate against multiple carburetors, fuel injection, and superchargers by NASCAR. So while the J-2 option remained available on Oldsmobile models in 1958, the brand pretty much disappeared from stock car racing. It wasn't until the muscle car era of the mid-1960s that the words Oldsmobile and high-performance were mentioned in the same sentence.

Cadillac

CLASS, STYLE AND PERFORMANCE GO HAND IN HAND IN THE MID-1950s.

Anyone who doesn't think of Cadillac as a car brand with a performance image to uphold has never heard the 1950s novelty tune titled "Little Nash Rambler." The lyrical theme repeated throughout the song states, "I'll show him that a Cadillac is not a car to scorn." In an era of automotive opulence when chrome and fins were in style, you should not be surprised that along with the other bragging rights afforded by Cadillac ownership, a powerful engine would be expected. While it was short-lived (just 1957 and 1958 models packed the extra punch), Cadillac offered high-performance engine options and adorned them with the class and style you would expect on a top-of-the-line automobile.

The 1957 Cadillacs were equipped with a 365-ci (4.00-inch bore and 3.62-inch stroke) engine that had a premium fuel–only compression ratio of 10.0:1. It pumped out an advertised 300 hp when equipped with the standard 4-barrel carburetor, and 335 ponies when fitted with the optional inline dual 4-barrel (Carter WCFBs) intake option. The 1958 version of the 365 V-8 had its compression ratio increased to 10.25:1, resulting in the standard version delivering 10 more horsepower (310) than in the previous model year.

The high-performance option for 1958 consisted of three Rochester 2-barrel carburetors that bumped the horsepower to 335 at 4,800 rpm. Following weak sales of the more powerful engines, the AMA ban, and the recession of 1958, Cadillac dropped any reference to performance from its line and seemed satisfied with producing cars with high-end style and comfort, leaving the hot rod pieces to other GM divisions.

Along with style, opulence, and a host of creature comforts, the 1957 Eldorado Biarritz showed that Cadillac was not a car to scorn when it came to performance that year. The nearly 5,000-pound behemoth relied on a 365-ci V-8 with two Rochester 4-barrel carburetors that pumped out 325 hp to achieve a top speed of approximately 120 mph. This engine was Cadillac's only effort at a performance car during the decade.

Those wealthy enough to afford the 1957 Cadillac Eldorado Biarritz traveled in the lap of luxury. The Eldorado's magnificently appointed dash even included dual ashtrays and cigarette lighters.

Ford

THE COMPANY THAT WAS ONCE THE BIGGEST NAME IN AMERICAN PERFORMANCE GETS A LATE START.

Somehow it took the folks at Ford a little longer to catch on to the concept that building performance and winning races sold cars in the 1950s. While the company was right on track for the future by introducing an OHV V-8 engine in 1954 to replace the aging flathead V-8 that (with improvements along the way) had been the company mainstay since 1932, it seemed that squeezing any serious horsepower out of the revolutionary new Y-block V-8 was not being taken into consideration. The new engine series debuted with the same displacement as the flathead that it replaced in the Ford line with 239 ci.

Mercury fared a little better, as its new V-8 came had 256 cubes and could be obtained with a 4-barrel carburetor, which was not an option on the Ford. While a couple of 1954 Mercurys were campaigned by independent racers on the NASCAR circuit with some success, it took until the latter part of the 1955 racing season for Ford and Mercury to get on the performance band wagon.

The top-of-the-line Lincoln models had achieved great success from 1952 to 1954 in the Carrera Panamericana road race, after being prepared by the West Coast shop of Bill Stroppe with factory assistance. But the publicity gained by winning seemed lost within the Ford Motor Company as a whole. The good news is that when Ford designed the Y-block OHV engine, they engineered it to be a "high futurity design," which planned for 10 years of progressive increases in cubic inches, compression, and power output.

Partway through 1955, Ford, perhaps taking a clue from rival Chevrolet who was publicizing their NASCAR stock car wins, introduced a dealer available stock car racing kit. It consisted of a BorgWarner T-85 close-ratio, heavy-duty 3-speed transmission; rear axle ratios from 4.57:1 for short tracks and 3.78:1 for longer courses; heavy-duty shock absorbers, springs, stabilizer bar, and radiator; and Lincoln spindles, hubs, and brakes.

This car, along with the now available 292-ci 205-hp version of the Y-block, made Ford a winner in both NASCAR (where the company scored several wins and numerous top-5 finishes) and the Midwest Racing Association for Race Cars (MARC; later, Automobile Racing Club of America, ARCA) series, where Iggy Katona, who had come over from Oldsmobile, took home the championship. Also in 1955, Ford introduced the Thunderbird, a two-seat vehicle described as a "personal car," powered by a 196 hp, 292-ci engine, which allowed a 3,240-pound, standard transmission T-Bird to hit 60 mph from a standing start in 9.6 seconds. While it had

Ford introduced its first OHV V-8 in 1954. At 239 ci, it was the same displacement as the flathead V-8 that it replaced. A strong, deep-skirted cylinder block gave rise to the engine series being called the Y-block. Although Ford showed little interest in performance in 1954, the new engine was a design that allowed for much larger displacements in the future.

The styling of the 1954 Ford was a carryover of what had debuted in 1952. While it was a pleasing look and generally durable, the 130-hp V-8 did little to thrill the performance-minded driver. New styling and more powerful engines were on the horizon for 1955.

Ford introduced the Thunderbird in 1955. The two-seat sports model was heavier than Chevrolet's new V-8 Corvette, yet the T-Bird was able to hold its own thanks to the Y-block V-8 that had been enlarged to 292 ci and put out 198 hp. It was offered with both a 3-speed standard and an automatic transmission. The new model outsold the Corvette and Ford's own expectations.

Some of the attributes that made the Thunderbird such a sales success were interior appointments that defined it as more than what was expected at the time in a sports car. A 150-mph speedometer and instrument panel–mounted tachometer added a high-performance feel.

slightly slower acceleration than the Corvette, now with its own 265-ci V-8 engine, the Thunderbird's amenities and production numbers allowed it to outpace Corvette in the sales arena for the year.

A landmark year for Ford performance was 1956, as the company signed on former Indy 500 winner Peter DePaolo to prepare cars for NASCAR. Ford's money was well spent as DePaolo's preparation and the handling of top drivers on his team handed Ford the NASCAR Manufacturer's Cup. Ford driver Buck Baker, who also drove Chryslers that year, won the driving championship and Iggy Katona claimed the MARC series championship once again for Ford that year.

Ford's successes for 1956 were aided in part by the increase in engine displacement to 312 ci and a dealer-available performance upgrade called the Super Power Pack, consisting of higher compression cylinder heads, a more aggressive camshaft profile, two Holley 4-barrel carburetors mounted on an aluminum intake manifold, and a special low-restriction air cleaner. Rated at 260 hp, the kit was available to both Ford and Mercury drivers after May 1956.

Ford prepared several 1956 Thunderbirds for the speed and acceleration trials held at Daytona Beach in 1956, including one highly modified car piloted by a team driver named Chuck Daigh, who cleaned the beach of all competi-

tion, including the factory Corvettes. While Ford did not support any drag racers in 1956, a top tuner and driver named Les Ritchey took advantage of the Super Power Pack pieces to turn his 1956 Fairlane into a dragstrip terror, winning 31 Eliminator titles on the West Coast that season. Ritchey was so successful at squeezing every ounce of power out of the Y-block Ford V-8 that *Rod and Custom* ran a series of articles showing Ritchey's techniques to fledgling drag racers using Ford products.

Ford came out swinging in 1957, offering a 270-hp version of the 312-ci Y-block that mounted two 4-barrel carburetors (there was also a 285-hp kit available in very limited numbers through the dealer parts network) and an even stouter version of the 312 that produced an advertised 300 hp, thanks to the addition of a McCulloch supercharger. Ford went on an immediate rampage with the newfound power, winning the Pikes Peak International Hill Climb, setting records at the Bonneville Salt Flats, and dominating in both the NASCAR and USAC stock car series, where Louis Unser won the championship.

Ford again prepared a series of Thunderbirds to compete on the sand at Daytona, this time going all out with two radically modified cars that were dubbed Battle Birds by the automotive press. One of them recorded an unofficial run of more than 200 mph on the beach, but an engine failure on the return leg negated any record. The Battle Birds were also entered in sports car races at Sebring, Florida, where one of the cars was withdrawn from competition, while the other bested the factory team Corvettes on the road course, finishing second to a Ferrari driven by Carroll Shelby.

In its third year of production, the Ford/Mercury Y-block had grown in displacement from 239 to 312 ci, and it was standard in the Thunderbird and optional as the Thunderbird Special V-8 across the Ford line. With a 4-barrel carburetor, the 312 produced 235 hp. With Ford now back in the performance game, aftermarket speed parts manufacturers had begun to take note of the Y-block engine and its potential.

On the West Coast, a future Indy 500 winner named Parnelli Jones won 21 consecutive feature races with his Ford-powered sprint car, and the team of Porter and Rourke won the National Short Track Championship.

But any hopes for fans of Ford performance were dashed on May 17, 1957, when a memorandum from Henry Ford II outlined the AMA edict calling for the end of factory participation and advertising of speed-related events. It appears that Mr. Ford intended to adhere to the mandate and had been led to believe that the other auto manufacturers would also comply. As of June 30, 1957, Ford officially pulled the plug on performance, and in the ensuing years between 1957 and 1960 any racing victories for Ford came through the efforts of independent racers with the parent company offering no support, development of technology, or sales advertising relating to performance.

Ford released a new engine series in 1958, the FE (Ford-Edsel), which was offered in 332 and 352 ci, but even with a rated 300 hp, the new 352 Police Interceptor Special V-8 with its single 4-barrel carburetor and mild hydraulic lifter camshaft fell woefully short of offerings from General Motors and Chrysler. Both of those manufacturers had, for the most part, just winked at the AMA ban and continued their performance programs unabated, while providing covert support for racers without advertising the fact. The

Both Ford and Mercury offered engine performance upgrade kits through the dealer parts network in 1956. Ford's Super Power Pack and Mercury's M-260 consisted of improved cylinder heads and camshaft, along with two Holley 4-barrel carburetors on an aluminum intake manifold.

The manufacturers of aftermarket speed equipment produced parts for the Ford Y-block engine in the 1950s; however, not at the prodigious rate that they did for the small-block Chevy that had been introduced in 1955. This particular Y-block, used to power a Modified stock car, is outfitted with mechanical fuel injection by Algon and other period speed parts.

Ford went after racing glory with great gusto in 1957, and the introduction of a McCulloch supercharger option for the 312-ci engine went a long way to prove it. Rated at 300 hp, these engines produced more. When Ford built a series of supercharged Thunderbirds destined to be used in competition, the horsepower was closer to 340, according to informed sources.

The model of choice when racing a supercharger-equipped Ford in 1957 was often the lighter, shorter wheelbase Custom two-door sedan. Fords similar to this one won races in nearly every form of competition in 1957, from the Pikes Peak International Hill Climb to the USAC, MARC, and NASCAR series. Supercharged 1957 Fords continued to win in drag racing into the late 1960s.

Stock car racing great Glen "Fireball" Roberts drove a 1957 Ford custom with supercharged 312 power for the Ford factory team of DePaolo Engineering on the NASCAR circuit with great success until the sanctioning body disallowed fuel injection, multiple carburetion, and superchargers partway through the season. This rules change coincided with the AMA ban on factory participation in racing. (Photo Courtesy Tom Kitchen)

only glimmer of hope for performance-minded Ford fans came in the form of a number of 1959 Thunderbirds prepared by Holman-Moody for NASCAR competition.

When Ford pulled its support in mid-1957, Peter DePaolo had sold his racing operation to a former employee, John Holman, and his partner, racing driver Ralph Moody. The duo formed Holman-Moody and did their best to compete without factory support. In 1959 they built a series of "race-ready" Thunderbirds for NASCAR competition, equipped with the optional 430-ci Mercury-Edsel-Lincoln (MEL) engine to be sold to independent drivers or teams, apparently with the unofficial blessing of Ford. A unique feature on some of these cars, dubbed Zipper Tops, was a removable hardtop that also allowed the car to compete in the NASCAR convertible series.

As it turned out, the Holman-Moody–prepared cars were successful in the hands of former factory drivers, winning a total of 11 NASCAR races in both hardtop and convertible configurations. Johnny Beauchamp, at the wheel of a Holman-Moody–prepared Thunderbird, lost a photo-finish decision to Lee Petty at the 1959 Daytona 500.

Ford also built a limited number of special 1957 Thunderbirds with the supercharged 312 engine for competition at the Daytona Beach Speed Trials and similar events. The performance records set by these factory race cars, along with the car's beautiful styling, led to a fair number of Thunderbirds being sold equipped with the supercharged 312 engine option in 1957. (Photo Courtesy Don Antilla)

The belt-driven McCulloch supercharger on the 312 Ford engine created boost that was forced into a Holley 4-barrel carburetor sealed under an aluminum bonnet. The supercharger option was available on all Ford models in 1957, including station wagons, of which at least two were built.

Lincoln-Mercury

FORD'S FANCIER COUSIN CARRIES THE COMPANY'S PERFORMANCE BANNER EARLY ON.

After receiving a 317-ci OHV V-8 in 1952, the Lincoln quickly became the darling of Mercury performance. Lincolns prepared by Bill Stroppe Engineering were a dominant force in the prestigious and rugged Mexican Road Race until 1954. While the Mercury division had received its first OHV V-8 in 1954 along with Ford, little attention was paid to any performance potential that the 256-ci Y-block V-8 might possess, aside from a few privateers who raced Mercurys in NASCAR with limited success.

That all changed when the 1955 Mexican Road Race was canceled due to several fatal accidents. It was at this point that Stroppe was tasked with making Mercury a winner in the performance arena, and by 1956 the Mercury factory team was in direct competition with their cousins at Ford on the NASCAR and USAC stock car circuits. The top engine offering from

Mercury, which received its first OHV V-8 in 1954, fared better than Ford in that its version of the Y-block V-8 displaced 256 ci, and with a 4-barrel carburetor the engine produced 30 more horsepower than the Ford 239. This additional power allowed for independent drivers to score several NASCAR stock car victories at the wheel of 1954 Mercurys that season.

Mercury in 1956 was the 312-ci M-260, which featured improved cylinder heads, a more aggressive camshaft, and a dual 4-barrel induction system similar to the Ford setup.

In 1957 the Mercury line was the recipient of not just a styling makeover but a brand-new engine design as well. To motivate the now-much-larger Mercury, a 368-ci version of the Y-block V-8 featured a conventional vertical intake port arrangement that differed from other Y-blocks, which had stacked or horizontal intake ports. From an engineering standpoint, the horizontal ports provided the advantage of a lower overall engine

The M-335 version of the new 368-ci Mercury V-8 provided plenty of power (335 hp) thanks to a hot solid lifter camshaft and two Holley 4-barrel carburetors mounted on top of a specially cast intake manifold. Legendary Bill Stroppe built 100 1957 Mercurys for stock car competition, and while they didn't have the success of the previous year, the larger Mercurys did score some impressive wins. (Photo Courtesy Ben S. Hammonds)

New styling made the 1955 and 1956 Mercurys popular with customizers, and the Mercury line shared powerplants with Ford in 1956, with the top offering being the M-260 package for the 312-ci Y-block V-8. Improved cylinder heads, a better camshaft, and two 4-barrel carburetors were part of a package available through the dealer parts network to make the option legal for stock car competition. The Bill Stroppe Engineering–prepared 1956 Mercurys did well on the NASCAR and USAC stock car circuit. (Photo Courtesy Ben S. Hammonds)

As a division of the Ford Motor Company, the strongest adherent to the AMA ban on performance, Mercury should have been expected to toe the line, but somehow an obscure performance engine option, the Super Marauder, slipped through the cracks in 1958. Based on the 430-ci MEL (Mercury, Edsel, Lincoln) engine series, the Super Marauder was topped with three Holley 2-barrel carburetors under a unique cast aluminum air cleaner. The engine produced 400 hp and was the first American production car engine to do so.

profile, allowing it to fit multiple models, including the new Thunderbird. A highly modified version of this engine had been performance tested in a Stroppe-prepared 1956 Mercury affectionately called Thumper for its unusual exhaust note. Based upon the success of this car, the engine series was slated to receive production high-performance parts when introduced in the 1957 models.

Mercury's new Turnpike Cruiser model was available at extra cost and included a 290-hp 368 engine that sported 10.0:1 compression, a solid lifter Iskenderian aftermarket camshaft with .468 inch of valve lift, heavy-duty valvesprings, and two 4-barrel carburetors. Also available through the dealer parts network for other Mercury models, the performance upgrade was referred to as the M-335 option.

A modified 1957 Mercury, dubbed the Mermaid, powered by a 368 that developed more than 400 hp and driven by drag racer Art Chrisman, posted a run of 159 mph at the Daytona Speed Trials. As he had done in 1956, Bill Stroppe again prepared cars for the Mercury stock car team in 1957. Stroppe received bodies in white (a bare shell on a chassis direct from the assembly plant) and set about modifying them for competition in NASCAR and USAC. The M-335 was the engine of choice and only differed from the production version in compression, which was increased to 10.8:1.

The Mercury team got off to a good start in 1957, with Tim Flock leading the way to the checkered flag in the NASCAR convertible series race in Daytona Beach. However, they had the rug pulled out from under them mid-season, when the company ceased racing support in compliance with the AMA ban.

While it was apparently all over from a performance standpoint for the entire Ford line by mid-year 1957, Mercury introduced a unique performance option to accompany a new engine series released in 1958 that, had it been advertised and developed for racing, could have perhaps been a record setter.

Ford introduced two new V-8 engine series in 1958, the FE and the MEL. At 430 ci, the MEL was a behemoth designed to move cars that weighed in excess of 4,000 pounds, such as the Lincoln. But at the same time, this engine was available in all Mercury models and, if a savvy buyer knew which option boxes to have the dealer check, this engine could be had in Super Marauder form. This meant having three Holley 2-barrel carburetors mounted on an aluminum intake manifold atop a 430-ci monster that developed 400 hp and an astounding 480 ft-lbs of torque.

In one magazine road test, a 1958 Mercury sedan powered by the Super Marauder engine, backed by an automatic transmission, recorded a 0–60 time of 6.5 seconds and clicked through the quarter-mile in 15.3 seconds at 93 mph. This was top-of-the-line performance from a company no longer in the performance business and not actively advertising one formidable engine option. It wasn't until 1962 that Mercury concentrated on performance, and found itself in the thick of things in short order.

Chrysler

HEMI HEADS PROVIDE THE POWER THAT MAKE TWO-TON BEHEMOTHS FLY.

In 1955, Chrysler Corporation introduced the 300 model, the first in a series of vehicles that came to be known as Letter cars, and in short order the title "World's fastest stock car" rested in Chrysler's hands. The 1955 300 model rode on a 126-inch wheelbase and had a shipping weight of 4,005 pounds. To motivate 2 tons of Detroit steel to the front of the pack, Chrysler installed a V-8 with 331 ci, 300 hp at 5,200 rpm, 345 ft-lbs of torque at 3,000 rpm that breathed deep thanks to cylinder heads that featured hemispherical combustion chambers. The big Hemi was potent enough to propel the Chrysler 300 from 0 to 60 mph in 10.2 seconds and through the quarter-mile clocks in 17.8 seconds at 81 mph. Factory driver Warren Koechling set a record of 127.58 mph for the Flying Mile at the Daytona Beach Speed Trials.

Most noteworthy was the manner in which the 300 was equipped as delivered from the factory. Dual 4-barrel carburetion topped an engine that sported a race-profile solid lifter camshaft, suspension far stiffer than normal, and an exhaust system greatly improved over other models. It was said at the time, and rightfully so, that Chrysler was selling race cars to the public for the purpose of homologating them as legal for NASCAR stock car competition. And the tactic certainly worked, as Mercury Marine engine magnate Carl Keikhaefer wasted no time in seizing the performance advantages built into the Chrysler 300 as he built a NASCAR team around them. Employing top drivers the Flock brothers and Buck Baker, Keikhaefer quickly built an almost insurmountable dynasty for the cars that became rolling billboards for Mercury Marine.

Along with his contribution to NASCAR stock car racing, Keikhaefer brought his apparently enormous ego and influence. He persuaded NASCAR to allow his Chryslers to be declared legal to run after having been converted to standard transmissions, even though the option was not offered by the factory, and other Chryslers in competition were forced to run with automatic transmissions.

For 1956 Chrysler upped the ante with the introduction of the 300-B. The engine had grown to 354 ci of displacement and two versions were offered, one producing 340 hp and the other a whopping 355, making it the first American car to produce one horsepower per cubic inch of displacement. Tim Flock took the new Chrysler through the Flying Mile clocks at 139.37 mph at Daytona Beach, and the Keikhaefer team cars continued their dominance of both the NASCAR and USAC stock car series races. The big Chryslers won both the NASCAR and USAC series championships in 1955 and 1956, accumulating 51 NASCAR wins along the way.

By the end of 1956, however, the competition was beginning to chip away at Keikhaefer's dynasty. With Ford scoring 16 NASCAR wins and the departure of top driver Tim Flock from his team, the man who wasn't used to losing folded his tents and departed from racing. Perhaps Keikhaefer felt that he had proved what he set out to prove. Or could it be that he realized the 1957 models from Chrysler, in spite of the fact that engine displacement would be increased to 392 ci, would just be too heavy to remain competitive, now that the other major Detroit manufacturers were throwing their hats into the stock car racing ring?

The Hemi engine in the 1957 Chrysler 300-C, with its increase in displacement and compression (9.25:1), pumped out 375 hp at 5,200 rpm and delivered 420 ft-lbs of torque at 4,000 rpm. It was enough to push a car that had an advertised shipping weight of 4,390 pounds, but arrived at the party weighing more than 4,500 pounds, went from 0 to 60 mph in 8.6 seconds, and through the quarter-mile in just over 16 seconds at close to 90 mph. It was obvious that lighter, more nimble cars would outperform them on the stock car tracks.

That is not to say that the Chrysler 300 did not have its moments in the sun for 1957. While they had dropped from the stock car tracks, two 300-C models were built specifically for the Daytona Beach Speed Trials, a venue that provided manufacturers with plenty of the "Sell on Monday" publicity they were clamoring for. Equipped with manual transmissions, a more aggressive camshaft, and limited slip differentials, bumping the horsepower to 390, the factory cars were driven down the beach by Chrysler test driver Brewster Shaw and stock car racer Red Byron. Shaw stopped the Standing Mile clocks at 86.9 mph, while Byron flew through the Flying Mile at 139.0 mph.

Chrysler also entered a highly modified version of the 300-C into the X-Class Flying Mile at Daytona that year with much fanfare. This entry produced more than 400 hp, thanks to the addition of ram intake manifold tubes that the factory had developed for a future fuel-injection unit, the removal of the exhaust system, and the featured rudimentary aerodynamic improvements made to the car using cardboard, clay, and tape. In testing, the car had run 145.7 mph and Chrysler's public relations firm hyped the car's performance potential heavily prior to the Daytona Speed Trials. The factory even hired top NASCAR driver Buck Baker to handle the car, paying him a reported $1,000, but Baker pulled out at the last moment to go with the Chevy camp. To salvage the day, the Chrysler team brought in talented female driver Vicky Wood to replace Baker, but it was all for naught as a clutch failure sidelined the car, and a Plymouth entry, powered by a Chrysler Hemi engine prepared by *Hot Rod* magazine, took home class honors at 159.9 mph.

In 1958, Chrysler Corporation winked at the AMA ban, actually withdrawing from the sponsorship of racing teams, while continuing development of performance engine options. The 1958 Chrysler 300-D picked up additional compression (10.1:1) and 5 more horsepower (380 at 5,200 rpm and 435 ft-lbs of torque at 3,600 rpm) over the 1957 model, enough to improve the 0–60 times to 7 seconds flat and the quarter-mile performance to 15.7 seconds at 89 mph. Very impressive for a car weighing nearly 4,500 pounds.

Chrysler did return to the Daytona Beach Speed Trials in 1958, but by that time Pontiac, which appeared to have completely ignored the AMA ban, had pretty much surpassed the other manufacturers in the field of performance.

Plymouth

VIRGIL EXNER DESIGNS A CAR WITH MOTION AND A V-8 ENGINE MAKES IT SPORTY.

The entire Plymouth line was redesigned for 1955, gaining 1 inch of wheelbase, 10.3 inches in overall length, and 2.5 inches in width over the 1954 models. But in the performance department, Plymouth got off to a slow start in 1955. The company actually sourced its first V-8 engine (a 241-ci polyspherical cylinder head design) from Dodge. With 7.6:1 compression and a 2-barrel carburetor delivering just 157 advertised horsepower, the Plymouth lagged behind the rest of the "Low Priced Three" (Chevrolet and Ford) in performance for the first half of the model year.

But the mid-year introduction of a 260-ci version of the Hy-Fire V-8, gained through an increase in cylinder bore size to 3.56 inches while retaining the 241's stroke of 3.25 inches, and an available Power Pack option consisting of a modern Carter 4-barrel carburetor and dual exhausts, brought

"Suddenly it's 1960" was the Plymouth ad campaign that accompanied the Forward Look styling for 1958. The upscale Fury model, introduced in 1956, was back with all its eye-catching trim enhancements, but it was the Savoy model that the serious racer or police agency sought out the high-performance 350-ci, 305-hp V-8 to take advantage of the model's lighter weight for enhanced acceleration.

According to Chrysler's advertising, the tailfins, shown on this Savoy owned by James Rawa, were vertical stabilizers. The Savoy was one step up from Plymouth's base model, the Plaza, and thus had a minimum of exterior trim. The unpopular taillight restyle, which was a departure from the 1957 version, was derisively called the "Lollipop." Plymouth's advertising called it a reflecting tower.

the horsepower numbers up to 177 with 231 ft-lbs of torque, and made the redesigned, re-engineered Plymouth a fair match with Ford and Chevrolet.

Plymouth finally caught on to the horsepower craze by 1956 and did its best to grab a share of the market with both styling and performance. Plymouth introduced a new sport model called Fury for 1956. Based on the Belvedere series, the Fury was available only in Eggshell white with gold anodized trim, including special gold turbine inspired wheel covers. While the rest of the Plymouth line had to get by with the 177-hp 260-ci engine as the top performance option, the Fury received something better to back up all that styling flash. The 3,650-pound 115-inch-wheelbase Fury was powered by a 303-ci Hy-Fire V-8, sourced from Chrysler of Canada, that sported domed pistons (9.25:1 compression), a solid lifter camshaft, a Carter 4-barrel carburetor, and dual exhausts that pumped out 240 hp at 4,800 rpm and 310 ft-lbs of torque at 2,800 rpm.

Also available for dealer installation was a $746 performance package that included two 4-barrel carburetors on an aluminum intake manifold, better cylinder heads for 10.0:1 compression, a more aggressive camshaft kit, and special low-restriction air cleaners that brought the horsepower up to 270. While the Plymouth brand remained mostly absent from the winner's circle in the NASCAR stock car series (the only exception being one win in the NASCAR convertible series), a preproduction model in the

hands of factory driver Phil Walters averaged 143.59 mph over the Flying Mile at the Daytona Speed Weeks, the fastest run ever by a Plymouth, and stopped the Standing quarter-mile clocks at 82.54 mph. Unfortunately, because the car was a preproduction model, it was not eligible to run in the Stock car class and had to run in the Experimental category, which was won by a factory-prepared Mercury that averaged 147.26 mph.

"Suddenly it's 1960." So stated one of the advertising buzz phrases for the redesigned 1957 model line at Plymouth. Virgil Exner's Flite Sweep styling brought "The Forward Look" to the Chrysler Corporation line and caught the competition completely by surprise. Not only was the Fury model back (still offered only in white with special gold anodized accents), but it came with a bigger engine and arguably the best automatic transmission of the era, the TorqueFlite. The Fury model offered heavy-duty suspension components, brakes, standard 3-speed transmission with a larger clutch, and a 150-mph speedometer. Power came from a 290-hp poly

In spite of the fact that the Plymouth Savoy was a base model in 1958, the interior was spacious enough for six adults and appealing to the eye.

One look at the instrument panel in Jim Rawa's 1958 Plymouth Savoy immediately reveals its utilitarian purpose. Devoid of radio, heater, clock, or any other accessories, this Plymouth is all business.

spherical 318-ci engine that sported 9.25:1 compression, twin Carter 4-barrel carburetors, and a solid lifter camshaft.

Chrysler Corporation decided to showcase the Plymouth line in the NASCAR stock car series for 1957, and to that end it hired Ronny Householder, "Spook" Crawford, and Bob Osiecki to manage the team and prepare the cars. Driving chores were assigned to Charlie Cregar, Johnny Allen, Everett Brashear, Dan Oldenberg, Jim Delany, Lem Svajian, and Pat Kirkwood. Unfortunately, the Plymouth teams were outclassed on the tracks by the Fords and Chevrolets, and by mid-season factory participation was halted due to the AMA ban.

For 1958, Plymouth wasn't advertising performance, but it was surely selling it. Still available was the 290-hp 318, but it was no longer the top offering.

New for 1958 was the Golden Commando option, a 350-ci version of the Chrysler B series engines. Topped with two new Carter AFB 4-barrel carburetors and 10.1:1 compression, the Golden Commando pumped out 305 hp at 5,800 rpm and 370 ft-lbs of torque at 3,600 rpm. As an additional option on the Golden Commando for 1958, Plymouth also listed Bendix "Electrojector" fuel injection, which bumped the horsepower rating to 315. Sadly the system proved to be troublesome as compared to GM's Bendix unit that had been released in 1957, so the few cars equipped with the fuel-injection setup that found their way into the hands of the public were soon recalled and replaced with conventional induction.

Another performance-enhancing option introduced for 1958 was the Sure-Grip limited slip rear, which went a long way in reducing wheel spin during hard acceleration from a standing stop. Comparison tests performed by *Motor Trend* that year showed that the new Plymouth was no slouch in the acceleration department, as a Golden Commando model bested both the 280-hp 348 and 300-hp 352 offerings from Chevrolet and Ford in both 0–60 and quarter-mile testing.

The optional Golden Commando engine grew again in 1959 to 361 ci, thanks to an increase in bore to 4.12 inches over the now-discontinued 350's 4.06 inches. The stroke remained the same at 3.38 inches, as did the compression ratio at 10.1:1. Equipped with a

Packing two Carter 4-barrel carburetors with low-restriction air cleaners, the Golden Commando 350-ci high-performance engine was based on the Chrysler B-block V-8, and with a compression ratio of 9.25:1, it developed 305 hp. A handful of these engines made it to production with an experimental Bendix fuel-injection unit, but all were recalled and replaced with the more conventional dual 4-barrel carburetor setup as a result of problems in the field.

high-performance camshaft and intake manifold mounting one Carter AFB 4-barrel carburetor, the engine delivered 305 hp at 4,600 rpm and a tire-shredding 395 ft-lbs of torque at 3,000 rpm.

Once again, Plymouth topped its rivals in magazine tests of the day, recording a 0–60 mph time of 7.8 seconds to best closest competitors Ford T-Bird at 9.9 seconds and the triple-carbureted 348 Chevy at 10.1. And all the while, big performance engineering was taking place behind the scenes at Plymouth and other manufacturers in preparation for a general rebellion against the AMA ban by most of the signers come 1960.

Dodge

MESS WITH THE RAM AND YOU'LL GET THE HORNS.

The Dodge Division of Chrysler Corporation got its very first OHV V-8 engine in 1953, putting the company ahead of sister brand Plymouth, along with competitors Ford and Chevrolet. The first Dodge V-8 was something very special, as the new 241-ci Red Ram powerplant was fitted with hemispherical combustion chamber cylinder heads that helped it punch out 140 hp. Pretty good numbers for an engine that was limited to 7.1:1 compression due to the low octane fuels available at the time. A bump in compression to 7.5:1 for 1954 boosted the output to 150 hp, and at the same time the Dodge boys decided it would be a good idea to market the Red Ram's performance potential by entering the cars into some high-profile racing events.

In September 1953, two 1954 Dodge sedans and two convertible models were prepared and taken to the Bonneville Salt Flats, where they promptly set 196 AAA–certified speed records, with one of the sedans recording a top speed of 108.36 mph in the Flying 10-Mile category. Dodge went all-out at the grueling Carrera Panamericana (Mexican Road Race), as well as taking home the first four places and six of the top nine finishing spots in the Medium Stock class. Dodge's top driver, Tommy Drisdale, won with an average speed of just under 90 mph, in a race where more cars routinely retired due to mechanical failures than actually finished.

Becoming aware of their main competition's (Ford and Chevrolet) efforts to grab some of the performance glory, in 1955 the Red Ram V-8 was enlarged to 270 ci, thanks to an increase in cylinder bore size to 3.63, while the advertised horsepower output remained at 150.

Performance-wise, 1956 looked to be a big year for the Dodge team with the introduction of the D-500 option. What the company hoped to accomplish was spelled out in an internal document dated prior to the release of the first D-500s on December 22, 1955. Dodge's goals were to provide a higher level of performance, accompanied by special sales literature to boost sales. The D-500 cars took advantage of heavy-duty parts sourced from the Chrysler and Imperial lines, including 12-inch brake drums, larger diameter exhaust systems, and suspension parts. Each D-500 Dodge also received special checkered-flag emblems to set the car apart from more mundane production models.

The 1956 D-500 received a 315-ci Hemi head V-8 courtesy of Chrysler of Canada and, with a compression ratio of 9.25:1 and a Carter WCFB 4-barrel carburetor, delivered 260 hp, which was sufficient to motivate the 3,550-pound Dodge from 0 to 60 in less than 10 seconds.

On January 12, 1956, Dodge released the D-500-1 version of the engine, which featured a more aggressive camshaft, an improved exhaust system,

Chrysler's Dodge Division received its first V-8 engine in 1953, and by 1954 the company had already started to think about establishing a performance image. This emblem announces that this particular 1954 Dodge has both the V-8 and the Powerflite automatic transmission.

The 241-ci Red Ram V-8 that powered the 1954 Dodge relied on a solid lifter camshaft and hemispherical chambered cylinder heads to produce 150 hp. Dodge was chosen to provide the pace car for the Indianapolis 500 in 1954, and a limited edition Royal 500 Pace Car edition was produced for sale to the public. While the actual pace car's engine was modified with two 4-barrel carburetors to make it more powerful, 150 hp was adequate for a production car in 1954 and substantially better than the recently introduced Ford OHV V-8.

and two 4-barrel carburetors mounted atop an aluminum intake provided by Mercury Marine. This version was described as "full race" and produced 276 hp. It is very likely that no full-race versions of the D-500 engine ever found their way into production cars, as the advertised availability was purely for the purpose of having the engine declared legal for competition in "stock" classes.

Dodge went on to score 11 NASCAR stock car wins in 1956, with ace driver Buck Baker delivering the lion's share of the victories, and added 9 wins in the NASCAR convertible series to the season total. On the dragstrips of the Midwest, Arnie Beswick, who went on to gain fame at the wheel of a series of Pontiacs beginning in 1958, was a consistent winner in the C/Gas class at Oswego, Illinois, with his 1956 D-500 Dodge. At Cordova, Illinois, Ed Lyons went undefeated on the season and claimed the track Super/Stock championship with his D-500 Dodge, turning quarter-mile elapsed times in the 14-second range.

The year 1957 saw sweeping changes in both styling and engineering across the Chrysler Corporation product line, and Dodge was no exception. The new "Forward Look" styling for 1957 included jet fighter–inspired tailfins that Chrysler referred to as vertical aerodynamic stabilizers and an ultra-modern torsion bar front suspension. The Dodge line also received a new 325-ci V-8 engine that featured poly-spherical chambered cylinder heads that produced 260 hp. But perhaps the greatest innovation from a performance standpoint came with the introduction of the TorqueFlite 3-speed automatic transmission that soon set the standard for the entire industry.

The D-500 option continued in 1957, and in spite of the new engine series introduction, the Hemi remained king for the D-500 with the single 4-barrel carburetor version delivering 285 hp at 4,800 rpm and 345 ft-lbs of torque at 2,800 rpm. The dual 4-barrel Super D-500 also had a more aggressive profile camshaft, pumping out 310 horses at 4,800

rpm and 350 ft-lbs of torque at 3,200 rpm. There was a rumor that some Super D-500s received the 354-ci Chrysler Hemi, but none are currently known to exist.

In 1958, the Hemi was dropped and the D-500 option was applied to the B-series wedge engine, which had been enlarged from the previous year's 350 to 361 ci by virtue of an increased cylinder bore size. With the conventional dual 4-barrel induction system, the engine produced 320 hp, but Dodge also listed a fuel-injected version of the engine rated at 345 hp. All indications are that the fuel-injection units immediately proved to be troublesome and few, if any, remained on the 1,163 production D-500 vehicles sold. Just the same, the new B-series powerplant was capable of moving an almost 3,800-pound Dodge from 0 to 60 mph in 8 seconds.

The 1959 D-500 stepped up its game again with the B-series engine growing to 383 ci, thanks to a 4.21-inch cylinder bore. With 345 hp on tap, the big Dodges could easily go from 0 to 60 mph in less than 8 seconds and stop the quarter-mile clocks in just over 15 seconds with a terminal speed of 89 mph. All in all, these performance numbers were not too bad for a company that was supposedly no longer in the performance business.

The Super D-550 produced 310 hp with 350 ft-lbs of torque, thanks in part to twin Carter WCFB 4-barrel carburetors, which gulped air through individual open-element air cleaners. The last year for the Hemi engine in the D-500 was 1957, but it was certainly not the last heard from this hot Dodge model.

Forward Look styling began in 1957 throughout the Chrysler line, and Dodge sprouted jet-like vertical fins from each quarter panel. The top performer was the D-500, a separate and distinct model first introduced in 1956 that featured its own special trim, heavy-duty suspension, brakes borrowed from the full-size Imperial model, a 325-ci Super D-500 engine with Hemi heads, dual 4-barrel carburetors, dual-point ignition system, and dual exhausts.

Hudson

HORNET PUTS THE STING ON "THE BIG THREE" IN PERFORMANCE.

The Hudson Motor Company was founded in 1909 by eight Detroit businessmen who named their company after Joseph L. Hudson, a Detroit department store owner who bankrolled their venture. Instrumental in the company's organization was the only partner with any automotive background, Roy D. Chapin Sr., who had previously worked for the auto manufacturer Ransom E. Olds. In 1954, Hudson merged with Nash-Kelvinator to form American Motors. After the 1957 model year, the Hudson name was discontinued from the product line.

In 1951, the "Fabulous Hudson Hornet" was America's top-performing and handling car, thanks to Hudson's designers having mounted the body over the frame for a lower stance and a powerful inline flathead 6-cylinder engine with twin carburetors.

With optional Twin H power and the dealer-available 7X Severe Usage engine package (consisting of larger valves with reliefs in the cylinder block to improve flow, an improved camshaft, the cylinder head from the 232-ci version of the engine for higher compression, and a split exhaust manifold). The Hornet's 308-ci, flathead-6 could produce 180 hp and 305 ft-lbs of torque.

What gave Hudson their performance edge over the competition? In 1948 the company introduced the concept of the step-down body, which was achieved by placing the car's passenger compartment down inside the perimeter of the frame rails. This in turn lowered the center of gravity and provided Hudson with superior handling characteristics over other production automobiles of the time.

In 1951 the company made improvements to the inline, flathead, 6-cylinder engine consisting of a new cylinder block with thicker cylinder walls for greater rigidity and a 4-speed Hydramatic automatic transmission that was sourced from General Motors. These improvements helped put Hudson in the forefront of the performance field at the time.

My favorite automotive author, Tom McCahill, writing for *Mechanics Illustrated* magazine, described Hudson cars like this: "Hudsons are ripping the feathers out of the other brands on one simple, but oh so vital, point. They are America's finest road cars from the very important standpoint of road ability, cornering, and steering. To stay with the Hudsons on a race course these other cars must literally pull themselves apart in corners, while the Hudsons sail around with effortless ease."

Hudson didn't depend entirely on superior handling to stay out in front of the competition. The 1951–1954 top-line model Hornet's powerplant had grown from 262 to a whopping 308 ci of displacement, making it the largest 6-cylinder passenger car engine of its time (3.812-inch bore and 4.500-inch stroke). With the standard aluminum cylinder head squeezing the compression ratio to 7.2:1, the Hornet Six pumped out 145 hp at 3,800 rpm. And it didn't end there.

In an example of what became common practice for Detroit's automak-ers a decade later, during the "Horsepower war," Hudson offered a performance upgrade package through its dealer parts network. The Twin H package (PN SP 306216) consisted of a cast-iron intake manifold mounting two Carter 1-barrel carburetors and fitted with two unique air cleaners that announced "Twin H Power." This upgrade cost the consumer $85.60 and bumped the engine's output to 160 hp at 3,800 rpm and an impressive 260 ft-lbs of torque at 1,800 rpm. So equipped, a Hornet could attain 60 mph from a standing start in 12.1 seconds and record a top speed of 107 mph.

Other performance improvements for the Hornet consisted of cold-air ducting to the carburetors via a styled horizontal leading-edge hood scoop on the 1952 and newer models. An increase in compression, along with improvements to the combustion chambers in the cylinder head for 1954, which increased horsepower to 170.

To ensure that America became fully aware of the performance capabilities of their cars prior to the era of mass media, Hudson took to the racetracks. Depending on the talents of top drivers such as Herb Thomas, Marshall Teague, and the Flock brothers (Tim and Fonty), the factory-supported Hudson Hornets set out to prove the brand's superiority on the stock car circuit against Detroit's best. It would be more than fair to say that Hudson got plenty of bang for its advertising buck from the racing efforts. Marshall Teague won the 1950 AAA Stock Car series championship and Herb Thomas took his Hornet to victory at NASCAR's Southern 500 in 1951 and 1954, with Indy car driver Dick Rathman taking home the gold at the 1952 race.

In what may have been the first ram air intake system on any American car, the 1953 Hudson Hornet's hood featured a leading-edge scoop, which allowed cooler outside air into the engine's open-element air cleaners to produce more horsepower.

This interior view of a 1953 Hudson Hornet shows the column-mounted gearshift selector that controls the GM-sourced 4-speed Hydra-Matic automatic transmission. This particular car has a drag racing history, thus the owner installed aftermarket tachometer and gauges under the dash to keep track of shift points, coolant temperature, and engine oil pressure.

Also in 1952, Teague took home the AAA series championship by a 1,000-point margin, winning 12 of the 13 events that year. Teague copped 14 more wins while on the NASCAR circuit, and Hudson team cars claimed an additional 27 wins out of 34 races that season.

In 1953 the Hudson team drivers took 22 of 37 NASCAR races and 17 of 37 for the 1954 season. So successful was the Hudson effort on the stock car tracks that Tim Flock's racer had its sides boldly emblazoned with lettering proclaiming it "The Fabulous Hudson Hornet." And fabulous it was.

The Twin H option wasn't all that Hudson brought to the party. A company technical bulletin dated February 2, 1952, described the 7X Severe Usage package. The 7X engines were each hand-built by the factory for the racing teams. In a move that was repeated by factories many times in the decades to follow, Hudson developed special racing parts for the engines and then, by making them available through their dealer parts network to the general public, had the parts declared legal for competition by the factory race teams. Racer Marshall Teague, along with Vince Piggins, set about modifying the 308-ci engine for all-out competition on the stock car racing circuit. This was accomplished by installing the 232 cylinder head on the 308 block, thus increasing the compression ratio to 9.2:1.

A "flat top" camshaft (PN 309742) featured .390 inch of valve lift and 268 degrees of duration (cost to the consumer over the parts counter was $32.50) as compared to the stock production camshaft's .356 inch of lift. Larger 2-inch intake and 1-11/16-inch exhaust valves were installed, and the cylinder block top surface was relieved.

Relieving is a process where an area of a flathead cylinder block (where the air/fuel mixture flows from the valves to the combustion chamber)

During the 1950s this Hornet emblem on a car from Hudson shouted performance to all who saw it and informed potential adversaries of the sting it possessed. The Hornet's successes on the NASCAR racing circuit, and later the dragstrip, became the stuff of legend.

is made deeper and wider using handheld grinding tools. The purpose of relieving was to create a Venturi effect, which reduced the pressure of the air/fuel mixture into the combustion chamber, allowing it to travel at a higher velocity, thus creating more power.

Also part of the 7X engine package was a split, dual-outlet exhaust manifold, which increased power by improving the scavenging effect on the spent gases leaving the engine. When all was said and done, the 7X engine produced 180 hp with 305 ft-lbs of torque at 3,000 rpm.

This custom-made badging announced that this particular Hornet was none other than Satan of Morimar, which made a name for itself on the hill climb circuit during the 1950s. Many Hudsons were class winners and record holders in various NHRA and AHRA classes into the 1970s.

Hudsons found success on the quarter-mile dragstrips of America as well, and this success extended into the mid-1960s, long after the Hudson brand had disappeared and the company's best drivers had abandoned the Hornet for more sophisticated and modern stock cars.

One of my favorite Hudson drag racing tales was related by Gaspar "Gas" Ronda, who went on to achieve fame as a driver of drag cars for Ford in the 1960s and someone who certainly learned his way around how to obtain the special parts reserved for the factory-supported teams at an early age.

By Ronda's account, he was feeling the stress of running a successful business and had complained of this fact to his doctor. The doctor's advice was that Gas take up a hobby to relieve his stress. Although it was probably not exactly the hobby the doctor had in mind, Ronda decided to take up drag racing, a sport that was growing in popularity in his native California. Seeing the racing successes of the Hudson Hornets on the stock car circuit, Ronda chose a Hornet as his mount, and off to the local dragstrip he went.

SMOKEY YUNICK'S TRICKS

Smokey Yunick, proprietor of the "Best damned garage in town," was a motorsports legend. And over the years the irascible, yet innovative builder of racing vehicles put his talents to work on behalf of several major auto manufacturers' performance efforts.

In the early 1950s, Smokey was the man behind the winning factory-supported Hudson Hornet driven by Herb Thomas on the NASCAR stock car circuit. Yunick was infamous for winking at the official rules governing the amount of modifications allowed to stock cars as set down by the sanctioning body, and his time with Hudson certainly kept his reputation for bending the rules intact.

In an interview given years later, Yunick provided insight into some of the tricks he employed to keep Thomas's Hudson out in front on the racetrack. While the official rules stated that engines had to use production camshafts, Yunick found those provided by the factory were not always of the best quality so he ground his own to ensure a degree of consistency.

While he was at it, he added mushroom-style tappets, which, while not changing the camshaft's listed specifications, quickened the valve action. He also added inserts under the valvesprings, which increased their rate as well. Nothing appeared in the official rules prohibiting that.

One area of the rulebook that was quite specific was the part that addressed lightening the engine's flywheel. This practice, which gave the car added inertia coming off the corners on racetracks, was forbidden. Yunick's solution was to remove the ring gear from the flywheel, drill a series of holes around the outside edge, then reinstall the ring gear, thus effectively hiding the modification from the prying eyes of NASCAR tech inspectors.

Another trick that went undiscovered was the offset grinding of the connecting rod journals on the crankshaft to attain a better rod angle and thus less internal engine friction. The rulebook left little room for interpretation in the area discussing the porting (enlarging) and polishing (smoothing by mechanical means) of the intake and exhaust ports of the engine. *Always the innovator, Yunick painted the port surfaces with multiple layers of hard lacquer, sanding each coat smooth between applications, until a mirror-like finish was achieved without the use of a grinder.*

An additional means of enhancing the flow of air in and out of the engine consisted of using an abrasive to remove casting imperfections, known as flash, from the inside of the intake and exhaust manifolds.

But perhaps the most interesting of all the modifications from "stock" pulled from Yunicks's seemingly bottomless bag of tricks was setting the engine up to run in reverse, or opposite to the normal direction of rotation. To do this, a special camshaft was ground and the car's differential was removed from its perches, turned upside down, and welded back into place. The result was that the engine's torque twisted toward the driver's side of the car instead of the passenger's side and by doing so loaded the driver's side, giving the car superior handling on circle tracks, which consisted of four left-hand turns.

The Twin H engine that powers **Satan of Morimar** *has been modified from stock through the addition of a Mallory dual-point ignition system, a "beehive" oil filter housing, and chrome air cleaners. All were popular touches found under the hood of many hot rods in the 1950s and early 1960s.*

This is a perfect example of how winning races equates to sales numbers at the dealer. Expecting the Hornet to be superior to all others on the track, Ronda was disappointed when he didn't realize the expected success with a car that in other venues of racing appeared almost invincible. Ronda made up his mind to go directly to the source for answers and he boldly contacted Marshall Teague.

The optional Hudson Twin H engine package included an aluminum cylinder head and unique dual, open-element air filters attached to twin carburetors.

The Twin H featured two single-throat Carter carburetors mounted on a cast-iron intake manifold. Note the heat shields between the carburetors and intake to isolate them from engine heat and prevent vapor lock.

After hearing of Ronda's lack of success, Teague provided the young hot rodder with a list of part numbers for the "good pieces" used by the factory teams and instructions to inform the men behind the local dealers' parts counter that Marshall Teague himself had referred him.

It wasn't long before Gas Ronda and his Hudson Hornet became a winning combination. Perhaps it was this experience that put Ronda on the path to becoming the drag racing legend that he is today.

While the power produced by a properly prepared Hudson Hornet engine made it a force to be reckoned with in the early days of drag racing, it was the superior power-to-weight ratio of one of Hudson's lesser models, the Jet, that delivered the greatest number of quarter-mile victories and records.

The Jet was a compact Hudson model that weighed 2,700 pounds as compared to the Hornet's 3,620, and while its 6-cylinder powerplant only displaced 202 ci (3.00-inch bore and 4.75-inch stroke), it was also available with the 4-speed Hydramatic automatic transmission and Twin H option. When combined with the optional aluminum cylinder head (8.0:1 compression ratio), it produced 114 hp at 4,000 rpm. The 400-pound weight advantage that the Jet enjoyed over comparable Ford and Chevrolet models of the time directly related to a performance advantage.

Speed Age tested a 1953 Super Jet Club Sedan, which recorded a very respectable 0–60 in 12.5 seconds, quicker than both the flathead V-8 Ford and OHV 6-cylinder Chevy. It was this power-to-weight ratio that kept the Hudson name alive in drag racing into the late 1960s, where Hudson Jets held NHRA elapsed time records in the lower stock classes. The late

American Motors, Rambler

THE COMPACT CAR WITH LIGHTNING UNDER THE HOOD.

The custom-made tubular exhaust header seen here in place of the Twin H Hornet's factory split exhaust manifold is evidence of this particular car's drag racing history. The free-breathing header could well have freed up an additional 15 hp from the engine.

Sloane McCauley was the American Hot Rod Association (AHRA) record holder in both the AHRA Formula 4 B/Altered and D/Altered classes with his Hudson Jet.

George Romney, president of the Automobile Manufacturers Association (AMA), became the architect of the infamous ban on factory participation in motorsports competition and the development of performance parts in mid-1957. Ironically it was his company, American Motors, that produced one of the most impressive performance cars of 1957, a year when Detroit built its best performing cars of the decade.

The 1957 Rambler Rebel laid claim to being the first American midsize production car with a big-block V-8. Now, let's take a look at the definition of a muscle car again, as it seems there were multiple claimants to the throne prior to the release of the Pontiac GTO in 1964. The Rebel, a four-door model in the Rambler line, was only available painted in metallic silver with contrasting gold anodized side-trim panels and weighed just 3,350 pounds, thanks to unit body construction, while riding on a 108-inch wheelbase.

With a Manufacturer's Suggested Retail Price of $2,786, the Rebel rolled out of Kenosha, Wisconsin, packing a potent punch in the form of a 327-ci V-8 that put a forged steel crankshaft and connecting rods and a solid lifter camshaft into a cylinder block with a 4.0-inch bore and 3.25-inch stroke. Topped off with a Carter WCFB 4-barrel carburetor and exhaling gases through dual exhausts, the Rebel's engine had a compression

Feast your eyes upon the unlikely car that was named "the fastest stock American sedan" in 1957, the Rambler Rebel. A limited production car with just 1,500 units built, the Rebel models were all very sedate-looking four-door sedans, the only giveaway being the special silver paint and gold side trim. With the capability to get from a standing start to 60 mph in 7.5 seconds, the Rambler Rebel checked in just a click behind the fuel-injected Corvette.

As was the style in the 1950s, the Rambler Rebel was adorned with miles of chrome. You can only imagine the performance potential of the Rebel V-8 had it been installed in a smaller, lighter vehicle.

The heart of the Rebel was this rather mundane-looking 327-ci V-8. But appearance aside, it was the internals that gave the Rebel its go. A forged-steel crankshaft and connecting rods, solid lifter camshaft, and a Carter WCFB 4-barrel carburetor provided 255 hp. When combined with a svelte 3,350 pounds, the power-to-weight ratio of the Rebel was impressive.

The interior of the Rebel was as spacious and as nicely appointed as any competitive cars in its field. The 3-speed manual transmission was controlled by a column-mounted shift, and had the factory linkage not proven to be so balky, there is a distinct chance the Rebel could have topped the Corvette's 0–60 time.

ratio of 8.7:1, and delivered 255 hp at 4,700 rpm and 345 ft-lbs of torque at 2,600 rpm.

The Rebel was available with either a 3-speed manual overdrive transmission or the optional GM Hydramatic automatic. With an outstanding power-to-weight ratio of 13 pounds per horsepower, the car that *Motor Trend* called "the fastest stock American sedan" stopped the 0–60 mph clocks in 7.5 seconds, making it second only to the fuel-injected Chevy Corvette among cars tested by the magazine that year.

And speaking of fuel injection, AMC had been experimenting with a Bendix Electrojector system featuring dual electronically controlled throttle bodies for the Rebel and, had this option reached production (development problems caused it to be scrapped), the Rebel's horsepower output was expected to jump from 255 to 288.

Although the Rambler Rebel was not a regular on the stock car circuit due to Romney's stance of factory participation in racing, the 1,500 cars produced certainly put American Motors on the map when it came to performance. Sadly, after 1957 the company focused almost entirely on stodgy, comfortable cars and economic cars, which were not well received in an era of inexpensive gasoline. It was until the late 1960s that the company attempted to avoid bankruptcy by marketing a line of exciting performance production and factory-supported drag cars that proved to be too little, too late to save the company from Kenosha.

It should be noted that if the parent company had listened to Bill Kraft, an enterprising AMC dealer from Norwalk, California, who championed performance with his own line of special parts and dealer prepared cars in the mid-1960s, it could have stayed in the performance market and kept the attention of America's youth.

Studebaker

FIRST WITH THE BIG-ENGINE SMALL-CAR CONCEPT.

Studebaker was a car company with forward-thinking ideas and styling ahead of its time in the 1950s, as evidenced by this 1955 Studebaker President Speedster sport coupe, which is finished in the two-tone paint scheme of this model.

Due to financial difficulties, Studebaker had merged with Packard in 1954, and that marriage produced a very unusual performance car in the form of the Studebaker Golden Hawk in 1956. Automotive writers of the time called the low-slung, stylish Studebaker Hawk the closest thing you could get to a sports car that would carry the entire family. In 1956, the 3,360-pound Hawk got a big boost in the form of a 352-ci Packard V-8 that punched out 275 hp, the most horsepower per pound of any American car, with the exception of the Chrysler 300. The car's performance seemed to prove that a big engine in a small car could put Studebaker in front of the competition, as on February 21, Wallace Chandler recorded a speed of 127.34 mph in the Flying Mile at Daytona Beach.

In July 1956, *Speed Age* tested the Golden Hawk against the Chevrolet Corvette, Ford Thunderbird, and Chrysler 300-B with some fairly astounding results. With a 0–60 mph time of 7.8 seconds and a quarter-mile time of 17.0 seconds, it bested the best with only the Corvette coming close to matching it. And if 275 hp wasn't enough, the discerning Golden Hawk owner could opt to have two 4-barrel carburetors installed by the dealer, which would bring the horsepower to 300. And if that still wasn't enough, the dealer parts network offered a McCulloch supercharger that boosted the horsepower to 360.

The biggest complaint about the 1956 Golden Hawk apparently arose from its nose-heavy attitude due to the big engine. Writing for *Popular Mechanics*, Tom McCahill said that he could not learn the car's full potential due to excessive wheel spin. *Motor Trend* stated that the Golden Hawk had the weight distribution of a black jack. These were hardly complimentary words for a struggling car company to hear about its product.

Studebaker set out to prove its critics wrong with the 1957 version of the Golden Hawk. Although the car was heavier overall than in the previous year, the installation of a 289-ci Studebaker V-8 in place of the Packard engine took 40 pounds off the front end of the car. The smaller engine, based on a bore of 3.56 inches and a stroke of 3.63 inches, could deliver 275 hp when equipped with the optional McCulloch supercharger. This, combined with redesigned rear leaf springs, allowed the 1957 Golden Hawk to have better road ability and handling, while delivering nearly identical performance numbers to the 1956 model.

But as previously stated, Studebaker was struggling financially during this time and obviously there was little money in the budget to go racing. Studebaker was heard from again, however, and in a big way in the early 1960s.

The colors on this car, called Lemon and Lime, went a long way to make the Speedster stand out in a crowd. This model was the forerunner to the successful Hawk series and one of the first V-8 engines in a small car model produced by an American car manufacturer.

Studebaker called the 259-ci V-8 engine that powered the President Speedster the Passmaster. Equipped with a Rochester 4-barrel carburetor, it pumped out 185 hp, which was the same as Ford's 272 Y-block V-8 of that year. When coupled with the Speedster's light body style, it had the capability of passing many cars on the highway.

CHAPTER 2

1960–1961: DETROIT GETS BACK INTO RACING WITH LIGHTWEIGHT PARTS

B y 1960, the Big Three auto manufacturers had pretty much come to the conclusion that to sell the maximum number of cars, they would have to appeal to all aspects of the market, and performance was once again popular with the American car buyer, making it part of that market. The horsepower war being waged by the manufacturers was about to escalate dramatically.

Chevrolet continued the 348-ci V-8 first introduced in 1958 until the 1961 model year. In 1960, horsepower ratings on the 348 ranged from 250 to 335. The top performer, called the Super Turbo Thrust Special 348, relied on 11.25:1 compression, a solid lifter camshaft, and three Rochester 2-barrel carburetors to punch out 335 hp at 5,800 rpm. California drag racer "Dyno Don" Nicholson first gained national attention in 1960, thanks to his preparation of and performance with a 348 1960 Biscayne. Chevrolet increased the horsepower rating on the top 348 engine to 350 for 1961, just before it disappeared from the lineup forever.

While NASCAR stock car racing series wins were more important to the manufacturers than drag racing, it wasn't long before they came to the realization that the youth market preferred the quarter-mile and largely based their brand preferences on what was happening there.

Chevrolet, 1960

PERFORMANCE AND STYLING COMBINE TO MAKE RACETRACK WINNERS.

Chevrolet toned down the styling of its cars and stepped up the performance program for 1960, again placing the emphasis on the 348-ci big-block engine for the full-size models and the high-winding 283 small-block in the Corvette.

Chevrolet offered four versions of the 348 engine in 1960 with horsepower ratings from 250 to 335. The top-of-the-line 335-hp Super Turbo Thrust Special 348 got its punch from a compression ratio of 11.25:1, a solid lifter camshaft, and three 2-barrel carburetors. Peak horsepower came at 5,800 rpm and 364 ft-lbs of tire-shredding torque came at 3,600 rpm. Combine this engine with a creature-comforts-deleted Biscayne body, back it with a 4-speed transmission, add a Dyno Tune at C.S. Meade Chevrolet, take her out to Pomona, and you might be rewarded with a 13.69-second elapsed time at 101.01 mph and a Super/Stock class win. This event became known as the NHRA Winternationals the following year.

This was just the beginning of the many racing accomplishments of Don Nicholson, who later became known as "Dyno Don" as a result of his expertise at performance tuning cars. In later years, Don related to me that he felt certain that had he traveled to Detroit for the NHRA Nationals that

The Corvette's cockpit remained all business for 1960, thoughtfully planned with performance in mind. The tachometer and 160-mph speedometer were easily read through the three-spoke steering wheel, and the short shifter handle was ergonomically designed to "grab a gear."

year, his Chevy would have prevailed over the best Super/Stock cars in the nation.

In spite of Pontiac and Ford seizing the majority of the publicity in the 1960 NASCAR series, it was Chevy driver Rex White who compiled the most points and was crowned series champion that year. Chevrolet teams visited the winner's circle 13 times.

Corvette continued to rely on several versions of the 283-ci small-block V-8 through the end of 1961. The 1960 Corvette could be optioned with either the dual 4-barrel carbureted, 270-hp engine or the fuel-injected 283 that now produced 315 hp, thanks to the addition of a new solid lifter camshaft and an increase in compression to 11.0:1. The last year for the 283 in the Corvette was 1961 when it was replaced by the larger 327-ci small-block.

Corvette continued to be the enduring symbol of Chevy performance in 1960 with three performance engine offerings. The dual 4-barrel carbureted 283 remained at 270 rated horsepower, while the fuel-injected version with 10.5:1 compression got a bump up to 290 ponies, and a special competition version that featured an improved cam and 11.1:1 compression delivered an astounding 315 hp. Coupled with a car that weighed just over 3,000 pounds, the Corvette was a formidable opponent on the street, strip, and sports car course.

Chevrolet, 1961

"She's real fine, my 409."

These lyrics, penned by the Beach Boys, were perhaps some of the best free advertising any auto company received during the 1960s and became one of the favorite anthems for a generation of Americans gone wild for performance automobiles. Interestingly, Chevrolet fitted fewer than 150 cars with the widely acclaimed 409-ci version of the "W" series big-block in 1961, but that did little to dampen the enthusiasm of America's youth.

Chevrolet started the year advertising the 348 Special Turbo Thrust V-8 as the top engine option, claiming it to be "sized and equipped for performance with wedge-shaped machined combustion chambers, high efficiency air cleaner, full flow oil filter, and dual exhausts. Triple 2-barrel carburetion adds extra muscle." But it wasn't long before the lucky few could step up to the 409 for an additional $484 over the base engine, and along with the added cubic inches came 360 (a mere 10 more horsepower than the top 348 engine) conservatively rated horsepower.

Chevrolet enjoyed another good year in NASCAR stock car competition in 1961, visiting the winner's circle 11 times, thanks to top drivers such as Ned Jarrett and Rex White.

NHRA and the Horsepower War

By 1961 the popularity of stock class drag racing was growing as fast as the auto manufacturers were introducing new performance-enhancing options to their respective models, in an effort to maintain the largest share of the market. As a result, by mid-year the NHRA established a new class, one step above Super/Stock, for top-line production cars that featured limited production performance parts or upgrades.

This class, called Optional/Super Stock, filled the void until rules changes sorted out how vehicle production numbers affected classification. In October 1961, the team of Strickler and Jenkins held the NHRA O/SS class elapsed time record at 13.24 seconds with their 409-powered Chevy Biscayne. Hayden Proffitt claimed the speed record at 109.22 in his Mickey Thompson–prepared Pontiac.

Pontiac, 1960

It's easy to be in the lead when you have a head start.

GM's Pontiac Motor Division showed that it was lightyears ahead of the competition, including its cousins at Chevrolet. By the time the dark cloud of the AMA ban had dissipated and the Detroit auto manufacturers realized that to grab their share of the growing youth market in America, they would have to build not just sporty-looking cars but cars that performed as good as they looked. As previously stated, the Super Duty Group

In 1961 Chevrolet released a new 409-ci engine in very limited quantities based on the 348. Conservatively rated at 360 hp, the few 409s available found their way into the hands of factory-connected drag racers such as Don Nicholson, Frank Sanders, and Dave Strickler. Strickler's Amon R. Smith sponsored a 1961 Biscayne, which was prepared by tuning ace Bill Jenkins, who held the national record in the new Optional/Super Stock class. This class was formed by NHRA to keep pace with the rapid release of limited production performance parts from the Detroit auto manufacturers. Optional/Super Stock became the A/Factory Experimental class in 1962. (Photo Courtesy Bob Wenzelburger)

Ace Wilson's Royal Pontiac made a big splash for the brand in drag racing, fielding Super/Stock cars in 1960. Jim Wangers drove his Catalina to class honors at the 1960 NHRA Nationals. While a Wide Track 1960 Pontiac is considered a huge automobile by today's standards, they remained a favorite among drag racers well into the late 1960s, thanks to the availability of high-performance parts direct from the dealer. (Photo Courtesy Bob Knudsen)

The 1961 Pontiac models were smaller and lighter than those of the previous year, making them even better performers. Not just another pretty face, the 1961 Catalina could be fitted with a full range of optional factory speed equipment, including aluminum bumpers and body panels, which often made them the class of the Super/Stock field at any dragstrip they frequented. (Photo Courtesy Mike Bretsch)

at Pontiac continued to develop bigger, stronger engines that produced more horsepower right through 1959 and had also forged an alliance with the aftermarket speed parts industry, something that no other manufacturer had done.

Pontiac's association with companies such as Iskendarian, manufacturer of high-performance valvetrain components, showed great foresight. After all, if speed parts already existed for your engine line, why reinvent the wheel by expending time, money, and resources to develop your own?

Ed Beyer's Scalper II was a frequent competitor at Vargo Dragway in Perkasie, Pennsylvania. (Photo Courtesy Ken Gunning)

Perhaps no alliance proved to be more beneficial to Pontiac than that with California racer Mickey Thompson. A pioneer in many forms of motorsports in America, Thompson put Pontiac on the performance map when he used four highly modified 389-ci Pontiac engines to power his *Challenger I* race car that made him the fastest man on wheels. He brought the World's Land Speed record home to the United States in 1960, courtesy of a run of more than 400 mph at the Bonneville Salt Flats. Thompson was also keenly interested in the quickly evolving sport of drag racing and to that end he developed performance parts to further his successes with Pontiac power.

These successes were not lost on the Super Duty Group, which later applied corporate part numbers to items developed by Thompson so that the pieces became legal for competition in stock class racing.

To aid the group's efforts on the stock car tracks that were once again becoming an effective means of showcasing Pontiac performance, an up-and-coming driver named Glen "Fireball" Roberts was hired on as a factory backed driver. The addition of Roberts and other top drivers paid dividends to Pontiac's performance image for several years.

What better way to get the word out about how your products perform than to have a professional ad man, who just happened to be an avid drag racer, do it for you? Enter Jim Wangers.

Originally hired by the marketing firm Campbell-Ewald to represent Chevrolet, Jim brought his professional mantra, "If you want to be perceived as a winner, you have to beat somebody" to Pontiac when he took on its ad account. Wangers not only capitalized on Pontiac's winning ways through advertising, he added some of his own to them.

The hood scoop on Mike Bretsch's 1961 Catalina was actually borrowed from Ford. The performance gurus at Pontiac adapted the scoop from a Ford heavy truck to feed cool outside air to its powerful V-8s and even assigned it a GM part number to ensure that it was legal for competition. (Photo Courtesy Mike Bretsch)

While the majority of high-performance 1961 Pontiacs received the 389-ci engine with three 2-barrel carburetors (left), select drag racers with factory connections were the recipients of the next great engine, the Super Duty 421, which mounted two 4-barrel carburetors, pumped out 405 hp, and became available toward the end of the year. (Photo Courtesy Mike Bretsch)

In a trend that carried over to other manufacturers later, Wangers was aligned with Ace Wilson's Royal Pontiac dealership as the sponsor of record for his drag racing efforts. Royal Pontiac soon became the factory's de-facto performance headquarters and one of the first to offer in-house performance modifications for customer cars. While fully supported by the factory, having the name of a dealer on the side of the car conveyed a message to potential buyers that they could easily obtain a comparable car from their local dealership and take it racing as well. By Wangers's admission, the 1960 Catalina that he drove to acclaim on the nation's dragstrips featured a few items that you couldn't buy right off the showroom floor.

While lightweight components from the factory were not publicized or even available on a limited basis on Pontiac vehicles until 1961, drag racers already recognized that getting weight off the car, particularly off the front of the car, related directly to increased weight transfer to the rear and the increased traction that came along with it. And for every 100 pounds removed, elapsed times decreased by .1 second in the quarter-mile.

From drag racing's earliest days, drivers removed excess weight from their vehicles, often rendering them almost unrecognizable from production cars, in a quest for quicker times. This didn't work if you were trying to showcase cars that could be purchased at your dealer and used as transportation. The manufacturers had to gain that performance advantage while keeping the outward appearance of the car stock.

To that end, Wangers's Royal Pontiac Catalina was fitted with an aluminum front bumper, chrome plated to give the appearance of a heavier production part. The car featured other weight-saving deletions such as radio, power steering, and other non-essential options. Wangers also used his connections within the industry to obtain tires from Goodyear that were

In the 1960s most serious drag racers soon replaced their cars' flimsy original equipment 4-speed shift linkage with a Hurst shifter. Seen in this 1961 Pontiac Catalina belonging to Mike Bretsch, the addition of an aftermarket tachometer to keep track of engine RPM was also a must. The device with the white knob just to the right of the steering column is a unique drag racer adaptation. Originally designed to help hold standard transmission cars of the 1940s and 1950s stationary while on a hill, it also provided a drag racer with a means to keep the car from rolling through the starting beams at the dragstrip. (Photo Courtesy Mike Bretsch)

Some of the most successful Pontiac drag cars of the 1960s hailed from Ace Wilson's Royal Pontiac dealership and were handled by GM ad man Jim Wangers. The Royal Pontiac cars always received the latest high-performance parts developed by the factory, which helped make them frequent winners on the track. After winning at the NHRA Nationals in 1960, Wangers was denied a second chance when it was reported that the two Royal Pontiac team cars had been making test runs on local streets before the event. This led to their disqualification. (Photo Courtesy Bob Knudson)

uncured, essentially removed from the line before hardening agents were added for tread life. The resulting much softer rubber compound gave the big Pontiac added grip off the starting line in a drag race in the days before drag slicks became readily available.

Pontiac released two options for 1960 that aided in both weight reduction and performance. The line received its first 4-speed manual transmissions with floor-mounted shifter to replace the standard column-shifted 3-speed, and the optional Kelsey-Hayes eight-lug aluminum brake drum/wheel combination, which resulted in an 80-pound weight savings over standard steel drums and rims when mounted with the same tires.

Wangers and Royal Pontiac delivered their first NHRA national drag racing title when Jim wheeled his Catalina to victory in the Super/Stock and Top Stock Eliminator categories at the

1960 NHRA Nationals in Detroit, Michigan. Wangers, who had run as quick as 13.89 seconds at 102.67 mph during the event, won the class with a 14.14 at 102.04 mph in the final round, and took home the Top Stock Eliminator title over a similar Pontiac.

A number of others who became some of the top names in drag racing came over to Pontiac around this time and became affiliated with dealerships that sold performance. Arnie "The Farmer" Beswick emerged victorious as the Overall Super/Stock Eliminator at the NASCAR Winternationals in Daytona Beach, Florida. Former Chevy racer Harold Ramsey, now driving for Union Park Pontiac, Bob Harrop from New Jersey, and Don Gay, the son of a Texas Pontiac dealer who won his first drag race with a 1958 Pontiac that he took from the dealership's showroom without permission, helped put Pontiac in the winner's circle in 1960.

Pontiac's powertrain lineup for 1960 consisted of four levels of available performance from the 389-ci engine: a 303-hp single 4-barrel version; a 318-hp triple-carbureted version; and when fitted with a slightly hotter hydraulic lifter camshaft, horsepower jumped to 333 and 348 hp respectively. The latter also featured improved cylinder blocks with four-bolt main caps and better flowing exhaust manifolds.

The ultimate in Pontiac performance that year came in the form of the Super Duty parts package (officially, the Tempest 425-A), which consisted of a four-bolt cylinder block with chamfered cylinder bores to clear larger 1.92-inch intake valves; forged crankshaft, connecting rods, and pistons (10.75:1 compression); a McKellar #7 mechanical lifter camshaft (.445/.447-inch lift, 300/304-degree duration); 1.65 ratio rocker arms; and two-plane aluminum intake manifolds mounting either one Carter AFB or three Rochester 2-barrel carburetors, respectively. The Super Duty 389 engines were cleverly underrated at 363 hp by the factory.

Thanks to numerous NASCAR and drag racing victories, performance-minded individuals all across the land flocked to their local

COMPARING THE 1960s

The following is a compilation of magazine road tests conducted on the popular performance cars available in 1960.

Car/Model	Engine/Transmission	Magazine	Performance (quarter-mile)
Chevy Impala	348/320 hp	Motor Life	15.36 at 92.78
Chevy Corvette	283/270 hp	Motor Trend	16.1 at 85
Chrysler 300F	413/375 hp	Motor Trend	16.0 at 85
Dodge Dart	383/330 hp	Motor Life	15.19 at 86.03
Ford Starliner	352/360 hp	Motor Life	14.81 at 94.71
Pontiac Catalina	389/348 hp	Motor Life	14.55 at 94.53
Pontiac Ventura	389/333 hp	Motor Trend	14.80 at 89

Pontiac dealers, boosting overall sales for the year to nearly 400,000, up by nearly 14,000 units from the previous year.

Pontiac, 1961

THE INDIANS RECEIVE SOME ALUMINUM PIECES

Pontiac took off the gloves in 1961, by reducing the wheelbase of the full-size model line from 122 to 119 inches and dropping the overall shipping weight by an average of 180 pounds across the board. The most popular model that year was the Catalina Sport Hardtop, or bubble top, the choice of NASCAR racers due to its aerodynamic design, and the one-year-only Style 61 Catalina Sport Sedan, or Batwing, the choice of many drag racers due to the fact that it offered a 30-pound weight advantage over the hardtop.

Pontiac took things a step further to ensure that their drag cars stayed out in front of the competition by producing a limited number of cars equipped with lightweight aluminum body parts right from the factory. The Special Purpose Equipment package consisted of aluminum front and rear bumpers and brackets, front fenders, inner fenders, and hood. An aluminum radiator that had been designed for Pontiac's stock car racing program was also made available.

The Super Duty 389 for 1961 featured the same beefy cylinder block and rotating assembly, an improved camshaft (McKellar #8), larger exhaust passages in the cylinder heads, twin outlet exhaust manifolds, deep-groove engine pulleys, and three Rochester 2-barrel carburetors mounted on an aluminum intake manifold. Horsepower was rated at a very conservative 363.

The Royal Pontiac team fielded two cars in 1961, a lightweight 4-speed Catalina bubble top piloted by Jim Wangers and an all-steel automatic transmission version driven by Winston Brown. Unfortunately, they were denied a shot to follow-up on the previous year's successes at the NHRA Nationals when both were disqualified for participating in unauthorized testing on local streets the night before eliminations.

Pontiac claimed victory at the Nationals just the same, as Hayden Proffitt took home the win in the newly formed Optional/Super Stock class (for cars with limited production factory options such as lightweight parts) with his Mickey Thompson–prepared Catalina, defeating Don Nicholson's Chevy in the final round with the best elapsed time recorded by a Super/Stock class car to date at 12.55 seconds. Arnie Beswick's all-steel Catalina copped Super/Stock class honors in an all-Pontiac sweep of the top stock categories, only to be disqualified due to a disputed over-bore of the engine's cylinder bores. Beswick was also a big winner at the NASCAR Winternationals in Daytona Beach, Florida, posting a best elapsed time of 13.78 seconds at 104 mph on his way to winning both the Super/Stock class and Super/Stock Eliminator titles.

Pontiacs dominated the NASCAR Grand National Stock car series in 1961 eclipsing the efforts of all other brands by scoring 30 wins.

Pontiac closed out a successful 1961 racing season with the introduction of a bigger, more powerful version of the Super Duty V-8. An increase in bore size to 4.09 inches and in stroke to 4.00 inches brought displacement up to 421 ci. Mickey Thompson–supplied pistons bumped compression to 11.0:1, a McKeller #10 camshaft bumped undercut valves, and a new intake manifold mounted two Carter 4-barrel carburetors in place of the previous 2-barrel Rochesters. Horsepower was rated at 405 and the engine was listed as a dealer-installed option for competition purposes.

It is estimated that just over 160 cars received the 421 in 1961, with most being placed into the hands of factory-supported racers. The prospects for a successful 1962 racing season for the Pontiac teams looked good.

Ford, 1960

DEARBORN BUILDS ITS FIRST DEDICATED HIGH-PERFORMANCE ENGINE.

Ford did a couple of things in 1960 that went a long way toward getting the company back into the performance business that it had abandoned in mid-1957. First, Ford introduced a restyled car line, and with it came the model known as the Starliner. Based on the Galaxie, the Starliner featured a beautifully styled roofline that gave the car a streamlined look.

Ford made both major styling and performance changes with the introduction of its 1960 car line. A new model, the Starliner, sported a sweptback roof design and unique badging. Ford also began to show an interest in stock car racing for the first time since mid-1957, using performance subcontractor Holman-Moody to prepare factory-supported cars.

While the interior of this 1960 Ford Starliner is well appointed, one of the biggest detriments to the car's performance was its steering-column-mounted shift linkage. Also, the only manual transmissions available from Ford in 1960 were 3-speeds, putting them at a disadvantage against other manufacturers' cars equipped with 4-speed transmissions and floor-mounted shifters.

Ford carried the Starliner model into 1961 and increased the displacement of the FE engine series to 390 ci by virtue of a 4.05-inch bore and 3.78-inch stroke. This step up in displacement went a long way toward keeping pace with the performance advances being made by rivals General Motors and Chrysler. (Photo Courtesy Zach Straits)

Having introduced the FE (Ford-Edsel) engine series in 1958, Ford used it as the basis for its first dedicated high-performance engine in 1960. With 352 ci of displacement, a specially cast cylinder block, 10.6:1 compression, solid lifter camshaft, improved cylinder heads, Holley 4-barrel carburetor, open-element air filter, aluminum intake manifold, dual-point distributor, and free-flowing cast-iron exhaust headers, the engine was rated at 360 hp.

Second, and perhaps most important, Ford engineers designed a dedicated high-performance engine based on the FE series that had been introduced in 1958. To complement the basic 352-ci FE cylinder block, inherently strong by virtue of a deep skirted design, the folks at Ford added a high nodular iron crankshaft, mechanical lifter cam, improved cylinder heads (that bumped the compression ratio to 10.6 to 1), an aluminum intake manifold mounting a Holley 4-barrel carburetor, a mechanical advance dual-point ignition, and free flowing, header style, exhaust manifolds. Backed by a heavy-duty 3-speed manual transmission, the high-performance 352 was rated at 360 hp and was available in all full-size Ford models with the exception of the station wagon.

While stock car racers opted for the aerodynamic Starliner body style, drag racers often preferred the lightest model available, which was the base Fairlane two-door sedan. In spite of being hampered by the lack of a 4-speed transmission and bulky column-shift linkage, the new high-performance Fords made themselves known on the streets and dragstrips of America. Proving that the company was interested in drag racing on a corporate level, Dave Evans of the Performance and Economy Division at Ford had a high-performance 352 Starliner prepared by his Experimental Garage Team. He then generated internal documents indicating that the car was on lease to an individual (a drag racer who evaluated the car in competition) and by doing so insulated the factory from any association with the effort.

The sloping roofline of the Starliner not only looked pleasing, it also provided improved aerodynamics and, along with the increase in engine displacement/horsepower, allowed Ford to become more competitive in stock car racing during the 1961 season. Company support of racing, although not overt, seemed to be gaining momentum. (Photo Courtesy Zach Straits)

Perhaps the best news performance-wise to come out of Ford for 1961 was the announcement that the BorgWarner T-10 4-speed transmission with floor-mounted shift linkage became available for dealer installation partway through the model year. Until the release of the 4-speed, Fords had been handicapped on the dragstrip by its 3-speed manual box and balky column-mounted shift linkage. (Photo Courtesy Zach Straits)

Along with increasing the maximum available displacement of the FE engine from 352 to 390 ci, in 1961 Ford again cast special high-performance cylinder blocks and heads. The high-performance 390 had beefier connecting rods, 10.5:1 compression, a solid lifter camshaft, dual-point ignition, and free-flowing cast-iron exhaust manifolds. Two versions of the engine were offered. One, which mounted a single Holley 4-barrel carburetor on an aluminum intake manifold, developed a rated 375 hp. The other, with three Holley 2-barrel carburetors on top, was rated at 401 hp. Cars competing in NASCAR stock car racing were limited to one carburetor, but the multi-carb version saw action at many dragstrips and delivered Ford numerous victories. (Photo Courtesy Zach Straits)

Ford was testing the waters but did not jump into the deep end of the pool for some time. In the meantime, some recognized the drag racing potential in Ford's new engine, and racers such as Californian Gas Ronda were making a name for themselves, and Ford, on dragstrips around the country. Thanks to the new engine and aerodynamic Starliner roofline combination, NASCAR teams, including Ford stalwarts Holman & Moody and the Wood Brothers, began to bring Ford to the forefront of stock car racing in 1960, where they scored the greatest number of victories by any manufacturer that year with 16.

Ford, 1961

A BIGGER, MORE POWERFUL FE ENGINE MAKES ITS DEBUT.

The year 1961 saw an increase in displacement for the FE-series Ford engine, which grew from 352 to 390 ci by virtue of an increase in cylinder bore size to 4.05 inches and a longer stroke of 3.78 inches. Once again Ford cast special high-performance cylinder blocks for the 390, as it had done for the 1960 352. A solid lifter camshaft, 10.5:1 compression, an aluminum intake manifold mounting a Holley 4-barrel carburetor, and special exhaust manifolds gave the high-performance 390 a horsepower rating of 375.

Each high-performance 390 Ford for 1961 came with a brochure that contained the part numbers of special service engine and chassis components available from Ford dealers informing the buyer, "Your new 390 High-Performance Special is the finest expression of Ford engineering. An unbeatable combination of blazing acceleration and safety, designed for the very ultimate in fast, confident motoring. We hope this booklet will better acquaint you with your new car and its components and assist you in the preparation of your vehicle for various supervised acceleration and drag racing trials, should you decide to participate in such activity."

In an effort to keep up with the competition, Ford introduced an optional three 2-barrel induction system that was advertised to deliver 401 hp just prior to the NHRA Winternationals. It was not until late in the model year, however, that Ford was able to strike a deal with BorgWarner to obtain a 4-speed transmission (listed as available for dealer installation). So, for most of the season Ford's drag racing efforts were hampered by a balky, column-shifted, 3-speed box, as it had been in 1960. In spite of this, rising stars in the Ford ranks such as Gas Ronda, Les Ritchey, Dick Brannan, Phil Bonner, and many others put Ford in the winner's circle on the dragstrip.

Of particular note was the fact that at the Winternationals Les Ritchey had run an elapsed time with his 3-speed 390 Ford that was quicker than the time recorded by eventual Super/Stock class winner Dyno Don Nicholson's 409 Chevy. Don Martin, driving for Ed Martin Ford, gave Ford a drag racing title in 1961 by taking home the class win in O/SSA (Optional Super Stock Automatic) at the NASCAR Nationals.

Thanks to the new, bigger displacement engine, Ford teams scored seven NASCAR stock car wins in 1961, the majority of which were delivered by a rising star out of Illinois named Fred Lorenzen.

Dodge and Plymouth, 1960

SONORAMIC IS THE NAME AND PERFORMANCE IS THE GAME.

Chrysler Corporation took several leaps forward in 1960 with the introduction of unitized construction, which replaced the previous perimeter frame, the optional TorqueFlite automatic transmission, and a revolutionary new performance intake manifold design. Dodge continued the D-500 performance option for 1960, offering both 361- and 383-ci versions. The 361 produced an advertised horsepower of 310 at 4,800 rpm with 435 ft-lbs of torque at 2,800. The top of the line was the 383-ci version with 330 hp at 4,800 rpm and 460 ft-lbs of torque at 2,800.

While Chrysler's Dodge line had shed its tailfins at the end of the 1959 model year, Plymouth carried the look into 1960. The top of the Plymouth line that year was once again the Fury. Miles of chrome, special badging, front fender covers, top, and trunk-mounted false spare wheel painted in contrasting colors to the body set the Fury apart from the rest of the Plymouth models that year. (Photo Courtesy Greg Cook)

The 1960 Plymouth line sported tall tailfins (vertical stabilizers, according to Plymouth's ad department), which by this time were becoming a dated look. The 1961 models underwent a radical redesign that is best described as one you either loved or hated. And 1961 was also the final year for a full-perimeter frame for the Plymouth and Dodge lines. (Photo Courtesy Greg Cook)

The feature that gave both D-500 options their punch was a unique ram-induction intake manifold mounting two 4-barrel carburetors. The manifold was designed to take advantage of the air pulsation within the manifold caused by the opening and closing of the intake valves. In a conventional intake design, this pressure wave bounces back and forth, creating a disruption in the air-fuel mixture. The ram manifold is "tuned like a pipe

The 1960 Plymouth Fury had one of the most visually attractive interiors of any American car that year. The Fury's outstanding 3-speed TorqueFlite automatic transmission was controlled by a bank of pushbuttons located on the instrument panel to the left of the steering column. (Photo Courtesy Greg Cook)

organ" to move the pressure wave away from the intake valve when it is closed and toward it when it opens, creating the "ram effect."

Plymouth used the same design on its optional engines, calling it the Sonoramic Commando. The lightest models of the Dodge and Plymouth for 1960 were the Phoenix and Savoy, respectively, and both weighed approximately 3,300 pounds.

Perhaps the biggest thing to happen from a street/strip performance standpoint from the Chrysler camp in 1960 came from the formation of a group of 20 to 25 performance-minded Dodge engineers known as the Ramchargers. The combination of these hot rodders, Chrysler's advertising department, and a company that understood the value of how winning races resulted in increased sales continued to pay dividends for more than a decade. While still behind their cousins at Dodge, the Plymouth Division was able to take full advantage of company-wide performance gains. Within two short years the division received its own version of the Ramchargers team.

Plymouth scored six victories on the NASCAR circuit in 1960; Dodge claimed just one. Racing veteran Lee Petty and his son Richard were now carrying the banner for Plymouth in what became a long and successful relationship for both.

Dodge and Plymouth, 1961

Cutting-edge styling combines with performance.

The new model year saw both the Plymouth and Dodge lines receive radical styling redesigns. On the powertrain front, the offerings remained unchanged from 1960. Both model lines lost a little weight, which equated to better performance, and the Ramchargers Dodge team began to come into their own, fielding a car that proved to be more than competitive against the Fords, Pontiacs, and Chevrolets that year.

At the 1961 NHRA Nationals, a 1960 Plymouth driven by Ray Christian took home the A/SA class victory and Frank Dade's Dodge took the A/Stock crown with an elapsed time of 14.51 seconds at 98.90 mph. At the NASCAR Winternational drag races in Daytona Beach, Florida, Grayson McClure wheeled his D-500-powered 1960 Dodge to a win in the S/SA automatic class.

The father-and-son team of Lee and Richard Petty gave Plymouth three NASCAR series wins in 1961. Buck Baker brought a 1961 Chrysler to victory lane for the only other corporate win that season.

The top-performing engine available from both Plymouth and Dodge for the 1960–1961 model years was the 330-hp 383 B-block V-8. Its unique cross-ram intake manifold mounting two Carter AFB 4-barrel carburetors developed 460 ft-lbs of torque. Dodge called this option the D-500 engine, as it had in previous years, while Plymouth called its version the Sonoramic Commando, a reference to the engineering theory of how the long ram intake manifold worked. The long ram intake manifold produced power in the mid-RPM range and was not considered particularly effective for drag racing. Chrysler corrected this shortcoming by 1962.

CHAPTER 3

1962–1963: DETROIT GOES DRAG RACING IN A BIG WAY

With the onslaught of new models and packages being developed in Detroit, the NHRA had to adjust classes yet again to keep pace. For 1962, the NHRA decided to drop the Optional/Super Stock class, replacing it with Super/Super Stock to cover the limited production but nonetheless available factory options such as lightweight body components and horsepower-adding parts. Super/Stock remained in place to provide the top cars from the previous years and those not equipped with the latest factory goodies a place to compete.

Chevy's 409 came into its own in 1962 and cars so equipped received badging to tell the world what lurked between the fenders of that particular Impala, Bel Air, or Biscayne. The engine series received a huge boost in popularity when pop music group The Beach Boys released its hit song titled "409," which spoke of saving nickels and dimes to buy a "brand-new 409." (Photo Courtesy CarTech Archive)

To support the latest trend of stuffing the biggest performing engine into a manufacturer's smallest body in extremely limited numbers, the NHRA developed Factory/Experimental, a class that became wildly popular with fans and led to even more radical combinations from manufacturers.

Chevrolet, 1962

CHEVY RACING TEAMS RIDE HIGH UNTIL A CORPORATE DECISION PULLS THE PLUG.

The 409 became even better in 1962 as Chevrolet achieved one horsepower per ci in the top powerplant, thanks to improved cylinder heads with improved intake ports and larger 2.20-inch intake and 1.70-inch exhaust valves. The shape of the piston dome was revised to increase the compression ratio to 11.4:1, and engine internals were strengthened to deal with the extra horsepower. Two Carter AFB 4-barrel carburetors fed fuel to the hungry 409 via a dual-plane aluminum intake manifold. These early-year improvements were quickly followed with a GM service package designed to aid high-RPM breathing in the 409, consisting of an improved-profile solid lifter camshaft (.480-inch lift, 322-degree duration), stiffer valve-springs, and improved exhaust manifolds.

Many of those who later became top names in Super Stock and Factory Experimental drag racing, such as Don Nicholson, Hubert Platt, Butch Leal, Ronnie Sox, Dick Harrell, and Dave Strickler, first gained national prominence behind the wheel of 409-powered Chevys in 1962. Although Hayden Proffitt's Pontiac claimed victory in the SS/S class at the 1962 Winternationals, the two cars that faced off in the final for Top Stock Eliminator were the 409 Chevys of Don Nicholson and Dave Strickler, with Nicholson taking home the win for the second straight year.

Chevrolet also climbed on the Factory Experimental bandwagon in 1962 by producing a dealer-available kit to upgrade the new compact model Chevy II from standard 4- or 6-cylinder power to the 327 small-block V-8. A four-door version of the Chevy II, powered by a fuel-injected Corvette engine, was in competition at the NHRA Winternationals, where it fell victim to the Mickey Thompson 421 Tempest.

A second Chevy II, a station wagon, was prepared and entered by Don Nicholson under sponsorship from Steve's Chevrolet. The added weight of the station wagon dropped the car into the B/Factory Experimental class, where Nicholson took advantage of the additional traction provided by the longer rear axle overhang to bring home the class win with an elapsed time of 12.55 seconds at 108.96 mph.

Californian Tom Sturm collected gold in the C/FX class with his full-size Chevy, which also used a fuel-injected 327 for power. Sturm went on to win the 1962 NHRA Championship with this car.

The lightest 409 offering from Chevrolet in 1962 was the Biscayne, and drag racers took full advantage of it because creature comforts and additional trim only resulted in slower elapsed times. The Tom Jacobson 409 Biscayne was dealer sponsored and had the additional advantage of being prepared by Hayden Proffitt, one of the top Chevy men in the nation. (Photo Courtesy CarTech Archive)

The 409 for 1962 stepped up in the power department thanks to 11.0:1 compression, and improved cylinder heads and camshaft. With a single Carter AFB 4-barrel carburetor, the engine was rated at 380 hp while the dual 4-barrel 409 produced one horsepower per cubic inch with 409 at 6,000 rpm and 420 ft-lbs of torque at 4,000 rpm.

Following the trend set by the competition, in August 1962, Chevrolet introduced a lightweight body kit consisting of aluminum fenders, inner fender panels, and hood, and yet another engine upgrade (the Mark 1) for the 409, which included raised port cylinder heads, a two-piece intake manifold, and revised piston domes that provided more compression. A 409 with this upgrade was rated at 425 hp, and while the number of cars

The Chevy Bel Air model, affectionately known as the bubble top, first released as a 1961 model, continued to be one of the most popular choices with performance-minded buyers for 1962. This was particularly true when the car was equipped with a 409.

Chevy built just a handful of cars with aluminum body panels in 1962, with others being retrofitted with the parts via the dealer parts network by independent racers. The Zintsmaster Chevy Impala from Kokomo, Indiana, was one of the factory-built cars. (Photo Courtesy Gary Atkins)

equipped with the lightweight components and new engine combination was rare with only 12 to 18 cars built by the factory, those produced were put to good use in the B/FX class by top drivers.

The majority of Chevy drivers stayed in S/SS class competition, and at the 1962 NHRA Nationals, the class runoff came down to Hayden Proffitt versus Dave Strickler, with Strickler getting the win at 12.83 to 12.97. Proffitt ultimately went on to win Top Stock Eliminator, stopping Jim Thornton in the Ramchargers S/SA Dodge in the final.

Chevy teams scored 11 victories in NASCAR competition during 1962, with the majority of the wins being delivered by drivers Rex White and Ned Jarrett. The Chevy teams, along with those of Chrysler and Ford, pretty much lived in the shadow of the series-dominant Pontiacs in 1962.

Chevy's sports car, the Corvette, received the newly introduced 327-ci small-block V-8 that was based on the original 265/283, and when equipped with fuel injection, it had a horsepower rating of 360. *Hot Rod* tested a "fuelie" Corvette, equipped with a 3.42-ratio rear and 4-speed transmission, posting 0–60 times of 5.9 seconds and a 14.12-second time at a 103.98-mph quarter-mile pass.

Proffitt and other top Chevy drag racers in 1962 squeezed more horsepower out of their 409s by replacing the factory air cleaner with a type that flowed more air. This one allows duct hoses to be attached to bring in cooler outside air during match races and in classes that allowed such modifications.

The interior of this 409-powered 1962 Bel Air shows that the buyer was interested in nothing but performance, as evidenced by the radio and heater delete and the addition of aftermarket tachometer, gauges, Hurst shifter, and, of course, seat belts, which were required to run the car in drag races.

Outwardly the 409 engine that powered Strickler's 62 Bel Air looked little different from any other drag racing that year, except for the tubular steel exhaust headers custom fabricated by Jere Stahl. But this engine had been prepared by the master, Bill Jenkins, and that, along with Strickler's prowess as a driver, made this car a winner.

Strickler and Jenkins were the recipients of one of the 50 factory lightweight Impalas powered by the Z-11 427 engine in 1963. Strickler took this car to victory in the AFX class and Little Eliminator category at the NHRA Nationals. It also realized much success as a match racer, winning 98 percent of its matches during the 1963 season. (Photo Courtesy Bob Wenzelburger)

Another very successful 1963 Z-11 Chevy was the Ronnie Sox–prepared Good Ole Mr. Wilson car of Larry Wilson, who raced this car in southern-style "run what ya brung" match races into the 1965 season. (Photo Courtesy Hank Gabbert)

As was the style at the time, Larry Wilson made up for the lack of tire technology by fabricating and installing longer than average traction bars in an effort to shift the Z-11's center of gravity and gain more traction off the starting line. (Photo Courtesy Hank Gabbert)

New York racer Bill Lagana made his mark in drag racing with a Z-11 Impala, and his original mount has now been restored to as-delivered condition. As with most of the factory-built lightweight drag cars of the time, little in its outward appearance gave any indication of the car's potential for brutal acceleration. The Z-11 cars did not even have badging to identify the engine size.

A look inside a 1963 Z-11 Impala's spartan interior reveals the factory-deleted radio and heater, standard bench front seat, factory tachometer but no other gauges to monitor the engine, and an anemic-looking factory shift lever, which drag racers soon replaced with a Hurst unit.

Although it is based on the 409 engine series, the Z-11 was quite a different beast in many ways. The Z-11 cylinder block had a special casting number. The crankshaft differed from the 409 by virtue of a 3.64-inch stroke. It had a specially ground camshaft, high-port 409 cylinder heads, an aluminum water pump, and a two-piece aluminum intake manifold. (Photo Courtesy Hank Gabbert)

The Z-11 engine also used two Carter AFB 4-barrel carburetors with larger venturis (higher-CFM airflow) than those on the 409 to feed the additional cubic inches and aid in the development of the engine's 430 advertised horsepower. (Photo Courtesy Hank Gabbert)

Z-11 Chevys had a unique air-cleaner arrangement, which ducted the cooler high-pressure outside air that accumulated at the base of the windshield into the carburetors for a ram air effect.

Chevrolet, 1963

Z-11 AND "MYSTERY" ENGINES CAUSE QUITE A COMMOTION.

RPO in GM jargon stands for Regular Production Option; the ultimate RPO available to Chevy racers for 1963 was designated Z-11. For the somewhat hefty additional cost over the base 1963 Chevy Impala of $1,237.40, the buyer received the Special Performance Package, consisting of 4-speed transmission, metallic brake shoes, Posi-Traction rear axle, aluminum fenders, gravel shield, fan shroud, bumpers, and hood. Deleting the radio, heater, and sound deadener made the Impala weigh 3,345 pounds, nearly 400 pounds lighter than the production version of the Impala.

The biggest bang for your buck came from the 430-hp, 427-ci engine that powered the Z-11. While based on the 409, the Z-11 engine block had a "QM" stamping that set it apart. The block shared its 4.31-inch bore size with the 409 but used a different crankshaft with a 3.65-inch stroke.

The engine featured its own special camshaft (.556-inch lift, 325 degrees of duration), high-port 409 cylinder heads, a unique two-piece intake manifold mounting two Carter AFB 4-barrel carburetors, an aluminum water pump, and a unique air cleaner designed to duct cool air from the base of the

car's windshield directly into the carburetors. With standard dragstrip modifications such as headers, deeper rear-end gears, a performance tune-up, cheater slicks, and an experienced driver, the Z-11 Impala could stop the quarter-mile clocks in the low-12-second range at 115 mph.

With just 50 produced, the Z-11 Chevys were first relegated by the NHRA to the short-lived Limited/Production class at the Winternationals, where the winning car was found to be illegal, and later to A/Factory Experimental, where it faced some very stiff competition.

Some of the nation's top Chevy racers received the new Z-11 cars and immediately became a force to be reckoned with. Along with winning more than 90 percent of his match races that year, Dave Strickler took home gold in the A/Factory Experimental class at the NHRA Nationals, with his Z-11 recording a 12.17-second elapsed time at 118.11 mph, and the Little Eliminator title with a 12.10 at 126.16 mph. "Dyno Don" Nicholson, Ronnie Sox, Hubert Platt, Butch Leal, and other top-name drivers who went on to great success in drag racing, all made their mark behind the wheel of 1963 Z-11 Chevy Impalas.

Often confused with the Z-11 427 engine is a second powerplant developed by Chevrolet in 1963, the Mark III, better known as the "Mystery V-8." This engine series, which gave rise to the 396/427 big-block V-8 that was introduced in 1965 bore no resemblance to the 409, 427 Z-11 engine at all. While the earlier W series engines featured a cylinder block angle that allowed for the combustion chambers to be at the top of the cylinder bores, the new engine used a conventional 90-degree bore-to-deck surface, which allowed for the combustion chambers to be in the cylinder heads. The cylinder heads were also completely different in design, with the Mark III having a splayed-valve arrangement and equally spaced exhaust ports.

The few similarities between the two engines are the bore size, connecting rods, and crankshaft. A newly designed 180-degree aluminum intake manifold mounted a single Holley 4-barrel carburetor and free-flowing cast-iron exhaust manifolds expelled burnt gases. Horsepower was estimated to be more than 500.

The biggest mystery surrounding the new engine was probably how Chevrolet convinced NASCAR to allow it to be used in competition at all. It was immediately announced that this engine was not available to the public and thus not a production option offered in any Chevrolet model that year. Availability aside, NASCAR did allow 1963 Chevys to compete with the Mark III engine, and factory drivers, while experiencing some reliability problems with the new design, scored eight series victories and set numerous track records along the way.

Chevrolet did a radical redesign of the Corvette for 1963, naming it the Stingray after the Ray Brock/Bill Mitchell/Larry Shinoda–designed Corvette concept car of 1957. The new look was an immediate success and the one-year-only split-back window on the hardtop made it an icon for collectors.

Four versions of the 327-ci small-block V-8 were available to power the new Sting Ray, along with three transmission choices. The top-performing engines for 1963 were the single 4-barrel, 11.25:1-compression, solid lifter camshaft 340-hp model and the 360-hp version that differed from the 340-hp engine only in that it was fuel injected. These powertrain choices were the same as on the previous Corvette, but the new Sting Ray gained performance due to a decrease in curb weight to 3,150 pounds.

When General Motors officially ended corporate support for racing midyear in 1963, the future looked pretty dim, but a clever performance strategy revealed itself over the next few years that proved to be more than effective while saving the company millions when compared to what the competition spent on racing programs.

Pontiac, 1962

A SUPER YEAR FOR THE SUPER DUTY.

The company that pioneered lightweight components as a means of getting full-size cars down the dragstrip quicker came out of the gate with guns blazing in 1962. Ordering the Catalina Super Stock package set the buyer back $1,334, with an additional $234 to upgrade from the standard 3-speed manual transmission to the more desirable 4-speed. The addition of aluminum front-end sheet metal shaved 159 pounds off the Catalina's 3,700-pound curb weight. But the heart and soul of the Pontiac performance program for 1962 was the Super Duty 421. Delivered from the factory with an NHRA-allowed .030 overbore of the cylinders, the engines were actually 428 ci in displacement.

On top of this, the Super Duty was stuffed with all the best parts: a forged-steel crankshaft, heavy-duty connecting rods, forged aluminum Mickey Thompson 11.0:1 compression pistons, a McKellar #10 camshaft, cylinder heads with undercut 1.92-inch intake, 1.66-inch exhaust valves, 1.65 ratio rocker arms, heavy-duty oil pump, and a 6-quart oil pan. Factory blueprinted with clearances on the high side of the specification, this formidable package was topped by two Carter AFB 4-barrel carburetors sitting on an aluminum intake manifold. Exhaust gases were expelled through high-flowing manifolds featuring cutouts that allowed the exhaust system to be bypassed and opened for competition. Ignition chores were trusted to a full centrifugal advance dual-point distributor.

Conservatively rated at 405 hp, with 605 ft-lbs of torque, the Super Duty 421 proved that Pontiac was dedicated to remaining ahead of the competition. Further proof was found in the release of an improved cylinder head (PN 541127) later in the year. These heads had larger valves (2.02-inch intake and 1.96-inch exhaust), and the compression ratio was increased to 12.5:1.

With Super Duty power on tap, Pontiac drivers went on the warpath on the dragstrip with Jim Wangers, Hayden Proffitt, Arlen Vanke, Arnie

Pontiac followed the great styling and performance of its 1961 models with more of the same in 1962. The Catalina was stylish, sporty, and one of the most capable performance cars of its day.

Beswick, Howard Maseles, and Harold Ramsey gaining national prominence for the brand. Hayden Proffitt drove a Mickey Thompson–prepared Catalina to victory in the S/SS class with an elapsed time of 12.75 seconds at 111.94 mph. Jess Tyree wheeled another Thompson Pontiac to the Super/ Stock class win with a 13.11 at 108.95 mph, making it a clean sweep for Pontiac in the top stock classes at the 1962 NHRA Winternationals. Proffitt also claimed the California State Super Stock Championship with a win over the Ford of Gas Ronda.

You would never guess from looking at the interior of this 1962 Catalina that it was not at the top of the Pontiac line that year. Pontiac had adopted the tri-color interior design several years before, and it carried over well on the 1962 models.

While the Super Duty 421-ci engine offered the most horsepower for 1962, the Tri-Power 389 cars were more numerous and could hold their own in most performance contests. The owner of this 1962 Catalina ditched the huge, unattractive factory air cleaner for three individual open-element air cleaners as seen on later GTOs.

The lightest full-size production car body style available from Pontiac in 1963 was the Catalina two-door sedan. This particular Catalina is even lighter yet, thanks to the addition of optional aluminum bumpers and brackets, fenders, inner fender liners, hood, and radiator supports. Seam sealer and sound deadener were also deleted from this special-order vehicle that was constructed with drag racing in mind.

The 1962 Super Duty Pontiacs may have been bumped from the Super/Stock class after the 1962 season and replaced by newer, more improved models, but that didn't mean they were no longer competitive. This Catalina continued to be campaigned successfully in the NHRA A/Stock class for a number of years. (Photo Courtesy Gary Atkins)

The Catalina's interior is strictly "no frills" with its bench seat, deleted radio, heater, and two-spoke base model steering wheel. Because this car was destined for the dragstrip, the owner added an aftermarket tachometer and gauges to monitor vital engine functions and a Hurst Competition Plus shifter for more positive gear selection in the T-10 4-speed transmission.

By the running of the NHRA Nationals held on Labor Day weekend, the Chevy, Ford, and Chrysler teams had begun, to some extent, to catch up. Proffitt had switched to Chevrolet, taking home the Super/Super Stock class win over the similar Chevrolet of Dave Strickler, but the Super/Stock class runoff was an all-Pontiac affair, with Bill Sassee winning over Bob Harrop's 1961 Batwing Catalina with a 13.48 at 108.43 mph. Carol Cox upset the Plymouths and Dodges that had become the cars to beat in the top automatic transmission classes as she took home the Super/Stock Automatic trophy with a 13.69 at 106.25 mph. In like fashion, Ralph Hardt wheeled his Pontiac to victory in the A/Stock Automatic class with a 14.43 at 98.79 mph, and Larry Leonard copped the B/Stock Automatic crown with his 1961 Catalina with a sub-national record blast of 14.51 seconds.

Already a drag racing legend, and Pontiac's top innovator, Mickey Thompson no doubt saw the time fast approaching when the full-size Pontiacs would no longer be competitive against the lighter cars offered by the competition, particularly the Chrysler products with their unitized construction. In true hot rodding fashion, Thompson and the Royal Pontiac team set out to offset any weight deficit by stuffing Pontiac's biggest engine, the Super Duty 421, into their smallest production vehicle, the compact Tempest. This proved to be a perfect fit for the Factory Experimental class.

While the Tempest was a compact model, there was ample room in the engine compartment for the largest V-8, thanks to the fact that the car's standard powerplant was a 4-cylinder derived by cutting the 389-ci V-8 in half down the middle. The one drawback to the design was that the car used a transaxle (differential and transmission in combination). Thompson remedied this situation by converting his Tempest to a conventional driveline featuring a 3-speed manual transmission connected to a narrowed conventional rear-axle assembly from a Catalina. Combining the Tempest's curb weight of 2,785 pounds with a 421 Super Duty engine resulted in what *Hot Rod* called "Thompson's terrible Tempest" in a 1962 article.

Hayden Proffitt wheeled the Tempest to the FX/A class win at the 1962 NHRA Winternationals (NHRA later changed the class designation to A/FX) recording low-12-second elapsed times. Proffitt defeated a unique Chevy entry, a 1962 Chevy II four-door powered by a 360-hp Corvette engine. At the only other NHRA national event that year, the Nationals, Lloyd Cox drove the Thompson entry to victory once again.

With 22 wins, 1962 was again a big year for Pontiac on the NASCAR circuit, which unbeknownst to them, was their last successful year in the series until the advent of the modern corporate engine era. Glen "Fireball" Roberts continued to deliver wins for Pontiac and Joe Weatherly took home the NASCAR series championship.

On the USAC stock car circuit, driver Paul Goldsmith delivered season champion honors to Pontiac. Pontiac Catalinas, powered by the 421-ci Super Duty engine and prepared for competition by legends of the NASCAR racing series such as Cotton Owens, Bud Moore, Ray Nichels, and Smokey Yunick, proved to be nearly invincible.

The king of all Pontiac engines for 1963, the Super Duty 421 (officially known as the Trophy 425-A), provides the power to move this 3,600-pound beast from point A to point B in the quickest possible fashion. This particular SD 421 has been fitted with the rare factory high-rise, tunnel-ram aluminum intake manifold known to racers as the "bath tub" due to its large plenum. By design it provided additional horsepower to the engine at high RPM.

The rarest of the 1963 Pontiacs, with just 13 or 14 produced, is the special lightweight Catalina drag car that came to be known as Swiss Cheese Catalinas. These cars were delivered into the hands of factory-backed racers to do battle with similar lightweight cars being fielded by Chevrolet, Ford, Dodge, and Plymouth during the 1963 season.

Since the cars were not built in sufficient numbers to be legal for the Super/Stock class, the NHRA classified them as Factory Experimental. With the addition of some weight, the cars fit nicely into the B/FX class, where Jim Wangers took his Royal Pontiac–prepared car to the class championship and a runner-up spot in Little Eliminator at the 1963 NHRA Nationals.

The only outward indication that this pedestrian-appearing Catalina could be anything out of the ordinary is provided by the 421 emblems that adorn each of the car's aluminum front fenders, which were stamped from even lighter gauge aluminum than those used on the previous year's lightweight cars.

The reason that the special lightweight Catalinas came to be known as Swiss Cheese cars is seen here. In an effort to shed every ounce of unnecessary weight, the bottom section of the frame rails was cut out and large holes were drilled every few inches along the sides. Unfortunately this attempt at losing weight caused structural problems, and most of the frames eventually developed cracks.

Power for the Swiss Cheese factory Super/Stock cars came from a version of the Super Duty 421 that was conservatively rated at 410 hp, as opposed to 405, thanks to an increase in compression ratio to 13.0:1. Actual horsepower numbers for this engine were closer to 500 by most estimates.

A closer look at the Super Duty 421 as delivered in this Swiss Cheese Catalina reveals additional weight saving and horsepower-building tricks such as the larger alternator pulley with an extra-deep groove. This slows its speed, reduces horsepower lost to parasitic drag, and helps keep the fan belt in place during high-RPM operation. The unique, free-flowing, cast aluminum exhaust manifolds helped shed many unwanted pounds from the front of the car. Unfortunately it was soon found that these manifolds had a propensity to melt if the engine was run for long periods of time.

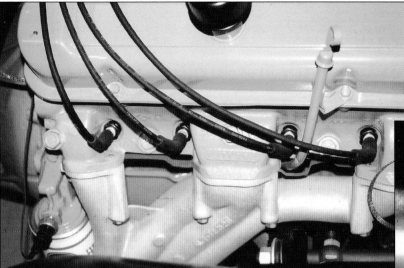

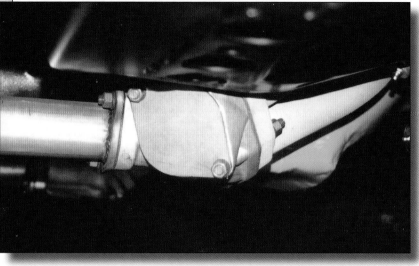

Another unique feature of the Super Duty's aluminum exhaust manifolds were the cutouts at their base. Removal of these caps bypassed the car's exhaust system for drag race use.

In their efforts to shave off every extra pound they could from the Catalina drag cars, Pontiac engineers went so far as to have an aluminum differential case cast to replace the usual cast-iron production part.

To do battle in the NHRA A/Factory Experimental class where the Mickey Thompson and Royal Pontiac–prepared Tempests had done so well the previous year, Pontiac built six special, lightweight SD 421 Tempest coupes as a follow-up for 1963. The Little Chief Tempest was prepared by Union Park Pontiac, one of the brand's top high-performance dealerships in the 1960s, and driven by Harold Ramsey. (Photo Courtesy Bob Wenzelburger)

Power for the A/FX Tempests came from the same 410-hp rated SD 421 that powered the Swiss Cheese Catalina drag cars. With the NHRA allowable .060 overbore, these engines actually displaced 434 ci. (Photo Courtesy Gary Atkins)

The A/FX Tempests and Tempest wagons were true factory light-weight race cars with aluminum front sheet metal and lightweight steel bumpers. The standard bench seat was replaced by two lighter bucket seats and radio; heater sealers and sound deadener were deleted. A floor shift controls the car's unique transaxle.

Arguably the most unique of all the factory-prepared drag cars of 1963 were the six lightweight SD 421-powered Pontiac Tempest station wagons. The theory behind the use of a station wagon for drag racing was that the additional rear overhang in the wagon would aid weight transfer and provide additional traction off the starting line.

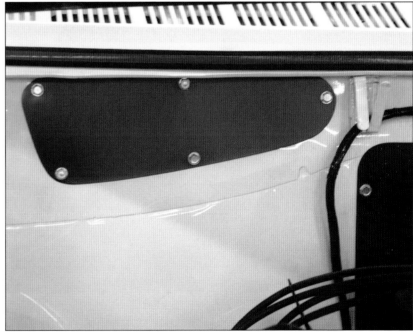

The SD 421 fits nicely between the front fenders of the A/FX Tempest wagon, leaving room for maintenance not found in many racing vehicles. Note the factory block-off plate where the heater box once protruded through the firewall. (Photo Courtesy Steve Savage)

With the access panel removed, the A/FX Tempest's 4-speed transaxle is revealed. A remarkable feat of engineering combined a standard cast-iron front transaxle section that housed the ring and pinion gears with a second aluminum transaxle case that added two additional gears, making the unit a 4-speed. A standard flywheel, clutch, and starter were mated to the rear of the unit and controlled by a hydraulic throw-out bearing. While the clutch pedal is required to move the car initially from that point on, the gears are engaged by manually moving the shift lever as they would be in an automatic transmission equipped with a manual valve body. (Photo Courtesy Steve Savage)

This view of the A/FX Tempest's aluminum hood from the underside shows the Ford truck accessed scoop that became a trademark on Pontiac race cars of the era.

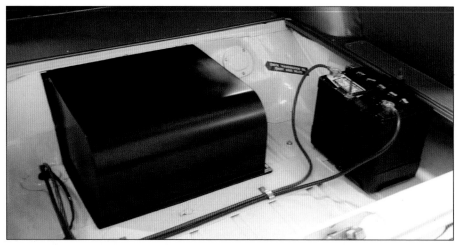

The cargo area in the rear of the A/FX Tempest wagon housed the battery and an access panel that allowed maintenance to be performed on the car's unique 4-speed transaxle, which took the place of a conventional-style transmission.

Pontiac, 1963

AN ALL-OUT EFFORT PRECEDES A BAN ON RACING BY GM BRASS.

Pontiac began the 1963 season with the advantage of not having to enlarge any existing engines or develop a new one to meet the 7-litre (427-ci) displacement limit imposed by the NHRA (Drag racing), NASCAR, and USAC (Stock cars). They already had the Super Duty 421 so all that was left to do was refine what was already a proven winner.

The Super Duty was available in three versions for 1963: a single 4-barrel 12:1 (Stock car) version putting out 390 hp; a dual-quad 12:1 version with 405 advertised horsepower for "limited street use"; and the Grand Daddy of them all, a mounted dual-quad, 13:1 dragstrip killer that was very conservatively rated at 410 hp while it actually made closer to 500, according to estimates.

Pontiac engineers improved the 421 Super Duty cylinder heads for 1963 by increasing the exhaust ports by 8 percent, streamlining the intake ports, and casting a smaller combustion chamber (64 cc versus 66.8 cc minimum in 1962 castings). Racers were given a choice between three McKellar camshafts (#10, #11, and #12), the difference being the RPM that the engine delivered maximum torque.

The dual 4-barrel engines received the Super Duty's signature aluminum exhaust manifolds. Single 4-barrel engines had free-flowing fabricated steel exhaust manifolds because these engines were more likely to be used for stock car racers, where long running times would cause the aluminum manifolds to melt. A transistorized ignition system also became standard equipment on all premium-fuel-burning engines for 1963.

It was obvious that Pontiac planned another no-holds-barred assault on the stock car tracks and dragstrips of America for 1963. In an effort to offset the weight advantage that the Plymouths and Dodges enjoyed on the dragstrip, Pontiac not only offered the weight-saving aluminum front end and bumper package for 1963 but also built a limited number (the accepted number is 14) of special Catalinas to be delivered into the hands of select factory-supported drag racers. These cars became known as Swiss Cheese Catalinas because the factory had drilled more than 100 huge, oblong holes through the inside and outside frame rails after cutting out the bottom rail completely, in an effort to shed pounds from the full-size Pontiac.

Also returning were the aluminum parts first introduced in 1961: hood, fenders, inner fenders, splash pan, radiator support, and front and rear bumpers and their brackets. For 1963 the aluminum parts were stamped from thinner material, making them 10 to 20 percent lighter when compared to the 1962 aluminum pieces, which had provided a weight savings of 159 pounds over the steel parts they replaced. The aluminum exhaust manifolds weighed a svelte 27 pounds when compared to the stock cast-iron manifolds, which tipped the scales at 72 pounds.

Replacing the cast-iron bellhousing with an aluminum version helped remove more excess weight from the front of the car. When equipped with the standard T-85 3-speed transmission, the racer realized some weight savings from an aluminum tail shaft, and when the optional T-10 was ordered, both the case and tail shaft were aluminum, saving 20 pounds over the 3-speed box.

An aluminum differential carrier was also available. The battery was moved to the trunk and mounted over the passenger-side wheel to aid in weight transfer. With all creature comforts deleted (radio, heater, sound deadener, seam sealer, etc.), the big Poncho weighed just over 3,300 pounds, 350 pounds lighter than the 1962 model.

The cars were delivered with suspension modifications for drag racing in place, making them race ready as delivered and capable of mid- to low-12-second quarter-mile elapsed times. NHRA rules at the time relegated the limited production Swiss Cheese Catalinas to Factory/Experimental classes and with the 421-powered Tempests dominating the A/FX ranks, the lightweight Catalina was a natural for the B/FX class after a bit of weight was added where it would do the most good to make it class legal.

Special Catalinas of Jim Wangers and other factory drivers were in great demand for match races (in best two of three, or three of five), pairing two cars from competing brands that were gaining popularity

END OF GM FACTORY PARTICIPATION

In January 1963, General Motors announced that there would be no further factory support of racing. This edict affected the company's Pontiac and Chevrolet Divisions only, as the Buick and Oldsmobile divisions had not participated in organized motorsports since 1959. On its face, considering that the dawn of the 1960s had proven that a strong performance image was a major factor in automobile sales, this decision appeared to be a huge financial blunder, particularly considering the successes of both Chevrolet and Pontiac on the racetracks of America. But if you take into consideration the fact that not only did General Motors continue building high-performance Pontiacs and Chevrolets, it wasn't long before both Oldsmobile and Buick found themselves back in the performance car arena.

As Ford and Chrysler continued to spend large portions of their budget developing and supporting various forms of racing, General Motors continued to develop and build high-performance automobiles and optional parts that could make those who chose their products successful racers on many levels. Looking back over GM's decision many years later, it occurred to me that perhaps the company had not blundered at all but instead had hit upon a great strategy based on deniability.

While both Pontiac and Chevrolet racers suffered in terms of overall numbers of races won against factory-sponsored teams in NASCAR, USAC, and drag racing, General Motors simply pointed out that the company wasn't involved in racing, and when it did win, General Motors could capitalize greatly by bragging that its products could beat the "factory teams," even without corporate support.

At the same time, Chevrolets were the most numerous cars in competition on dragstrips and the company continued to offer showroom-available high-performance cars that could be easily modified with inexpensive and plentiful corporate and aftermarket parts. Chevrolet seemed to suffer very little as a result of the decision.

I had the occasion to ask one of Chevrolet's most successful drag racers, "Dyno Don" Nicholson, about the withdrawal of factory support from General Motors and his ultimate decision to sign on with the fledgling Mercury drag team in 1964. Don indicated that he could have continued to receive "back-door" support from Chevrolet had he stayed but chose Mercury based on a more financially attractive offer at the time.

At one point Ed Cole, executive vice president of the Chevrolet Division, seized the moment when Ford executives announced that they had opened a new test track for the development of racing vehicles. He responded by saying that his company saw fit to spend its money building safer cars for the public. And although General Motors officially stayed out of the racing business for the remainder of the decade and into the next, the company continued to pump out some of the most radical high-performance street cars through its dealer network.

nationwide. Jim Wangers claimed B/FX class honors at the NHRA Nationals with his Royal Pontiac–sponsored Swiss Cheese Catalina posting an elapsed time of 12.59 at 110.83 mph. Wangers later lost to Dave Strickler's Chevy in the Little Eliminator runoff by virtue of a foul start. The all-steel Pontiacs also acquitted themselves well at the 1963 Nationals, with Don Gay bringing home class honors in A/Stock and Bill Abraham copping the A/Stock Automatic crown.

Following Mickey Thompson's and the Royal Pontiac team's successes with 421 Tempests the previous year, Pontiac decided to build a series of cars for the 1963 season to retain dominance in the Factory Experimental classes. The factory produced 12 Tempests with 421 Super Duty power for 1963. Six of these cars were two-door coupes and six were station wagons. Although the station wagon at 3,305 pounds was 200 pounds heavier than the coupe, it was hoped that the additional overhang behind the rear wheels would provide a traction advantage that would offset the weight. The cars were equipped with aluminum front ends, the early-production cars also received aluminum front bumpers, and later cars received acid-dipped steel bumpers.

As expected, the Super Duty Tempests went to the top Pontiac teams, with Arnie Beswick receiving both a coupe and a station wagon. Not to be left out, Arlen Vanke built his own coupe when the factory didn't come through on his behalf. When the cars debuted at the NHRA Winternationals, they did not disappoint. Bill Shrewsberry, driving for Mickey Thompson, won the A/FX class going away with a 12.04 at 116.29, nearly .5 second quicker than his closest competitor. Arnie Beswick later drove his Super Duty Tempest to an 11.89 elapsed time at 123.11 mph and a new NHRA A/FX class record. Beswick continued to race his A/FX Tempest into the 1964 season, competing and winning in the A/Modified Production class.

One of the Super Duty Tempest coupes was delivered to the shop of Ray Nichels in Merrillville, Illinois, where it was prepared for a completely different type of competition. Chassis reinforcement, beefier brakes, oil coolers, a full roll cage, boxed control arms, and heavy-duty springs and shocks were added to make the Tempest a handler, while its lightweight body components were retained. The aluminum exhaust manifolds were replaced by the unique double-stacked production Tempest transaxle that was unique to the Super Duty cars but replaced by many of the drag racers (the doubled two-speed units providing four forward speeds) was retained.

Entered by Pontiac in the 250-mile Challenge Cup race at Daytona International Speedway, the car was driven by top USAC and NASCAR stock car pilot Paul Goldsmith, who promptly put the car on the pole against some of the best racing sports cars in the world, including several Z-06 Corvettes. At the green flag, Goldsmith proved that the Tempest was no fluke as he literally ran away with the race, eventually lapping second-place finisher A. J. Foyt's Corvette twice in the process.

The history of this car from that point became the stuff of legend. It is reported that after dropping out of its next race due to a blown engine,

the car was purchased by the Mercedes-Benz Company and spirited off to Europe, where it could be dissected in an attempt to discover its secrets. Years later when attempting to learn the car's ultimate fate, automotive historians were told that the car had been destroyed.

The future for Pontiac performance looked very bright for the 1963 season until General Motors issued a mandate that essentially cut off any overt support for racing from any of its divisions. Although many Pontiac stalwarts soldiered on, things were never the same.

On the NASCAR circuit, Pontiac's fortunes suffered due to the cessation of factory support as the brand scored just four victories in 1963; three were credited to 1962 series champion Joe Weatherly and one to Buck Baker. This can be at least partially credited to many of the top Pontiac drivers leaving for other factory-supported teams. Weatherly won the 1963 NASCAR Championship, with three of his nine wins in a Pontiac, but he also drove for Mercury and Chrysler during the year, adding to his season point total.

Ford, 1962

STILL PLAYING CATCH-UP IN THE PERFORMANCE MARKET.

Using the catch phrase "The Lively Ones from Ford" to describe the 1962 models, the folks in Dearborn seemed to have grasped the concept of

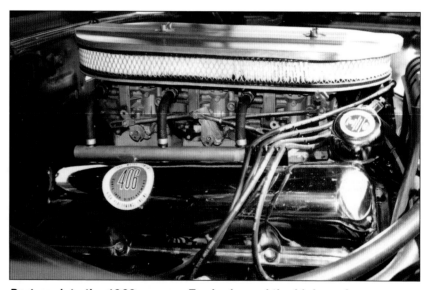

Partway into the 1962 season, Ford released the high-performance 406-ci FE engine to counter increases in displacement by General Motors and Chrysler. With 10.9:1 compression, solid lifter camshaft, and aluminum intake with a Holley 4-barrel carburetor, the engine had 385 advertised horsepower. With three Holley 2-barrel carburetors the horsepower jumped to 405.

Although some of the factory-built lightweight Galaxies in 1962 retained the bench seat, Dick Brannan's car received two bucket seats, which saved additional weight. Block-off plates cover locations where the radio and heater controls would have been.

To squeeze more horsepower from the 406 engines that powered the factory lightweight Galaxie drag cars, the cast aluminum intake manifolds accommodated two Holley 4-barrel carburetors. However, due to the limited production numbers of these special Galaxies, they were forced to run in the NHRA A/Factory Experimental class against the lighter Pontiac Tempests, which had larger engines. Steel versions of the 406 Galaxie fared somewhat better, as they were classified in the Super/Stock class.

Ford kicked off 1963 with the 406 engine as its top performance offering again. With 405 hp on tap, the 406 had little trouble moving a 4,000-pound Galaxie such as this top-of-the-line 500XL convertible, but that wasn't going to cut it on the racetrack and Ford engineers knew it.

appealing to youthful buyers, but in the performance department the company apparently got caught napping. While the competition stepped up their game with cubic inches and/or horsepower advances, Ford began 1962 with the 401-hp 390-ci engine as the top option. That, coupled with the heavy car, put Ford at an immediate disadvantage.

By midyear the company had stepped up with the third dedicated high-performance engine of the FE series, the 406. Using the 3.78-inch stroke of the 390, the newly cast block featured a 4.13-inch bore, 10.9:1 compression, solid lifter camshaft, full centrifugal advance distributor, free-flowing cast-iron exhaust manifolds, and a choice of either a single 4-barrel or three 2-barrel Holley carburetors mounted atop an aluminum intake manifold. Ford rated the single carb version at 385 hp and the triple carb engine at 405. With a 119-inch wheelbase, 209.3-inch overall length, and a dry shipping weight of 3,616 pounds, Ford's Galaxie model tipped the scales at close to, and in some cases more than 4,000 pounds in street trim.

A few months into the 1963 season, Ford unleashed an improved, stronger, and more powerful high-performance FE engine. The engine's displacement had been increased to 427 by virtue of an increase in bore size to 4.23 inches, while the stroke remained at 3.78. The new cylinder block casting featured cross-bolted main bearing caps on #2, #3, and #4, an improvement previously developed for 406 engines running in the NASCAR circuit. The cylinder heads were also improved, along with the exhaust manifolds, which were now more header-like with longer runners. Rated at 410 hp with a single Holley 4-barrel carburetor and 425 with twin Holleys, the 427 quickly put Ford performance on the map.

On a bright note Ford did offer an optional 4-speed manual transmission for the first time. In the negative column, Ford's Equa-loc limited slip differential was too anemic for duty behind the 406, so customers were stuck with an open rear, unless they opted for a dealer-offered Detroit Locker unit. *Car Life* tested a Ford Galaxie with the 406/405 option, 4-speed transmission, and 3.56 open rear. Handicapped by skinny bias-ply tires and an engine that was not yet broken in, the test car still managed a 0–60 time of 6 seconds flat and cleared the quarter-mile clocks in 15.3 seconds at 93 mph.

Longtime Ford racer Les Ritchey's Performance Associates in California prepared several 406 Ford Galaxies that *Hot Rod* reported "showed great promise." Another West Coast Ford ace, Gas Ronda continued his winning ways in 1962 with a new 406 Galaxie finishing runner-up in the California State Super Stock Championship.

Closer to the factory, the folks at Ford had begun to dabble with a couple of Galaxie drag cars, prepared at Ford's Performance and Economy Division, and handled by company test drivers Bill Humphries and Len Richter. But it wasn't until the factory boys got shown the short way home by a young man named Dick Brannan, racing a dealer-prepared Galaxie out of South Bend, Indiana, that Ford's drag racing program really got off the ground. Brannan was on a tear with his *Lively One* 406 Galaxie, and after he defeated many of the top-running Super Stock cars in the nation at Detroit Dragway, Ford offered him the position of Drag Racing Coordinator.

In May 1962, Henry Ford II saw the error of the path that Robert S. McNamara had sent the company down with his signing of the AMA ban on racing in 1957 and "The Deuce," as he was known, announced that Ford was back in the racing business. It was painfully obvious that the full-size Galaxie was at a weight disadvantage against the cars fielded by Chevrolet and Chrysler, so the factory embarked on a program to put a handful of

Not wanting to be last out of the gate for the 1963 drag racing season, Ford re-bodied the majority of the 1962 lightweight Galaxies of its Drag Council members with the new 1963 Galaxie sports roof (also known as the 1963-1/2 body). Production lines were set up to accommodate a run of at least 100 lightweight cars to make the cars legal for NHRA Super/Stock class competition. The 1963 cars were fitted with lighter frames; fiberglass hood, fenders, inner fenders, and deck lid; aluminum bumpers and brackets; and carpet, sound deadener, seam sealer, radio, heater, clock, and spare tire deletes.

Dick Brannan, Ford's Drag Racing Coordinator, had two lightweight Galaxies in 1963. The #823 car, which was re-bodied from his 1962 mount, and the #824, which was a later production line lightweight.

The 1963 Galaxie lightweight raced by Wes Dawson and Jim Brady of Front Royal, Virginia, was one of the just over 100 lightweight cars built at Ford's Norfolk assembly plant. All the production line lightweight Galaxies were painted Corinthian White and had red vinyl interiors. The Dawson and Brady car raced successfully in the eastern United States during the 1963 season.

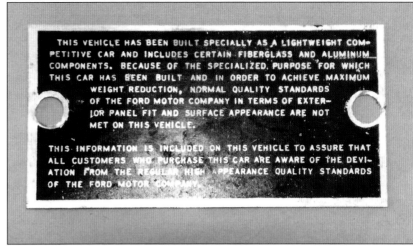

Each lightweight Galaxie had a special disclaimer tag riveted to its glove box door. The disclaimer explains the car's lightweight components and competition purpose. Those who purchased these purpose-built race cars were required to sign an acknowledgment that they would not be used as passenger cars.

Lightweight Galaxies were fitted with front seats supplied for Ford fleet vehicles, such as taxicabs and police cars, by subcontractor Bostrum. Carpet was replaced with a light-gauge rubber mat; radio, heater, clock, and armrests were deleted. The normal padded sun visors found in Galaxies were replaced by a lighter cardboard type used in lesser Ford models.

The next lightest body style in the full-size Ford line for 1963 was the Custom two-door sedan. The 410- and 425-hp versions of the 427 engine were also available in this model, making it a potentially strong competitor in NHRA's A/Stock or B/Stock classes.

Thanks to some employees at Shelby American, love of drag racing the Ford-powered sports car was no longer confined to winning in sports car competitions when they convinced their boss to allow the modification of several Cobras into Drag Snakes, or Dragon Snakes. Soon, the Dragon Snakes were winning class Eliminator titles and setting records across the country. (Photo Courtesy Carl Mentz)

drag cars on a diet and into the hands of select drivers of their newly formed Drag Council.

Ten Galaxie two-door sedans, sans seam sealer, sound deadener, radio, and heater, with 406 engines and 4-speed transmissions (an 11th car was built later) were shipped from the Wayne, Michigan, assembly plant to Ford's high-performance subcontractor Dearborn Steel Tubing Company. There, chassis were lightened through the removal of some bracing, steel fenders and hoods were replaced by fiberglass pieces, and aluminum inner fender panels, front bumpers, and associated brackets were installed. Some of the cars retained their production bench seat while others received lighter bucket seats.

With very little preparation time, after completion the cars were delivered into the hands of Drag Council members for competition at the NHRA Nationals on Labor Day weekend. Due to the low production numbers, the NHRA promptly classified the lightweight Galaxies in the A/Factory Experimental class, where they faced Mickey Thompson's 421 Pontiac Tempests and the 413-powered Dodge Lancer from Chrysler. To counter the disadvantage, some of the lightweights had their steel parts reinstalled to compete in the S/SS class, where they at least had a fighting chance. Brannan's lightweight car was fitted with a 380-ci engine, which put it down into the B/FX class.

A lack of preparation time and mechanical maladies sidelined all the Fords early on, with the exception of Brannan's steel car. By virtue of his performance in the S/SS class, Brannan was selected to be the lone Ford entry in a special eliminator category for the quickest cars in competition.

Heavily outnumbered, Brannan used his driving skills to keep hope alive before being eliminated by the Ramchargers' automatic transmission Dodge.

What could have been a bright spot for Ford at the 1962 Nationals was dashed when the Dearborn Steel Tubing Company's 1962 Galaxie was declared illegal due to shimmed valvesprings after winning the A/Stock class. But if nothing else, Ford learned quite a bit about drag racing from the members of the Drag Council in 1962, and the guys at Dearborn Steel Tubing had begun to dabble in the smaller, lighter car/big engine concept by stuffing a 406 engine backed by an automatic transmission into a 1962 Fairlane body. This car passed into the hands of Rhode Island Ford dealer and proponent of Ford performance, Robert F. Tasca Sr., who had his drag team in limited A/FX class competition with the car.

The extra factory support provided to NASCAR stock car teams didn't pan out as well as expected, as the formal roofline of the 1962 Fords put the cars at an aerodynamic disadvantage when compared to the previous sloping roof of the Starliner model. Ford's products did better in USAC stock car competition, winning the Pikes Peak Hill climb and other events where the boxy roofline wasn't as much of a factor. Indy car driver Troy Ruttman, receiving support from Ford's Lincoln-Mercury Division, put a Mercury stock car back in the winner's circle for the first time in five years with his victories on the USAC circuit.

As a harbinger of things to come in the world of Ford performance, a former sports car racer and visionary named Carroll Shelby, after being turned away by Chevrolet (which already had a performance sports car, thank you), convinced Ford to supply him with engines to mate with an English sports car from AC. Shelby employed a group of California hot rodders who modified the AC to accept a warmed-over 260-ci small-block V-8 that Ford had just introduced to see if they could build a world-class sports car and perhaps a Corvette killer.

Car Life was provided with the car Shelby named the Cobra for testing, and recorded a blistering 13.80 quarter-mile elapsed time at 112 mph on street tires with 3.54 rear-end gearing. Shelby had done what he set out to do, and Ford soon began to reap the benefits.

Ford and Mercury, 1963

THE GLOVES HAVE FINALLY COME OFF WHEN IT COMES TO PERFORMANCE.

Ford looked to expand its horizons across multiple racing venues for 1963. The company took its new 260 V-8 Falcon Sprint to Monte Carlo and topped Europe's best in Rally racing. Ford returned to the Indianapolis 500 and USAC Champ car racing with revolutionary, rear-engine cars using a stock-block V-8; raced to the top of Pikes Peak; and assaulted the USAC and NASCAR stock car tracks with a never-before-seen fervor.

Ford was positioned to become an international racing powerhouse. The area in which Ford seemed to lag behind the other Detroit manufacturers was in the ever-growing sport of drag racing. If ever there was a venue where racing victories equated directly to sales, it was drag racing.

The September 1962 introduction of the new Ford models and engines for 1963 did little to impress the youth market, who eagerly awaited the latest sporty models producing more horsepower than the previous year. While Ford's styling changed for the 1963 model year, the top engine offering at the start was still the 405-hp 406, and it was several months before the company gave performance fans something to be excited about. The good news came several months into the model year with the introduction of a stronger, more powerful version of the FE engine and a new roofline that increased the appeal of Ford's cars to the youth market tenfold.

The hot new offering from Dearborn for 1963 was the 427. Not merely an over-bored 406, the 427 received an improved cylinder block featuring cross-bolted caps on numbers 2, 3, and 4 main bearings. This strengthening came about as a result of improvements made the previous year on 406 engines being used in NASCAR competition.

The 427 was again a dedicated high-performance block with a beefier casting, stronger connecting rods and crankshaft, and no provisions for hydraulic valve lifters. The new engine had a cylinder bore of 4.23 inches, while sharing its 3.78-inch stroke with the 406. Compression was now up to 12.0:1 and two Holley 4-barrel carburetors on an aluminum intake manifold replaced the previous three-carb setup. In this configuration, the new engine was rated at 425 hp and, as before, a single 4-barrel version was rated at 410. Longer free-flowing cast-iron exhaust manifolds developed for the later 406 engines became standard equipment on all 427s.

Having learned from its aerodynamic mistake on the stock car tracks in 1962, Ford was hard-pressed to remedy this situation before the kick-off of the NASCAR racing season in February 1963. The stylists responded by designing a sloped roofline for the Galaxie body that was advertised as the Sports Roof. These Fords are commonly referred to as 1963½ models due to their delayed release.

The Ford Drag Council still had some work to do to remove weight in the effort to gain parity with other manufacturers on the dragstrips. While the initial plan was to construct a limited number of lightweight Galaxies for members of the Drag Council to compete with in 1963 as they had done in 1962, Rhode Island Ford dealer Robert F. Tasca Sr. strongly suggested to his contacts high up in the company that an actual production run of cars equipped with lightweight components be considered. To that end Ford decided to produce 100 Galaxie 500 Sports Roof models with

SNAKES ALIVE, IT'S A DRAGON SNAKE

Some enterprising young men working for Shelby American Company had begun harping on Carroll Shelby to take one of his hot little Cobra sports cars drag racing where they could perhaps show the Corvettes a thing or two. Shelby relented late in the 1963 season, authorizing the preparation of a Cobra that had originally been used as the company's Public Relations car, and later on loan to a movie company for use in the film *Viva Las Vegas,* for drag racing.

The car's 260 engine had barely been replaced with a dual 4-barrel carbureted high-performance 289 and had other minor modifications completed before it was thrown into competition at the NHRA Nationals in the A/Sports class, where it posted a 12.69-second elapsed time in a losing effort against a top-running Corvette.

The car then returned to Shelby American, where it was repainted and the engine fitted with improved cylinder heads, drag shocks, a heavier clutch, Hurst shifter, and 5.14 rear-end gears. The car was put into the hands of Shelby team driver Tony Stoer, and from that point forward, the Dragon Snake, as it had come to be known, was seldom if ever bested by any Corvette. Stoer set the NHRA A/SP class record at 12.26 seconds at 114.06 mph and later the AA/SP class record at 11.73 seconds at 119.20 mph.

This car, the first to run with factory support, was later followed by a second car, which California drag racer Ed Terry took on a nationwide tour with more winning results.

427 engines and lightweight components specifically designed for drag race competition.

Upon learning that it would be some time before the assembly lines at Ford could start producing the lightweight Galaxies, members of the Drag Council took matters into their own hands. The 1963 Galaxie Sports Roof bodies were shipped to a number of the racers who had received the 1962 lightweight cars and the new bodies, 427 engines, and associated lightweight components were swapped onto the 1962 chassis, which were already set up for competition.

In the meantime, two 1963 lightweight Galaxie "Mules" were built at Ford's Wayne, Michigan, plant to test the feasibility of the concept. The assembly plant at Norfolk, Virginia, was ultimately chosen for the production run of the special lightweight cars, and each one was configured in the same fashion with no deviations allowed. Special components and/or deletions were a lightweight chassis (designed for Galaxies equipped with 6-cylinder or small V-8 engines, due to the lighter gauge of steel) and a two-door sports roof, painted Corinthian white with red interior trim. All sound deadener and seam sealer were deleted. Radio, heater, and clock were deleted. Carpet was replaced with a lightweight rubber floor mat. The front seat was replaced with fleet vehicle–style bucket seats by Bostrum. Aluminum bumpers, brackets, and NHRA-approved bellhousing were included. Fiberglass was used for fenders, inner fenders, hood, deck lid, and doors. Most cars did not receive the fiberglass doors due to problems with the subcontractor and concerns on the part of Ford's lawyers about the liability should the cars be driven on the street and involved in an accident.

Power was provided by the 425-hp 427 engine backed by a BorgWarner T-10 4-speed, aluminum-case transmission. By all accounts, just over 100 lightweight Galaxies were delivered to select Ford dealers to be sold with the understanding that the cars were intended for use in "timed competition events" and not as passenger vehicles.

Mercury, now sponsoring teams in both the USAC and NASCAR stock car series, was also beginning to discover drag racing in 1963, and one enterprising dealership, Sachs and Sons Lincoln-Mercury, of Long Beach, California, was the pioneer for Mercury performance cars in drag racing. Tom Sturm, who had driven his B/FX Chevy to an NHRA Championship in 1962, was selected to take the reins of a unique Mercury for 1963. Sachs and Sons sponsored Sturm's efforts with a 1963 Mercury Marauder powered by the same 427 engine that had been introduced in Ford cars that year.

By virtue of its additional weight, the big Mercury had what might be considered an advantage over its Ford cousins, as it fit very nicely into the NHRA A/Stock class. Sturm took full advantage of the A/Stock competition as he went on a nationwide tear with the Sachs and Sons car, setting and then bettering his own A/Stock national record. One automotive publication described how Sturm had brought his Mercury to the East Coast, where he promptly "Gave the Chevys, Mopars, and Pontiacs fits."

A magazine road test of a stock 427 Mercury Marauder equipped with a 4.11 open rear resulted in a quarter-mile elapsed time of 15.1 seconds. This proved the 427's capability to rapidly move cars weighing more than 4,000 pounds even when hampered with skinny bias-ply tires and no limited slip differential.

Ford introduced the Falcon Sprint model for 1963, powering it with the 260-ci version of the new small-block V-8 introduced in 1962. The Falcon proved to be a good fit for the NHRA J/Stock class, and Les Ritchey delivered the win with his Falcon at the NHRA Nationals.

Introduced in 1962, the midsize Fairlane, was the recipient of the stoutest member of the new small-block engine family, the high-performance 289 in 1963. At 271 hp, the high-winning little V-8 in the light Fairlane proved to be a good performer, and Milo Coleman showed just how good it was by taking home the D/Stock class win at the NHRA Nationals. In the class final, Coleman defeated a full-size 330-hp 390 Galaxie, which fit into the same class by virtue of ratio of horsepower to advertised weight.

Ford's high-performance subcontractor Dearborn Steel Tubing Company was tapped to again shoehorn Ford's biggest high-performance V-8, in this case the 427, into a midsize Fairlane. Now equipped with revised cylinder heads and intake it became known as the High Riser (based on the configuration of the taller intake and cylinder head intake ports), the 427 was backed up with an aluminum case BorgWarner T-10 4-speed transmission and a heavy-duty rear axle housing fitted with specially fabricated traction bars.

The modified Fairlane had all sound deadener, seam sealer, and creature comforts deleted. Then it was fitted with fiberglass fenders, hood, doors, and front bumper to make it a perfect candidate for NHRA's A/Factory Experimental class. The car, painted with Tasca Ford livery, made its debut at the NHRA Nationals, where Ford test driver Bill Humphries was eliminated from competition as a result of a missed shift.

The car was then turned over to the Tasca Ford team. With their input, driver Bill Lawton set the NHRA A/FX class speed record before the end of the season. In an apparent effort to see just how interested other teams might be in obtaining a limited production 427 Fairlane drag car, Ford had prepared a dealer window sticker for the car describing all its attributes and even assigned a DSO (District or Domestic Special Order) number to the package.

Ford had its biggest year in the NASCAR and USAC series in 1963. On January 20, Dan Gurney won the NASCAR Riverside 500 for Ford and the Ford teams never looked back, scoring 21 more victories, including the first 5 finishing positions at the Daytona 500.

On the USAC circuit Don White drove his Ford to the 1963 series championship, Parnelli Jones conquered at Pikes Peak with his Bill Stroppe–prepared Mercury, and AK Miller won the Sports Car class with his 406 Ford-powered Devin racer. Ford advertising made great use of Miller's victory by pointing out that the engine that powered his racer to the win was a stock production 406.

On the American road race circuit, a Shelby Cobra driven by Dan Gurney scored a win at Bridgehampton, Connecticut, in July 1963, a harbinger of the wins and championships to come for Shelby in the future.

Whether by design or not, Chrysler's new midsize car line received a big boost in performance through the introduction of unitized body construction in place of the previous year's cars, which had a full-perimeter frame. This saved hundreds of pounds on the base Plymouth Savoy and Dodge Dart models, and when equipped with new high-performance engines, they were approximately 300 pounds lighter than a comparable Ford, Chevrolet, or Pontiac.

Dodge and Plymouth, 1962

SUPER STOCK AND RAMCHARGER 413S UNDER THE HOOD.

The Mopar camp had several distinct advantages over the competition in 1962. First, due to unitized construction, their cars were lighter than those of Ford, Pontiac, and Chevrolet, even when the latter were equipped with lightweight body components. Second, the TorqueFlite automatic transmission was superior to those available elsewhere and allowed drivers to take advantage of quicker starts on the 7-inch-wide cheater slicks (the maximum allowed by the NHRA for Stock and Super/Stock class competition). Third, Chrysler sealed the deal with a high-performance 413-ci engine that was a match for the best that Detroit had to offer.

The maximum performance 413, available in both Dodge and Plymouth models, sported a cylinder block that had notches at the top of its cylinder bores to accommodate 2.05-inch intake and 1.88-inch exhaust valves that were being bumped by a solid lifter camshaft with .510 inch of lift and 310 degrees of duration. The 3.75-inch-stroke, forged-steel crankshaft swung connecting rods that had been individually checked at the factory to

ensure durability. Two sets of forged aluminum pistons were available for the Max Wedge engine, as it was called.

The first set squeezed out a compression ratio of 11.0:1 and delivered a horsepower rating of 410; the second set bumped the horsepower to 420 by virtue of an increase to 13.5:1. On top was a redesigned cross-ram intake manifold with 15-inch runners mounting two Carter AFB 4-barrel carburetors that flowed 650 cfm each. Huge, specially designed free-flowing

Automotive magazines took great interest in factory drag cars in 1962 with several taking on project cars to test their performance potential in competition. Motor Trend prepared a 1962 Dodge Dart powered by the 413 Ramcharger engine and entered it into NHRA SS/SA class competition with good results.

cast-iron exhaust manifolds sent gases out through cutouts that eliminated the factory exhaust.

Since Chrysler lacked a 4-speed transmission at the time, the only manual available was a 3-speed. While some, including Tom Grove, could get the manual-equipped Mopar figured out and performing, most racers opted for the TorqueFlite. Grove recorded the first official sub-12-second run by a full-size car equipped with a factory option engine with an 11.93 on July 15, 1962, with his Melrose Missile Plymouth.

Although the Virgil Exner styling and taxi cab amenities found on the hottest models turned off some buyers, the car magazines went wild for the new Plymouths and Dodges. *Hot Rod* prepared a 410-hp, automatic transmission Plymouth and *Motor Trend* prepped a similar Dodge with blueprinted engines and other allowable modifications for NHRA SS/SA class competition. At the same time the factory teams, Ramchargers (Dodge), and Golden Commandos (Plymouth) fielded their own versions with great success. Ray Brock, at the wheel of the *Hot Rod* Plymouth, recorded an elapsed time of 12.37 seconds at 114.79 mph, which turned the heads of the factory teams to the point that the Ramchargers announced that they were out to "Beat Brock" with their Dodge.

The crew at *Motor Trend* took things a step further in an attempt to show the factory racers how things should be done. Their 1962 Dodge Dart was touted as a special "public relations vehicle," which translates to "prepared with all the best the manufacturer had to offer," to impress the magazine slated to test the car. Apparently Roger Huntington, writing for *Motor Trend,* was sufficiently impressed as he penned, "Dodge's new Ramcharger 413 package gives more performance per dollar than any other factory assembled car in America."

Plymouth and Dodge shared their top-line 413-ci, 410-hp high-performance engines for 1962, with the only outward difference being the labeling on the valvecovers. The Dodge received the Ramcharger logo matching the factory drag team of the same name. The lightweight body styles and superior automatic transmission in combination with the 413 engine made Chrysler a force to be reckoned with on the dragstrips of America in 1962.

The Motor Trend *1962 Dodge Dart certainly stood out in a crowd thanks to its Chrysler design guru Virgil Exner's "love it or leave it" styling. But styling aside, the magazine team let the car's performance do the talking, and it spoke loudly.*

A race-prepped and -tuned 410-hp Ramcharger 413, backed by a TorqueFlite automatic transmission, powered the Motor Trend *Special Dodge Dart. Removing the twin unsilenced air cleaners revealed that the beast was fed copious amounts of high-octane gasoline via two big Carter AFB 4-barrel carburetors mounted on a unique cross-ram intake manifold.*

To efficiently remove spent gases from the high-performance 413 engine, Chrysler engineers designed a magnificent set of free-flowing cast-iron exhaust manifolds that left very little clearance in the car's engine compartment. While efficient, these manifolds were very heavy.

The interior of the Motor Trend *Special Dodge Dart* featured all the weight-saving deletes, such as radio, heater, etc., and in the styling department, it did any taxicab of the day quite proud. But options, aside from the engine and transmission, did little to win drag races.

The 413 Ramcharger's exhaust manifolds had cutouts installed on each side, which allowed easy access to bypass the car's exhaust system, and resulted in power-robbing back pressure when drag racing.

The Dart's TorqueFlite automatic transmission was controlled by push-buttons on the instrument panel just to the left of the steering wheel.

Chrysler continued to promote a performance image for its full-size "letter cars" in 1962, and driver Bud Faubel set records at the Daytona Beach Speed Trials with this specially prepared, manual transmission Chrysler 300C. A drag racer at heart, Faubel found time to set the NHRA B/Factory Experimental class record with the car during the season. (Photo Courtesy Bob Wenzelburger)

In an attempt to stay ahead on the dragstrip, Chrysler built its first Plymouth and Dodge lightweight models for 1963. Using aluminum components in place of steel fenders, gravel shield, and hoods with ram air scoops to feed cool air to the engine, along with lighter gauge steel bumpers, the Mopars retained the weight advantage over the competition for the second year running. The Stage III Max Wedge–powered Big Bad Dodge out of Ohio was one of the cars equipped with special lightweight components for 1963.

"Meet the Orange Monster" was Chrysler's advertising slogan for its newest dragstrip warrior in 1963. The top-of-the-line high-performance engine had grown to 426 ci and other improvements such as cam-shaft and cylinder heads led this version to be dubbed the Stage III. Rated at a conservative 425 hp, the Stage III 426 Max Wedge featured exhaust manifolds that were even more outrageous, and by design more efficient, than those on the previous 413 powerplant. (Photo Courtesy Bob Wenzelburger)

Longtime Pontiac racer "Akron Arlen" Vanke was one of many lured to the Chrysler camp in 1963 by the obvious advantages offered by the lightweight 426-powered cars and the company's full-on commitment to racing.

Tommy Grove was a former GM racer who switched to the Chrysler camp with great success. Teaming with Melrose Motors, Grove became a force to be reckoned with in a 1962 Plymouth and won the NHRA Winternationals with this 426 Max Wedge Plymouth in 1963. Grove chose to run his Mopars with a 4-speed transmission rather than the popular TorqueFlite automatic. (Photo Courtesy CarTech Archive)

4-speed transmission, the Dodge fell short against the Mickey Thompson Tempest. But that certainly wouldn't be the last time Chrysler was heard from in the F/X classes as things were just starting to heat up.

Plymouth accounted for all 11 wins by Chrysler Corporation cars in NASCAR during the 1962 season with 10 grabbed by a young man from Randleman, North Carolina, named Richard Petty behind the wheel of a Plymouth Belvedere powered by a single 4-barrel 413-ci engine. The combination of the new Plymouth's unitized body construction and Petty's driving skills proved to be a winning combination.

Petty's father, Lee, winner of the 1959 Daytona 500 in an Oldsmobile, drove his last race in a 1962 Plymouth before retiring to devote all his efforts to the preparation of team cars for Petty Enterprises. The collaboration between the Pettys and Chrysler Corporation proved to be one of the most successful in NASCAR racing history.

After only minor performance modifications, the car covered the quarter-mile in 13.44 seconds at 109.76 mph, causing Huntington to report, "The Dodge loaned to me was about as close to an out-and-out production race car as you can come." After receiving an engine blueprint and other NHRA class legal modifications, the *Motor Trend* car lasted through four rounds of Super/Stock Eliminator competition at the 1962 NHRA Nationals, recording a best elapsed time of 12.65 seconds at 113.20 mph before losing to Jim Thornton of the Ramchargers. Thornton went on to the final round in Super/Stock Eliminator, ultimately losing to the Chevy of Proffitt.

While Pontiacs and Chevrolets once again proved to be the class of the Super Super/Stock and upper stock class field at the Nationals on Labor Day weekend, the SS/SA class had become an almost entirely Mopar show. The Dodges and Plymouths had at it until the class final, where the victory went to Al Ekstrand's Lawman Dodge with a 12.72 elapsed time over the similar 413 Dodge of Bud Faubel.

In spite of the fact that they enjoyed a weight advantage over the competition in the Super/Stock classes, the Chrysler teams recognized the attention being paid to the up-and-coming Factory/Experimental classes. To that end, a compact model 1962 Dodge Lancer was prepared using the 413-ci Ramcharger engine for A/FX competition. Hampered by the lack of a factory

Dodge and Plymouth, 1963

MEET THE ORANGE MONSTER.

So said the two-page advertisement for "Plymouth's explosive Super Stock 426 III" in *Hot Rod*. The Mopar camp, Plymouth and Dodge, came out with guns blazing for 1963 with the new 426-ci (4.25-inch bore and 3.75-inch stroke) Max Wedge engine that was offered in two versions: Stage II included 415 hp, 470 ft-lbs of torque, and 11:1 compression; the optional Stage III included 425 ponies, 480 ft-lbs of torque, and 12.5:1 compression.

Aluminum front sheet metal (including a scooped hood that ducted air directly into the carburetors) gravel shield, and bumper in place of steel was optional and reduced the weight to 3,200 pounds. This was a nearly 300-pound advantage over the lightweight Ford Galaxie and 100 pounds lighter than the Swiss Cheese Pontiac Catalina.

Improved cylinder heads, new intake and exhaust manifolds (which still featured exhaust cutouts), a hotter camshaft, larger Carter AFB carburetors, and a 4-speed manual transmission (available for the first time) to supplement the TorqueFlite automatic all helped Plymouth set seven NHRA class records in 1963.

Ray Brock of *Hot Rod* was provided a 1963 Plymouth equipped with the Stage II engine and automatic transmission for performance testing. After swapping out the 3.91 rear gears for a 4.56 set, doing a performance tune, some minor suspension modifications, mounting Casler 7-inch cheater slicks, and uncapping the factory exhaust, the mighty Mopar posted a best quarter-mile elapsed time of 12.69 at 111.97, which led Brock to declare the car, "the hottest car you can buy."

At the NHRA Winternationals, Tom Grove proved that you didn't need an automatic transmission to win with a Mopar as he rowed his 4-speed Plymouth to the top spot in the Super/Stock class, recording a winning elapsed time of 12.37 seconds at 114.94 mph. The Super/Stock Automatic crown went to another Plymouth as Bill Hanyon put his 1962 model out front with a 12.30 elapsed time at 115.38 mph. The Top Stock Eliminator Crown went to Al Ekstrand's Dodge, winning with a 12.44 at 115.08 over the Golden Commandos Plymouth.

At the NHRA Nationals on Labor Day, it was Jim Thornton in the Ramchargers Dodge claiming the top spot in the Super/Stock Automatic class with an elapsed time of 12.23 at 116.42 mph.

The Stock Eliminator crown came down to Al Ekstrand in the Lawman Dodge against Herman Moser in another Ramchargers car, with Moser taking the win with a 12.22 to Ekstrand's 12.23.

As of September 1963, Tom Grove held the NHRA Super/Stock class elapsed time record with his Plymouth at 12.50 seconds, while Bob Simerly's Dodge had the speed record at 115.32 mph. Tom Ritchie's Plymouth had both ends of the Super/Stock Automatic record at 12.53 seconds at 115.03 mph.

Studebaker

ONE LAST GASP FROM SOUTH BEND BEFORE THE LIGHTS GO OUT.

Perhaps some of the biggest performance innovations on any 1963 production car came out of the Studebaker Corporation in South Bend, Indiana. That year the company introduced a fiberglass-bodied sports car named Avanti, powered it with a supercharged engine of proven strength and reliability, and had one of the biggest names in Indy car racing set records with their products on the Salt Flats of Bonneville, Utah.

Billed as "the most advanced car of its time," the Studebaker Avanti had features that were indeed years ahead of the competition. With its fiberglass body, reinforced steel frame, and 109-inch wheelbase, the Avanti weighed 3,195 pounds. Three V-8 engines were available, all based on the original 289-ci design that the company first introduced in 1957 with a 3.56-inch

The fiberglass-bodied Studebaker Avanti for 1963 was a car considered by many to be ahead of its time. The new model's great styling, innovation, and performance put Studebaker ahead of many competitors that year. Sadly the company only hung on for one more year before financial woes caused its demise.

The Avanti's great exterior styling carried over to its aircraft-inspired interior, which was designed for the performance-minded driver. The full array of gauges included one that recorded hours of operating time on the engine. Both 4-speed manual and automatic transmissions were available, along with two versions of the sturdy 289-ci V-8 engine.

The secret to Studebaker's performance successes came in the form of the Paxton supercharger. The company had bought the rights to Paxton, and as part of the deal it acquired the famed Andy Granatelli who knew a thing or two about performance thanks to years of preparing cars for the Indianapolis 500. The 289 engine's low-profile intake manifold allowed it to fit under the sleek hood of the Avanti with no problem. The belt-driven Paxton supercharger blew through a Carter AFB 4-barrel carburetor.

First introduced in the 1950s with ahead-of-its-time styling, the Studebaker Hawk had received numerous upgrades along the way, which allowed it to remain a viable model into the 1963 model year.

bore and 3.62-inch stroke. Referred to as an under-square engine, its strong but not the best design for out-and-out performance.

The R-1 version came with a 4-barrel carburetor, 10.25:1 compression ratio, 260-degree duration camshaft, and dual-point ignition with horsepower rated at 240.

The R-2 version came with 4-barrel carburetor, Paxton Supercharger, 9.0:1 compression, 260-degree duration camshaft, and dual-point ignition with rated horsepower at 289.

The R-3 version received overbored cylinders, which increased displacement to 304 ci. The R-3 was a factory-blueprinted engine with 4-barrel carburetors, Paxton

Along with the Avanti, the Hawk was also available with the optional Paxton supercharged 289-ci V-8 in 1963. Although heavier than the Avanti, the Hawk was still a good performer when so equipped.

supercharger, 9.5:1 or 9.75:1 compression chamfered cylinder bores, 276- or 288-degree duration camshaft, special cylinder head castings with larger valves, Isky valvesprings, forged pistons, header-style exhausts, transistorized ignition, and 400 hp at 6,000 rpm rating. R-3 cars also received heavy-duty suspension pieces, a Dana 44 rear axle, and choice of either a BorgWarner T-10 4-speed manual or a BorgWarner automatic transmission. The Avanti, when fully loaded, cost the consumer a hefty $5,980.

The experimental R-4 engine variant was planned for production in 1964. At 304 ci, it shared the attributes of the R-3 but differed in the fact that it had a compression ratio of 12:1 and relied on two 4-barrel carburetors in place of the R-3 supercharger.

Studebaker had purchased the Paxton supercharger company from Andy Granatelli in 1962 and the Indianapolis 500 Race stalwart and long-time automotive innovator came along with the deal, becoming president of the Paxton Products Division. Granatelli had come a long way in improving the reliability of the Paxton supercharger, and he set about establishing a reputation for performance for the Studebaker line.

Studebaker had introduced the compact Lark model in 1959 and for the first time a restyled sporty performance version known as the Daytona became available in 1963. Optional at extra cost on the Lark were the R-1 and R-2 engines, 4-speed manual transmission, and disc brakes. An even rarer version, known as the Super Lark, or Super Performance Package, featured the R-3 engine and suspension upgrades.

Always ahead of the curve when it came to styling, Studebaker had introduced the Hawk in 1956 and with a redesign in 1962, the model received a new name, Gran Turismo Hawk, or GT Hawk. In similar fashion to the Lark, the GT Hawk was offered with performance upgrades in the engine (R-1 or R-2), suspension, and brakes. Either an automatic transmission or BorgWarner T-10 4-speed box was available as well.

After having taken a preproduction Avanti to Bonneville and setting 29 USAC speed records late in 1962 (recording a top speed of 170.78 mph), Andy Granatelli prepared 12 Studebakers, including Avantis, Super Larks, and Super Hawks, for runs at the Bonneville Salt Flats in 1963. The 12 cars set 72 USAC records in September and an additional 337 records in October. Among the cars were two Super Hawks, one fitted with the R-3 engine ran 157.29 mph, while another with an experimental R-4 setup posted a speed of 147.86 mph, proving to the world that the combination of a dedicated racer and the company from South Bend equaled performance.

When it came to drag racing, Studebaker's new cars found themselves on the short end of NHRA rules, which called for classification of cars based on an advertised horsepower-to-weight ratio because the company was late in publishing the output of its available engines. In spite of that, Ted Harbit had been making a name for himself in NHRA stock class competition with his 1951 Starlight coupe, powered by a 232-ci

Studebaker included its compact economy model, the Lark, in the 1963 performance lineup. Best known for its low price and good fuel economy, the boxy Lark proved to be a big surprise to drivers of other brands that year.

The performance version of the Lark received an interior upgrade for 1963 with bucket seats and a redesigned instrument panel. A previous owner of this car replaced the factory shift linkage with a sturdy Hurst Competition Plus shifter. While the 3-speed manual transmission was standard on the Lark, an automatic and a 4-speed manual were options.

V-8 (predecessor of the 289) and winning multiple class championships over several years. Another competitor, Ray Tanner, a Studebaker dealer from Phoenix, Arizona, took advantage of the AHRA rules and set the A/Compact Stock class record with his R-3-powered Lark at 13.52 seconds at 104.52 mph. Tanner's Lark had run a best elapsed time of 13.40 seconds at 108.64 mph.

Sadly, all the performance gains made by Studebaker in 1963 proved to be too little, too late as the financially strapped company went belly up in 1964 after producing only nine R-3 Avantis and no R-4 models.

Failure on the part of drivers of other performance cars to notice this unobtrusive badge on the Lark sitting next to them at the stoplight could lead to some degree of embarrassment as the Lark showed its taillights when the light turned green.

The available Paxton supercharged 289 turned the Studebaker Lark into the perhaps the biggest "sleeper" performance car of the early 1960s. Although few in number, the supercharged Larks made a big splash that year.

CHAPTER 4

1964: CHANGE IS ON THE HORIZON: ENTER MUSTANG AND GTO

Factory-backed Hemis and High Risers did battle on dragstrips and circle tracks as Ford and Chrysler went all out to win. At the same time midsize performance defined the term *muscle car*.

While General Motors had pulled the plug on its racing program in 1963, the 425-hp 409 was still available in 1964. Ranking at the top of the class of 1964 was the Impala SS convertible powered by the legendary 409. (Photo Courtesy CarTech Archive)

Chevrolet, 1964

A NEW MIDSIZE MODEL KEEPS THE COMPANY IN THE LIMELIGHT.

Chevrolet gave America its first look at the midsize Chevelle Malibu in 1964. Designed to compete with the Ford Fairlane and similar Chrysler models, the factory kept within the 330-ci engine limit by offering the new model with the tried-and-proven 327 in two flavors. The lesser of the two, rated at 250 hp at 4,400 rpm, featured small-valve cylinder heads and a Rochester 4-barrel carburetor; the sportier 327 at 300 hp at 5,000 rpm mounted a set of cylinder heads with larger valves, an improved intake manifold, and Carter AFB 4-barrel carburetor. Back all this up with the optional 4-speed transmission, Posi-Traction rear axle, and the Malibu SS trim upgrades, and you had a well thought out, fine performing car that would appeal to the younger buyer.

Although Chevrolet didn't take the Chevelle drag racing in 1964, the availability of numerous over-the-counter high-performance parts, coupled with those already in the performance aftermarket, meant that thousands of young people took the new Chevelle to the track every weekend. Among them you found Chevy stalwarts such as Malcolm Durham and Dick Harrell, who prepared their Chevelles for F/X and match race competition against the factory-supported cars of Ford, Mercury, and Chrysler by stuffing them full of 427 Z-11 engines they had used in the previous year with great success. And it wasn't long before the company that wasn't in racing made available a version of the "Mystery" racing engine that had made quite a splash on the NASCAR circuit in 1963 for production vehicles that any enthusiast could afford.

The full-size Chevy models for 1964 were still available with the 409-ci engine as well. The sedate version was rated at 340 hp at 4,000 rpm, thanks to 10.0:1 compression and hydraulic valve lifters. The other version allowed your 3,700-pound Impala to stay right with the competition. One came rated at 400 hp at 6,000 rpm and the other sported 425 ponies at 6,000 rpm. Both high-performance 409 engines featured solid lifter cams and 11.0:1 compression, the only difference was found on top, as the 425-hp 409 mounted two Carter AFB 4-barrel carburetors and the 400 just one.

Chevrolet recorded no NASCAR stock car wins during 1964, but taking into consideration the fact that the youth market for which it was aiming was more geared toward street performance and drag racing, it seemed to have little impact on the overall sales for the year.

And Chevrolet still had the Corvette. America's sports car underwent only minor styling changes for 1964. Gone was the split rear window in the hardtop, but the big news came in the form of engine options.

The base 250- and 300-hp 327 engines were still in the lineup, but the real awakening came in the form of the L76 version. With a solid lifter camshaft, 11.0:1 compression, improved cylinder heads, and a new aluminum

The last year for the 425-hp version of the 409 was 1964; it was to be replaced as Chevy's top high-performance engine by the 396-ci "porcupine head" big-block in 1965. The 409 soldiered on into 1965 in a de-tuned version that was a shadow of its former self. (Photo Courtesy CarTech Archive)

The Corvette's top engine option for 1964 remained the fuel-injected 327 packing 360 hp, which was more than enough to keep the Corvette in the fight as one of America's quickest and fastest production cars.

intake manifold mounting a Holley 4-barrel carburetor, this new offering topped out at an advertised 365 hp at 6,200 rpm and delivered 350 ft-lbs of torque at 4000 rpm. This placed the L76 second only to the king of them all for 1964, the fuel-injected L84, which delivered an additional 10 hp.

Combine either of these potent options with a 4-speed transmission and a curb weight of less than 3,200 pounds that was capable of 0–60 times in less than 6 seconds and could cover the quarter-mile in just a click over 14 seconds at 100 mph, and you have yourself one of the quickest cars on any street.

Pontiac, 1964

WE ARE NO LONGER INVOLVED IN RACING (WINK).

Pontiac had introduced the compact Tempest model in 1961 to compete with the Ford Falcon, Mercury Comet, Chevy Corvair, Buick Special, and Olds F-85. The Tempest featured a unique drivetrain that replaced the conventional transmission with a rear-mounted transaxle. Originally offered with a 4-cylinder engine, the Tempest received a 260-hp, 326-ci V-8 (a de-stroked version of the 389) late in 1962. But for 1964, Pontiac engineers John DeLorean, Russell Gee, and Bill Collins had other ideas. The team designed a new version of the Tempest with a conventional drivetrain that was approved by Pontiac General Manager Pete Estes. Then, in complete violation of a companywide edict stating that no A-Body cars were to be powered by engines exceeding 330 ci in displacement, the team hatched a plan for an optional version of the Tempest powered by the 389 Trophy V-8 that proved to be one of the greatest automotive coups of the decade.

For an additional $295, you could obtain the Tempest GTO package. GTO stood for Gran Turismo Omologato, or Grand Touring Homologation, which paid homage to an exotic Ferrari model of the same name. The GTO option consisted of the 389-ci engine with 10.75:1 compression and a single 4-barrel carburetor that delivered 325 hp at 4,800 rpm and 428 ft-lbs of torque at 3,200 rpm. Also included were a seven-blade de-clutching fan, 3-speed

The GTO as a tiger of a car image was another part of Wangers's aggressive ad campaign to establish the GTO as the performance car to buy in 1964. The car's size, styling, and host of available options that enhanced both performance and handling made it the car that every young person desired. (Photo Courtesy Don Salisbury)

Pontiac hit a home run in 1964 with the introduction of the GTO. Based on the midsize Tempest model, the GTO was an instant sales success and exceeded all expectations. While it can be said that Pontiac did not invent the muscle car, or even the big-engine, small-car concept, the publicity campaign launched by Pontiac ad man Jim Wangers soon had the public believing it. Wangers took things a step further by putting some specially prepared GTOs into the hands of car magazines for test purposes that immediately established the GTO as one of America's top performers in an era where performance sold cars. (Photo Courtesy Mike Champion)

manual transmission with Hurst shifter and heavy-duty clutch, heavy-duty springs and stabilizer, 7.5 x 14–inch wheels mounting Red Line tires, and an engine chrome dress-up package.

Optional at extra cost were Tri-Power induction consisting of three Rochester 2-barrel carburetors (348 advertised horsepower at 4,900 rpm and 428 ft-lbs of torque at 3,600 rpm), 4-speed manual or automatic transmission, 3.90 rear axle ratio, Safe-T Track limited-slip differential, metallic brake linings, heavy-duty shock absorbers, quick-ratio steering, transistorized ignition, tachometer, and a sport steering wheel.

It would seem that those in charge of the GTO's main in-house GM competition at Buick and Oldsmobile weren't quite as adventurous as DeLorean and company at Pontiac, as both camps abided by the "no more than 330 ci of displacement" rule when powering their restyled and upsized Buick Special and Olds Cutlass 4-4-2 (which stood for 4-barrel carburetor, 4-speed transmission, and dual exhaust) for 1964. As a result, both lagged well behind the GTO in sales and performance for the year.

How did the car known as "the great one" perform? Well, that would be according to whom you asked and who prepared the car to be tested. In another stroke of marketing brilliance, Jim Wangers provided test cars to major automotive publications that can only be described as "ringers."

When a Royal Pontiac–prepared GTO test car, secretly packing a 421-ci engine and being tested by *Car and Driver,* stopped the quarter-mile clocks in 12.8 seconds at 112 mph when equipped with cheater slicks, the magazine scribes collectively lost their minds. *Motor Trend* tested a base-engine GTO and it covered the quarter mile in 15.8 seconds at 93 mph. *Road & Track* coaxed a Tri-Power model to a very respectable, and infinitely more realistic 14.1-second quarter-mile time at 104.2 mph.

Needless to say, the GTO exceeded all sales estimates and gave Pontiac a huge shot in the arm when it came to performance. A perfect fit for the NHRA B/Stock class, GTOs soon lined the pits of dragstrips across the land. While the company no longer officially supported racing, several racers with corporate connections were able to obtain GTOs with deleted sound deadener, and in at least one case, sheet metal stamped from lighter-gauge steel, keeping Pontiac in the performance limelight. Most notable was perennial campaigner of Pontiacs, Arnie "The Farmer" Beswick, who rolled out a 1964 GTO fitted with aluminum front sheet metal and a supercharged 421 engine. Beswick was, as always, a top performer and his car was constantly in demand to match race against the "factory cars" from Ford and Chrysler.

This emblem, when affixed to a 1960s-era Pontiac, indicated that the car had received the special touches available from Ace Wilson's Royal Pontiac. Various levels of Bobcat kits were available, from performance tuning to internal engine modifications. A GTO that had received the full Bobcat treatment from Royal was said to be capable of producing up to 50 additional horsepower over stock. (Photo Courtesy Ken Skistimas)

ROYAL BOBCAT KITS

While other Pontiac dealers around the country recognized and capitalized on the performance craze of the 1960s, few could compete with Royal Pontiac of Royal Oak, Michigan. If you wanted your GTO to run quicker than the competition, it was well known that a Royal Bobcat kit was just the ticket. Royal marketed and, if you were lucky enough to live nearby, installed its performance-enhancing parts and tuning tricks that were said to increase the output of the GTO's famed 389 engine by 30 to 50 hp.

Customers could opt for lesser versions of the kit, but the ultimate package included a modified advance curve in the distributor, thinner head gaskets, which bumped the compression ratio to 11.23:1 (100-octane fuel required), blocked heat-riser passages to the intake manifold, larger carburetor jets, a high-capacity oil pump, and Poly-Locks installed on the rocker arms allowing for maximum travel without valve float. If you were beaten in a street race or at the dragstrip by a GTO, chances are it had the Bobcat kit installed.

Ford, 1964

THE "TOTAL PERFORMERS" FIND THEMSELVES IN THE WINNER'S CIRCLE.

The performance fortunes of the Ford Motor Company took a major leap forward in 1964. Tired of playing catch-up, the company pulled out all the stops, winning many and various racing titles as well as launching what became the most successful new car model in history, the Mustang.

While 1963 had been a banner year for Ford in the NASCAR and USAC stock cars series, where the Sports Roof Galaxies powered by the 427-ci engine dominated, Ford found itself at a disadvantage in drag racing due to its products giving up as many as 300 pounds to the competition. Careful examination of the NHRA rules for Super/Stock (the premier class for showroom-type vehicles) of 7 pounds of vehicle weight per advertised horsepower made it abundantly clear that the full-size Galaxie would not be a factor. But, with special modification, the midsize Fairlane model fit the class perfectly.

The company had also caught on to the trick of underrating horsepower figures to gain an advantage that had previously been used by General Motors and Chrysler with much success. As a result, the version of the 427 featuring improved cylinder heads, intake manifold, and carburetors introduced late in 1963 retained the advertised horsepower rating (425) of its predecessor, in spite of the fact that actual numbers were closer to 500. To achieve parity with the competition and increase their chances of a winning season on the nation's dragstrips, the folks at Ford contracted Dearborn Steel Tubing to prepare 100 Fairlane two-door sedans for Super/Stock competition. The decision to build 100 units was based on the NHRA rule that stated to be legal for Super Stock class racing, 100 needed to be produced.

Having previously built the 1963 Fairlane 427 "mule" car, the team at Dearborn Steel Tubing set about modifying the first 11 1964 Fairlane 427s (to be delivered to the members of the Ford Drag Council) to accept the 427 High Riser engine and installing lightweight body components to achieve the minimum allowable weight. Drag racing coordinator Dick Brannan was charged with aiding in the development of the new cars, ultimately dubbed Thunderbolts, to make them winners right out of the box. And win they did.

Drag Council members Gas Ronda and Butch Leal were the class of the Super Stock field at the NHRA Winternationals in Pomona, California, with Ronda emerging victorious in a winning streak that resulted in his being crowned one of two NHRA World Champion Ford drivers that season. Leal put his Thunderbolt in the winner's circle at the NHRA Nationals on Labor Day 1964, and Ford test driver Len Richter wheeled the Bob Ford Thunderbolt to the AHRA championship.

The ultimate in Ford performance for 1964 came in the form of 100 Fairlanes modified by Dearborn Steel Tubing Company for competition in the Super/Stock class. The first 11 cars, delivered to the members of the Ford Drag Council, were painted vintage burgundy, while the remainder were delivered in white but often painted other colors by dealers or owners. The first Thunderbolt was delivered to Ford drag racing coordinator Dick Brannan. The Alderman Ford car was raced with sponsorship from a dealer with ties to Ford performance dating to 1960.

Fairlane Thunderbolts were available with either an aluminum case BorgWarner T-10 4-speed or modified Lincoln automatic transmission. The automatic cars relied on the production column-mounted shift lever, while the 4-speed versions had a floor-mounted factory shifter. Most of these were soon replaced by more reliable Hurst linkage.

GETTING THE WORD OUT TO THE DEALERS: PERFORMANCE SELLS

It wasn't just the Drag Council members who scored big for Ford in 1964. On February 21, 1964, the parent company notified all district dealers of the "availability of Ford products for 1964 drag events," stating that the purpose of the communication was to explain the products offered by the company to take advantage of several important classes. The specially constructed and equipped cars were the Super Stock 427 Fairlane sedan and the A/Stock Galaxie 500 Tudor hardtop.

Officially 100 Fairlane Thunderbolts were produced for sale through Ford dealers in 1964. Due to an NHRA rules change allowing limited production cars to be declared legal for competition after 50 such units were produced, just 50 lightweight Galaxies were built, 25 equipped with the automatic transmission and 25 with the 4-speed.

Although Ford had produced the Galaxies with an eye toward the NHRA A/Stock class, the sanctioning body wasted little time in creating a separate class, designated AA/Stock or AA/SA, where the Fords, including the previous year's lightweight Galaxies, along with 1963 426 Max Wedge Mopars equipped with lightweight components, did battle. Mike Schmitt of Ridgecrest, California, took his Desert Motors–sponsored AA/SA 64 Galaxie to one of three drag racing World Championships won by Ford drivers that year.

Ford offered a performance car for just about every taste and budget in 1964: The Falcon Sprint (first introduced in 1963) with its 260-ci small-block V-8; the standard production 1964 Fairlane, which could be optioned with the high-winding 271-hp high-performance 289 (newly introduced for 1963); and full-size Fords at every trim level, except the station wagon could be purchased with either the 410-hp (single 4-barrel carburetor) or 425-hp (two 4-barrel carburetors) 427 Low Riser engine, which had also undergone several engineering improvements in the area of camshaft and cylinder heads since its 1963 introduction.

Although previous models equipped with the high-performance big-block V-8 had suffered with the break-prone BorgWarner T-10 4-speed transmission over the three previous years, Ford introduced its own, all-new, 4-speed box for 1964. The beefy new transmission, developed by Ford's engineers, became known as the Toploader by virtue of the case design, and it went on to gain a reputation for strength and reliability.

MEMO:

Super Stock: A 427 Fairlane Two-Door Sedan

This unit is available on special order only, directly from the office of the Special Vehicles Manager. Orders may be submitted by letter or wire, and should specify whether the 4-speed or automatic transmission is required. All other specifications are the same for all cars and are as follows with no additions or deletions allowed:

- Fiberglass hood, front fenders, and front bumper [fiberglass bumpers were soon replaced by aluminum stampings due to an NHRA ruling]
- Plexiglas windows (except windshield)
- Lightweight seats
- Revised drag suspension
- Drag racing tubular headers
- Forced-air induction system
- Tachometer and oil pressure gauge

- 4-speed or automatic transmission
- Ratios of 4-speed transmission: 1st 2.20, 2nd 1.43, 3rd 1.19, 4th 4.57:1
- Drag tires
- Special wheels, 4-inch front, 7-inch rear
- Heavy-duty brakes
- Oversize fuel line
- Aluminum transmission housing
- 427-ci High Riser type of engine

Upon delivery of these vehicles the customer must sign an acknowledgment of his understanding of the vehicle he has purchased, and an agreement attesting to his understanding of the lack of warranty on the car.

These cars are all-out vehicles, not for operation on streets, and capable of running in the low-11-second bracket. As supplied from the factory, the cars are ready for the strip. Dealers should be cautioned that these fine cars should only be sold to the knowing, capable enthusiast. This Super Stock car, as furnished, is capable of running the quarter mile in less than 12 seconds, the present world's record.

Price: Wholesale to dealer. Fairlane two-door sedan with 4-speed transmission $3,780 plus Detroit D&D. With automatic transmission $3,980 plus Detroit D&D.

A/Stock: A Galaxie 500 two-door hardtop with the 427 8-V engine

This unit is available on DSO through normal channels. Car is equipped as follows and should be ordered under DSO number 84-0018 for the 4-speed transmission and 84-0007 for the automatic transmission. The cars are to be furnished as follows and no additions or deletions are allowed:

- 427 8-V High Riser engine
- Forced-air induction
- Heavy-duty automatic transmission or
- Manual transmission: 1st 2.36, 2nd 1.76, 3rd 1.23, 4th 1:1. Other ratios are available.
- Drag clutch
- Aluminum bellhousing
- Rear axle 4.71-1 automatic, 4.57-1 manual
- Limited-slip differential

- 31-tooth axle shaft
- Lightweight frame
- Trunk-mounted battery
- Lightweight bucket seats
- Lightweight floor mats
- Modified grille to allow maximum airflow to ram air induction
- Fiberglass hood with bubble
- Complete sound package omitted

This car is a maximum performance vehicle and should only be sold to the knowing customer who understands the warranty implications if the car is used in competitive events.

Price: wholesale to dealer. With 4-speed $3,940 plus normal D&D. With automatic $4,150 plus normal D&D.

A version of the 427-ci FE introduced in 1963 provided the power for the Thunderbolts. It featured improved cylinder heads, improved intake manifold, and larger carburetors but was still rated at 425 hp. (Photo Courtesy CarTech Archive)

Known as the High Riser by virtue of the tall intake manifold that required the car have a hood scoop to provide clearance, the engine was fed cool air via large duct hoses that replaced the inner headlamps in the car's grille. It was estimated that the 427 High Riser produced 500 hp. (Photo Courtesy CarTech Archive)

The interior of a Thunderbolt was appointed in a fashion typical for factory drag cars of the 1960s. Heater, radio, armrests, one sun visor, carpet, sound deadener, and sealer were deleted. Side glass was replaced by lightweight Lexan and rear quarter glass was fixed in place. Bostrum bucket seats replaced the stock bench seat. Dearborn Steel Tubing also included an aftermarket tachometer and oil pressure gauge as part of the Thunderbolt package. (Photo Courtesy CarTech Archive)

The other factory drag car package offered by Ford in 1964 was the A/Stock Galaxie, and while the 1964 version of the factory drag car did not feature as many lightweight components as the 1963 model, it was powered by the same 427 High Riser engine as the Thunderbolt, making it a formidable package. Just 50 were produced: 25 4-speed and 25 automatic transmission 1964 lightweight Galaxies. Apparently the NHRA recognized the advantage of this package and immediately moved these cars into new classes, AA/Stock or AA/Stock Automatic. The Welsh Motors car ran out of Springfield, Ohio.

Not only was factory driver Mike Schmitt successful with his lightweight Galaxie in the AA/SA class, he took home an NHRA World Championship title with the car. Schmitt, along with Gas Ronda and his Super/Stock Fairlane Thunderbolt, gave Ford Motor Company its biggest year yet in NHRA drag racing, while factory driver Len Richter won the AHRA title with his Thunderbolt. Total Performance was the slogan at Ford, and it was working.

Instead of routing cool outside air through deleted inboard headlamps, as was done on the Thunderbolts, the lightweight Galaxies for 1964 used fiberglass ducts that picked up air through the car's grille and carried it to the air box mounted on top of the carburetors.

Ford's Lincoln Mercury Division had become deeply involved in performance by 1964 and offered the 410- and 425-hp versions of the 427 Low Riser in its full-size models. By virtue of being heavier than a comparable Ford Galaxie, they fit into a lower NHRA Stock Eliminator class. The Mercurys had no exterior badging to indicate the engine size, making them a "sleeper" at a stoplight.

On April 17, 1964, the top man at Ford, Lee Iacocca, introduced the greatest thing to hit the market since the Ford V-8 of 1932, at the Ford Pavilion of the New York World's Fair: the Mustang. The car that went on to be the best-selling new introduction in automotive history began as a fairly benign vehicle. Based on the Falcon platform and initially offered with no better powerplant than the 164-hp, 260-ci V-8, the Mustang hardly appeared ready to uphold any part of the Total Performers image that the company was touting.

But it wasn't long before the pleasing styling and low price point that launched the Mustang were followed by two versions of the 289-ci V-8,

Forewarned that Ford's new Mustang would be the focus of the company's drag racing efforts for 1965 and unable to obtain a preproduction model for testing, Drag Racing Coordinator Dick Brannan had Dearborn Steel Tubing Company convert a 1964 Falcon into an A/FX drag car.

FLYING FALCONS

Although he had been a member of the Ford Drag Council since 1962, southern racer Phil Bonner, when not selling cars, made his living on match racing. Southern track owners had pioneered the concept of offering appearance money and purses to Super Stock and Factory Experimental racers who faced off against one another in what came to be called "run what ya brung" match races. Nothing would fill the seats at a dragstrip on a weekend better than an advertised match race between representatives of the Detroit brands. Ford versus Chevrolet versus Mopar match races exploded in popularity by the mid-1960s and Phil Bonner was one of the best at the game.

Always looking for an edge over his competition, Bonner set out to build a Falcon powered by the same 427 High Riser engine found in his Fairlane Thunderbolt. Bonner figured that the lighter weight and shorter wheelbase of the Falcon would provide just what he needed to stay on top. Ford eventually sanctioned Bonner's efforts with the Falcon, and in very short order the car's wheel stands off the starting line had it gracing the pages of car magazines, not to mention top billing at numerous dragstrips.

Shortly after the debut of Bonner's Falcon, the Ford Drag Council's racing coordinator, Dick Brannan, caught wind of the pending release of Ford's newest model, the Mustang. Realizing that the company's youth and performance image would soon be built around the Mustang, Brannan sought to obtain a preproduction version of the new model for modification into a drag car, as was done with the Fairlane before it. When no examples could be readily obtained, Brannan did the next best thing: he used the platform on which the new model would be based, the Falcon, for a test bed.

Once again, Dearborn Steel Tubing Company was given the task of modifying a small Ford to accept a huge engine. The resulting highly modified 1964 Falcon provided Brannan with helpful information on the modifications that would be required to make the new Mustang a winner on the dragstrip. Running into the 10-second elapsed-time range with the Falcon very early on, Brannan rolled up event and match race wins that went a long way to further Ford's performance image that year.

Because the Mustang would be built on the Falcon platform, Brannan was able to gain valuable knowledge prior to the release of the Mustang by racing this 427 High Riser compact. Phil Bonner, a Drag Council teammate of Brannan, also built a 1964 Falcon that was very successful as a match racer and A/FX class competitor.

including the performance-proven 271-hp high winder, which when coupled with the car's curb weight of just over 2,500 pounds and the 4-speed transmission, made for a hot street or strip combination. As predicted, the Mustang went on to be the flag bearer for Ford performance, a trend that continues today.

Shelby's Cobras only got better in 1964 with both the Dragon Snakes and the SCCA versions tearing up the competition nationwide. Tony Stoer set the NHRA A/SP record at 12.26 seconds at 114.06 with his factory team car and after swapping the induction system he also claimed the AA/SP record at 11.73 seconds at 119.20 mph. Ed Terry, driving the Shelby team car, won the A/SP class at the NHRA Nationals and Hans Schmitt drove his *El Cid* Cobra to victory at the NASCAR Winter Drags in Daytona Beach, Florida, with an elapsed time of 11.31 seconds at 131.22. Over the 1964–1965 seasons, Schmitt held four class records with his car, losing just two rounds of competition in the process.

Plymouth and Dodge got all the attention on the NASCAR stock car circuit due to the release of the 426 Hemi engine for competition, but Ford capitalized on engineering advances in its proven 427 engine, the preparation of their cars by Holman-Moody, and top drivers like Fred Lorenzen to score the highest number of series wins with 29 checkered flags. The dominance shown by the Chrysler Hemi on the longer tracks did not necessarily carry over to shorter venues, which gave the Ford teams a fighting chance.

Two of the most successful Comet drag team members were former Chevy racers "Dyno Don" Nicholson and Ronnie Sox. Nicholson set a new A/FX class record early in the season and Sox claimed the title of Mr. Stock Eliminator at the NHRA Winternationals. Like the Ford Thunderbolts, the Comets were fitted with lightweight components and powered by the 427 High Riser engine.

In response to the dominance displayed by Chrysler's 426 Hemi engine at the NASCAR Daytona 500, Ford engineers developed a Hemi of their own. The SOHC 427 Ford engine featured cylinder heads with hemispherical combustion chambers and a single camshaft in each. Rated at 615 hp with a single 4-barrel carburetor and 647 when equipped with dual Holley 4-barrels, NASCAR immediately passed restrictive rules that precluded the engine from stock car competition. Rather than being shelved, the engines found their way into the hands of drag racers by early 1965 and continued to deliver racing victories for Ford into the early 1970s.

Lincoln-Mercury formed its own drag team in 1964 and in a similar fashion to the Ford Drag Council, it contracted Dearborn Steel Tubing Company to modify 21 Mercury Comets (20 coupes and 1 station wagon) for competition in the A/Factory Experimental class.

FORD FIRES BACK WITH A HEMI OF ITS OWN

By allowing the Chrysler teams to compete with the 426 Race Hemi engine, NASCAR had put them at a distinct disadvantage in a market where they had invested a large sum of money. After realizing that, Ford put its engineers to work on an engine package to counter the Hemi. Ford's engineering department provided more than their money's worth as, using the 427-ci FE engine as a starting point, they developed new cylinder heads with hemispherical combustion chambers and overhead camshafts. Dubbed the SOHC 427, the engine developed an incredible 615 hp with a single 4-barrel carburetor and 657 hp when fitted with two 4-barrels.

In an effort to keep things from spiraling out of control, NASCAR was quick to disallow the engine from competition, but in very short order it was welcomed with open arms by Ford drag racers. In 1965, NASCAR banned the Chrysler teams from competing with the 426 Hemi, which resulted in the factory-supported Mopar teams sitting out the year, allowing Ford to run rampant.

Mercury, 1964

THE CALIENTE IS HOT AND THE CYCLONE WHIPS UP QUITE A STORM.

Having found success in 1963 with the Bill Stroppe–prepared stock cars, Mercury decided to expand its motorsports program and go drag racing in 1964. Dearborn Steel Tubing Company was tasked with building 21 specially modified Mercury Comets for competition in the A/FX class. Twenty coupes and one very unique station wagon were constructed using many of the same weight-saving steps, unique modifications, and of course the 427 High Riser engine, applied to the Fairlane Thunderbolts.

Mercury was able to lure top name racers such as "Dyno Don" Nicholson, Eddie Schartman, and Ronnie Sox away from Chevrolet, and George Delorean from Pontiac in the hopes of building a winning team. And win they did. From the time of their debut at the NHRA Winternationals, the Comets cut a swath through all comers, winning the A/FX class title.

The Mr. Factory Stock Eliminator title came down to two Comets, the station wagon of Don Nicholson, and the more conventional coupe of Ronnie Sox. While Nicholson turned the quicker elapsed time, the Burlington, North Carolina, ace left the starting line first and claimed the honors.

The next scheduled stop for the fledgling Comet drag team was to be the AHRA Winter Nationals at Bee Line Dragway in Arizona. However, the team ended up boycotting the race when Nicholson's wagon was not allowed to participate due to protests from the factory Chrysler teams over

what they believed was an unfair traction advantage the wagon had due to its long overhang behind the rear wheels.

Some years back "Dyno Don" told me of this incident and how very shortly thereafter he received one of the Comet coupes and promptly set both ends of the NHRA A/FX class record before the car had even been lettered. As Dyno put it, "I guess the Mopar guys should have quit while they were ahead." Nicholson went on to win over 90 percent of the match races he participated in with the Comet in 1964 and had the car running in the high-10-second range before the end of the season.

The station wagon was placed in the capable hands of Eddie Schartman, who match raced the car very successfully but did score a big win at the NASCAR Winter Drag Races to add to the Comet win total for the year. According to official Ford Motor Company documents, during the period from January 1 to May 31, 1964, the Comet team scored 29 NHRA A/FX class victories, an enviable record indeed.

Bill Stroppe of Long Beach, California, was recognized as the man who put Mercury in the winner's circle prior to the 1957 competition ban. After returning to the team in 1963, he fielded a number of top-running Mercurys and prepared cars that made an even better showing in 1964, winning five NASCAR races and dominating the USAC Stock car series, with driver Parnelli Jones taking home the championship. Many top names, some more recognizable from Indy car and sports car racing than stock cars (such as Jim McElreath, Dave MacDonald, and Jones) complemented Billy Wade, Darrel Dierenger, and Rex White, who all successfully wheeled Mercurys that year.

In a stroke of marketing brilliance, Mercury had Dearborn Steel Tubing Company prepare a number of Comets that were subsequently taken to Daytona International Speedway and run nonstop for 100,000 miles at an average speed of more than 100 mph, to prove the reliability of the model and the 289 V-8 engine. And to top it off, several of the durability run Comets were later converted into lightweight drag cars for competition in the NHRA B/FX class. The best known of these cars, handled by Doug Nash, was very successful nationally and held the class record for a time.

Plymouth and Dodge, 1964

AS IF THE STAGE III 426 MAX WEDGE WASN'T ENOUGH, MOPAR INTRODUCES THE RACE HEMI.

Chrysler Corporation started the 1964 season by improving upon the very successful 426 Max Wedge engine. The Stage III Max Wedge benefited from improved cylinder heads, larger carburetors, and an ever hotter camshaft profile than its Stage II predecessor. The 1964 offering was again available in two flavors: a docile 410-hp version with 11.0:1 compression and

the maximum Max Wedge, still rated at 425 hp in spite of all the improvements, which squeezed the mixture at 12.5 to 1.

Once again a lightweight package was available featuring aluminum fenders, hood (with scoop), bumper brackets, acid-dipped front bumper, doors, deck lid, and Plexiglas windows. The addition of these parts, along with the deletion of creature comforts, took close to 300 pounds from the all-steel Plymouth or Dodge model so equipped. Later in the year aluminum doors and door hinges also became available.

Hot Rod tested an all-steel version of the Plymouth Savoy equipped with the 425-hp engine, backed with a TorqueFlite automatic transmission and 4.56 Sure-Grip differential. With open exhausts, 102-octane gasoline, and cheater slicks, the car stopped the quarter-mile clocks at 12.69 seconds at 112 mph.

Another addition to the Mopar lineup for 1964 was the all-new A833 4-speed manual transmission. Period advertising for the manual box announced, "We used to win automatically. Now you have a choice." Plymouth and Dodge were on track for another big year on the nation's dragstrips.

The Max Wedge wasn't all that the Mopar camp had to offer for 1964. On December 23, 1963, Chrysler announced Engine Package A864, the 426 Hemi. An internal company document indicated that 10 blocks had been shipped to Ray Nichels for preparation to equip drag cars at the upcoming NHRA Winternationals, as well as stock cars for the Daytona 500.

The second-generation Hemi engine from Chrysler was designed as a race-only piece initially, with 4.25-inch bore and 3.75-inch stroke, 12.5:1 compression, solid lifter camshaft, and either single 4-barrel induction (stock car racing) or two 4-barrels mounted on an aluminum cross-ram intake manifold (for drag racing). Initially the engines mounted Carter AFB carburetors, which soon proved to be inadequate for the task, and were replaced by Holleys. While the horsepower rating for the two engines was 410 for the single carburetor and 425 for the dual-carburetor version, dynamometer tests revealed that they easily produced 550 and 565 hp, respectively.

Dodges and Plymouths proved themselves to be at the top of the class in both the SS/A and A/FX categories in 1964, with the factory teams

These were race-only cars built to compete against the A/FX Comets and Ford Thunderbolts. They were built in limited numbers and devoid of any factory warranty.

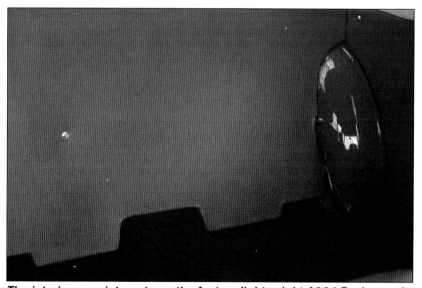

The interior appointments on the factory lightweight A864 Dodge and Plymouths were pure business with all comforts deleted, including the back seat. Automatic transmission cars were fitted with a manual valve body and race-only TorqueFlite transmission that had no Park position. Dodge A100 van seats replaced the stock bench and a thin rubber mat replaced the carpeting.

scoring big victories at national events and match races. Lesser known, but no less successful, competitors were winning local and regional events week after week.

Reflection on the 1964 NASCAR season seems to reveal that the Chrysler teams performed the same chicanery that Chevrolet had in 1963, where an engine that was not available in a production automobile, let alone produced in the required number of 500, was allowed to participate in competition. NASCAR seemed to turn a blind eye to the lack of 426 Hemi engines in production and also that the Plymouth and Dodge teams might enjoy an unfair advantage over the competition by the fact that their cars were intermediate-size models with unitized construction, while the other manufacturers raced full-size, perimeter-framed vehicles. Second-generation driver Richard Petty took full advantage of the rules and his considerable driving talents to win his first of seven NASCAR championships in 1964 in a 426 Hemi Plymouth.

While early versions were fitted with Carter carburetors, the race Hemis soon received larger Holley 4-barrel carburetors on their cross-ram intake manifolds. The Holleys, along with a race-profile solid lifter camshaft and a 12.0:1 compression ratio, moved a ton of air through the hemispherical combustion chambers. The burnt gases were sent downstream through custom-built exhaust headers with equal-length tubes for maximum power.

FUNNY CAR ORIGINS

The Super Stock Plymouths (116-inch wheelbase) and Dodges (119-inch wheelbase) gained a traction advantage through the use of rear leaf springs that had a 20-inch front section, as opposed to the standard 22 inches. This resulted in the rear wheels being moved forward approximately 1 inch, which increased the amount of rear overhang behind the tires, providing more traction off the starting line.

Later in the 1964 season, two Plymouths (Tom Grove and Al Ekstrand) and two Dodges (Ramchargers and Dave Strickler), were shipped to the Alexander Brothers Custom shop, where the wheelbases were radically modified. All the cars had their front suspensions relocated forward of the stock position, the Plymouths were moved 3 inches and the Dodges 4 inches. The rear wheels on both Dodges got moved ahead 5 inches. The results caused observers to exclaim that the cars looked "funny" and the term funny car was born. While these cars are referred to as "2-percent cars," simple math reveals that the wheelbases had been altered by 3 percent.

The term 2 percent comes from an NHRA ruling issued prior to the 1965 racing season, limiting A/FX cars to a wheelbase alteration of not more than 2 percent. This ruling initially caused much controversy with the factory teams but was soon worked out through rules changes that came about almost as rapidly as the cars were being modified as the season progressed.

Production figures for 1964 Plymouth and Dodge models equipped with the A864 426 Hemi were 55 Dodge sedans, 2 Plymouth sedans, 2 each Dodges and Plymouths with factory wheelbase alteration (2-percent cars), 4 Preproduction Development cars, and 35 each Dodge and Plymouth hardtops.

CHAPTER 5

1965–1966: THINGS GET "FUNNY"

There is little connection between showroom and race car as the focus shifted away from production-based drag cars. New engines and models out of Detroit proved that midsize muscle cars for the street were the latest rage.

The big news from Chevrolet in 1965 came in the form of an all-new big-block engine series to replace the 409, which was still available in 1965 but in a very watered-down form. The new engine series was born of the 427 Mystery engine run in NASCAR during the 1963 season and debuted at 396 ci. A particularly great performance version of the mid-size Chevelle, designated Z-16, was a true performer with 375 hp, heavier chassis design, and better suspension and brakes. Just 200 of these rare Chevelles were built in 1965, but they gave birth to a successful line of midsize Chevys with high-performance big-block engines that lasted into the 1970s. (Photo Courtesy CarTech Archive)

Chevrolet, 1965

HOW ABOUT THAT NEW ENGINE WITH THOSE "PORCUPINE" CYLINDER HEADS?

By 1965, the day of the 409 as a performance engine had passed, and while it was still listed as an option in its mildest form, the big news for Chevy fans came in the form of a brand-new engine series born of the Mark III, 427 Mystery engine, developed in 1963. The new cylinder block featured four-bolt main bearing caps, with a 4.094-inch bore, and when fitted with its 3.76-inch stroke crankshaft, it delivered 396 ci.

But the big news sat on top of the new engine in the form of completely redesigned cylinder heads with a splayed valve arrangement that gave rise to the nickname "porcupine heads." The new high-performance 396 was available in two versions, RPO L-37 and L-79. The L-37 boasted 11.0:1 compression, a hot hydraulic lifter camshaft, a Holley 4-barrel carburetor mounted on an aluminum intake manifold, and was rated at 375 hp at 6,500 rpm, with 420 ft-lbs of torque at 3,600 rpm. The L-37 was fitted to the Z-16 Chevelle, a very rare model with only 200 built.

It appears that Chevrolet had taken a look at what its cousins over at Pontiac had achieved with the GTO and decided to field its own midsize super car, one with more horsepower, of course. The Z-16 Chevelle was special in many ways, aside from the engine. To handle the additional horsepower and torque of the 396, the bodies were mounted on reinforced frames designed for convertible models and, along with other heavy-duty components, the Z-11 received 11-inch rear brakes to add some whoa to all that go. The only available transmission was the 4-speed manual and with its street tires and standard rear-axle ratio, the Z-16 Chevelle proved itself worthy of supercar status by covering the quarter-mile in 14.5 seconds at 100 mph.

A dual-snorkel air cleaner, chrome valvecovers, Holley carburetor, and a hot hydraulic lifter camshaft made the 396 a good-looking, as well as good-performing, engine when part of the Z-16 package. (Photo Courtesy CarTech Archive)

The interior of the Z-16 Chevelle enhanced the car's sporty performance image with two-tone vinyl bucket seats, console, sport steering wheel, floor-mounted 4-speed shifter, and dash-mounted tachometer. This particular Z-16, which belongs to Kayo Erwin, is even more rare thanks to its optional tilt steering wheel. (Photo Courtesy CarTech Archive)

The new big-block engine series had its own name, the 396 Turbo-Jet, and special fender emblems announced its arrival.

Chevrolet now had an answer to the GTO and 4-4-2, and it didn't take long for drag racers, including Dick Harrell, Huston Platt, and Malcolm Durham, to put the new engine into match race action against the factory-backed teams.

While the limited production Z-16 Chevelle was an impressive performer, for slightly more money you could step up to the ultimate asphalt shredder from Chevrolet in 1965, the L-79 Corvette. The fuel-injected 327 engine remained on the option list, but it was the new big-block Corvette that had all the car magazines talking. The Corvette L-79 engine differed from the Chevelle's L-37 only in that it had a solid lifter camshaft. Advertised horsepower was 425 at 6,400 rpm, with 415 ft-lbs of torque at 4,000 rpm.

Although the big-block V-8 added 200 pounds to the Corvette, the power produced more than made up for that fact in straight-line acceleration. *Car* tests conducted at the time indicated that the fuel-injected small-block Corvette could run the quarter-mile in 14.1 seconds, just slightly faster than the Z-16 Chevelle. An L-79 model was a full second quicker. With more than 2,000 Corvettes optioned with the L-79 that year, Chevrolet was well represented on the streets and dragstrips of America.

The owner of this big-block 1965 Corvette performed the always-popular swap from stock Muncie shift linkage to the more reliable Hurst unit. While it may hurt the car's originality factor, it sure makes shifting a lot easier. (Photo Courtesy Bob Wenzelburger)

The new high-performance 396 from Chevrolet was also available in the Corvette, giving the model its first big-block engine. The Corvette version of the engine was essentially the same as the one that powered the Z-16 Chevelle, except that the Corvette engine received a solid lifter camshaft that resulted in it being rated at 425 hp. (Photo Courtesy CarTech Archive)

It is likely that pound for pound, dollar for dollar, there was no better street and strip GM performance car than the L-79 Chevy II Nova in 1966. Affectionately known as the "Box Nova" by its fans, the Chevy II, which up to this point was little more than an economy model, was deceptively quick when optioned with the 350-hp 327 small-block engine.

Although racers such as Bill Jenkins, who won the 1966 NHRA Winternationals with his L-79 Nova, usually opted for the basic model bench seat interior, the sportier SS package was available and it went a long way toward turning the mundane Box Nova into a sporty performance car for the street.

The heart of the L-79 Nova was a wonderfully thought-out engine that produced 350 hp from 327 ci, thanks to improved cylinder heads, a hot hydraulic lifter camshaft, aluminum intake manifold, and Holley 4-barrel carburetor. A dual-snorkel air cleaner fed fresh air to the engine and the chrome dress-up package provided visual impact.

Chevrolet, 1966

THE "BIG-BLOCK" GETS BIGGER WHILE THE "SMALL-BLOCKS" STILL FLY.

Chevrolet turned its compact economy car, the Chevy II Nova, into one of the best deals for the customer dollar when it came to street performance in 1966. Chevrolet stuffed the L-79 engine with 327 ci, 11.0:1 compression, double-hump cylinder heads (2.02-inch intake, 1.60-inch exhaust valves), a hot hydraulic lifter camshaft, aluminum intake, Holley 4-barrel carburetor, and dual-snorkel air cleaner, and instantly turned the 3,000-pound Nova into a force to be reckoned with on the street and strip. If the hot little Nova had one drawback, it was the mono-leaf rear suspension, which cried out for the addition of traction bars before any full power starts were attempted.

Aside from that, and a few car magazine tests that criticized the handling and braking characteristics, the L-79 Nova may well have been, pound-for-pound and dollar-for-dollar, the best performance car on the market in 1966. Bill "Grumpy" Jenkins, who had come back to Chevrolet after a stint with Dodge (1964–1965), fielded one of the quickest NHRA A/Stock class racers in the nation in the form of his *Grumpy's Toy* L-79 Nova. His 11-second quarter-mile elapsed times in race trim spoke to the performance potential of the package.

The Chevelle received a facelift for 1966 and the 396 that had been so rare in 1965 became a readily available option in the line. Initially available in two versions, 325 and 360 hp (the L-34 360-hp engine had an improved camshaft profile and larger carburetor), it didn't take long for Chevrolet to turn the Chevelle into a true muscle car with the introduction of the L-78 engine option in the spring of that year.

The L-78 had an advertised horsepower rating of 375 at 5,600 rpm with 415 ft-lbs of torque at 3,600 rpm. It revved higher, thanks to a solid lifter camshaft, and breathed better, due to larger valve cylinder heads and improved exhaust manifolds. Capable of mid- to low-14-second quarter-mile elapsed times at 100 mph in stock form, the L-78 Chevelle was right in the thick of the battle for dealer-available muscle car supremacy.

Of course, the Corvette stepped up in the optional power department as well. The 300-hp 327 remained the base engine and the outstanding 350-hp 327 was the next option up the ladder, but the big-block V-8 got most of the attention. It had grown from 396 to 427 ci by virtue of a 4.25-inch bore and 3.76-inch stroke and was offered in two versions. One was rated at 390 hp at 5,400 rpm with 460 ft-lbs of torque at 3,500 rpm with a hydraulic lifter camshaft and 10.25:1 compression. The other belted out an advertised 425 hp at 5,600 rpm and 460 ft-lbs of torque at 4,000 rpm. This version was based on a beefier cylinder block with four-bolt main bearing caps, 11.1:1 compression, a solid lifter camshaft, and larger Holley 4-barrel carburetor on an aluminum intake manifold.

MR. USA #1, BRUCE LARSON

The national attention gained by driving the Jim Costilow and Bruce Larson Ford Cobra in 1965 surely had some bearing on why Sutliff Chevrolet, Bruce Larson's employer, extended an offer of sponsorship should he consider switching to Chevrolet for 1966. Not only did Bruce switch camps, he built and successfully raced a one-of-a-kind Chevelle-bodied match racer that had Chevy fans cheering from coast to coast.

Bruce contracted a local company to build an all-fiberglass body to the dimensions of a standard 1966 Chevelle. A combination boxed-rail tube chassis was built to carry a heavy-duty Dana rear axle and 427-ci Chevy engine that had been stroked to 454 ci. Hilborn fuel injectors with unique forward-leaning stacks fed a mixture of nitromethane and alcohol fuel to the engine. Originally equipped with a Muncie 4-speed transmission that proved unreliable, the car soon received a modified TH-400 automatic.

Weighing just 2,200 pounds, Larson's Chevelle, dubbed USA 1 and painted in a patriotic red, white, and blue scheme, quickly proved to be not only in demand for match race bookings, but a winning combination.

It is easy to claim that the 427/425 Corvette was the top performer in the Chevrolet line that year, as proved by a *Car and Driver* road test where the test on a big-block Corvette with a 3.36 rear-axle ratio showed the car capable of covering the quarter-mile in 12.8 seconds at 112 mph.

It was also in 1966 that a Chevrolet dealer in Canonsburg, Pennsylvania, by the name of Don Yenko, who had more than a passing interest in racing, decided that he would use his dealership to further the performance image of his favorite brand by doing some in-house modifications to Chevy's unique compact car, the Corvair. Yenko labeled these cars Stingers and offered them in three stages of modification, from the 160-hp Stage I for increased street performance, to the 240-hp stage IV, which was stripped of most creature comforts and ready for competition in the SCCA D/Production class as delivered. The sales successes realized with the Stinger Corvairs led Don Yenko to produce some of the most iconic Chevy performance cars.

Pontiac, 1965

THE GTO REMAINS EVERYONE'S DARLING, BUT DON'T COUNT OUT THE CATALINA.

While the engine options remained the same, the GTO received a restyle for 1965, and its popularity continued, with many more enthusiasts finally being able to buy the car that Pontiac couldn't seem to build enough of in the previous year. *Car Life* tested a 4-speed, 360-hp model that apparently had not been provided by Royal Pontiac and recorded some very believable performance numbers of 0–60 mph in 5.8 seconds and a quarter-mile time of 14.5 seconds at 100 mph.

Super Stock and Drag Illustrated prepared a GTO weighing 3,541 pounds for B/S class competition. With NHRA-legal modifications consisting of a Bobcat kit by Royal Pontiac, a Hurst shifter, 3.90 rear-end gearing, slicks, and tubular steel exhaust headers, the test car recorded a best quarter-mile elapsed time of 13.19 seconds at 105.88 mph, an improvement of more than 1 second when compared to a showroom-stock vehicle.

Pontiac also introduced what could best be described as the GTO's big brother for 1965, the Catalina 2+2 sport package. And for $425 above the base Catalina, you received both a good-looking and potentially strong-running full-size car. The 2+2 package included the 335-hp 421-ci engine, 3-speed manual transmission, heavy-duty suspension, special interior and exterior badging, and wheel covers. Optional at extra cost were the 4-speed manual and automatic transmissions.

Although a bit slower through the quarter-mile than the much lighter GTO, the big Catalinas proved themselves to be spirited performers and very popular with the motoring public, as 11,510 units were sold that year. *Car Life* tested a Catalina 2+2 equipped with the 421 engine, 4-speed transmission, and 4.11 rear axle. The car went from 0 to 60 mph in 7.2 seconds and covered the quarter-mile in 15.5 seconds at 95 mph.

In spite of having been signed on as a member of the Mercury Comet A/FX team for 1965, Pontiac man Arnie Beswick continued to supplement his income by match racing his 1964 GTO. Beswick made the long tow from Illinois to Daytona for the NASCAR Winter Drags and, after dropping a valve in his SOHC 427 Comet, he unloaded the GTO and won the Unlimited Class title. This raised the ire of the brass at Mercury and Beswick

STOCKPILED RACING PARTS

In keeping with Pontiac's long history of performance and building special vehicles, approximately 52 Catalina 2+2 models were built with specially prepared 421 Super Duty engines. These rare cars can be identified through the special VK/XX-coded cylinder blocks, which were, in essence, left over from the company's stock car racing program. These engines sported a steel crankshaft, 11.5:1 compression ratio, McKellar #11 camshaft, and special long exhaust manifolds.

The 20 cars built with automatic transmissions were equipped with a TH-400 from Cadillac for superior strength. All had the Saf-T-Trac differential, and two were equipped with 3.91:1 gears.

The GTO remained a part of the Tempest line for 1965, and although the wheelbase remained the same, the overall length of the car grew by 3.1 inches. The hood received a non-functional scoop, but a rare dealer option converted the scoop to an actual ram air system, which sealed to the top of the carburetors via a metal pan and foam ring. The 389 engine received a boost in power thanks to improved cylinder heads, intake, and camshaft. Rated horsepower for the standard single 4-barrel engine was 335, while the optional Tri-Power version jumped to 360. Capable of low-14-second quarter-mile elapsed times in stock form, the installation of the Royal Bobcat kit and cheater slicks shaved 1 second off that with ease. (Photo Courtesy Keith Seymore)

The GTO's big brother in 1965 was the Catalina 2+2. This full-size model lived in the shadow of the widely publicized GTO, although the big Catalina was powered by a standard 338-hp 421 with the Tri-Power 421 engine optional. With Tri-Power, the 421 produced 376 hp at 5,000 rpm and 461 ft-lbs of torque at 3,600 rpm. A Catalina 2+2 with 3.42 rear axle tested by Car and Driver recorded a 0–60 time of 3.9 seconds and topped out at 130 mph. Very impressive numbers but it was discovered that the team at Royal Pontiac had worked their magic on the car before delivery to the magazine. (Photo Courtesy Lea Huetteman)

responded by resigning his Comet commission and returning to his original love, the GTO, full time. Arnie continued to race a series of cars with Pontiac power based on the GTO body style for several years, much to the delight of hardcore Pontiac fans.

The interior of the Catalina 2+2 was both sporty and luxurious with bucket seats and console standard. A console-mounted tachometer was optional. Buyers had the choice of the new Turbo-Hydramatic automatic or a 4-speed manual transmission. (Photo Courtesy Lea Huetteman)

Pontiac, 1966

THE GTO CARRIES PONTIAC'S PERFORMANCE BANNER FORWARD.

The GTO did a couple of things for 1966. First, it became a model unto itself and no longer just a Tempest option. Second, an increase in performance served to offset the increase in overall size. While the horsepower rating for the GTO's 389 when equipped with three 2-barrel carburetors remained at 360 at 5,200 rpm, the addition of a #744 camshaft, which had the same lift as the previous cam at .400 inch, enjoyed an increase in duration from 288 to 302 degrees, which no doubt helped the power output.

Also optionally available for the first time was the XS option, which consisted of a functional hood scoop that ducted cool, horsepower-enhancing outside air to the carburetors, which were isolated from engine heat by an aluminum pan. *Car and Driver* recorded a quarter-mile time of 14.1 seconds at 105 mph with a showroom-stock GTO.

Longtime Pontiac racer "Akron Arlen" Vanke came back from the Chrysler camp in 1966. Vanke prepared two 1966 GTO sport coupes that had deleted the radio, console, and any deluxe trim; added 4.33 rear-end gears and an M-20 wide-ratio 4-speed transmission; and included other class-legal modifications such as headers, drag shocks, and slicks. Vanke's magic touch put the Knafel Pontiac–sponsored GTO, *Tin Indian,* in the winner's circle at the NASCAR Winternationals and NHRA Springnationals, recording a best elapsed time of 12.20 seconds, and compiling 27 class wins for the season.

Remaining faithful to Pontiac power as he had for years, drag racer Arnie Beswick went the tube chassis funny car route for 1966, using a fiberglass body that copied the production GTO.

Olds, 1965

4-4-2 NOW STANDS FOR "400 CI, 4-SPEED, AND DUAL EXHAUST."

In an effort to crash the GTO party, Oldsmobile engineers equipped the second-year 4-4-2 with a 400-ci (4.00-inch bore x 3.975-inch stroke) engine. Fitted with hydraulic valve lifters, 10.25:1 compression, and a Rochester

Bill Huetteman's Catalina 2+2 is even more rare thanks to the special order of this VK XX-stamped 421 engine that was essentially a leftover engine destined for NASCAR stock car competition before Pontiac pulled the plug on racing. One of the many unique features on these rare engines is the special high-flow exhaust manifold. Thanks to this speed parts–packed 421, the big Catalina can clear the quarter-mile traps in 12 seconds. (Photo Courtesy Lea Huetteman)

4-barrel carburetor, the engine produced 345 hp at 4,800 rpm and 440 ft-lbs of torque at 3,200 rpm. Available with the base 3-speed manual, 4-speed, or automatic transmission, and a host of available comforts, the 4-4-2 was a bit hefty, with a curb weight of 3,735 pounds.

Car and Driver tested a 4-speed 4-4-2, with 3.55 rear gears, but for some reason chose the convertible version that tipped the scales at 3,960 performance-robbing pounds. In spite of the weight deficit, the torquey 400 pulled the 4-4-2 through the quarter-mile traps in 15.0 seconds at 98 mph, pretty close to GTO numbers.

Modern Rod proved without a doubt that the new 442 could hang with the GTO as the magazine's team performed the same basic modifications that weekend racers could do on their test car. With good tuning, headers, and a set of slicks on the rear, the car stopped the quarter-mile clocks in 13.78 seconds at 102.73 mph.

Olds, 1966

A SERIOUS ASSAULT ON THE PERFORMANCE MARKET.

For 1966, the "W" in W-30 stood for winner. While one of the rarest of all Olds performance cars with just over 50 examples built, the 442s equipped with the W-30 option that year were true GTO, Fairlane, Chevelle, and Comet killers, thanks to the fact that these were the closest thing to a factory race car Olds had ever produced. The 400-ci engines that powered these special cars were factory blueprinted to exacting specifications, fitted with a hotter camshaft, bigger valves, heavier valvesprings, and three Rochester 2-barrel carburetors mounted on a cast-iron intake manifold that featured a special heat riser block-off. Cool outside air was ducted to the carburetors via large, vacuum-operated, intake tubes that were mounted under the front bumper.

To save weight and provide additional traction, the battery was mounted in the trunk over the right rear wheel and the steel front inner fender panels were replaced with plastic versions. Delivered into the hands of serious drag racers, the W-30 Oldsmobiles made believers out of many, recording 12-second quarter-mile elapsed times when properly tuned and equipped with headers and slicks.

Ford, 1965

THE MUSTANG GRABS THE SPOTLIGHT AND TOTAL PERFORMANCE MARCHES ON.

Ford continued corporate participation in all forms of motorsports for 1965, and the re-engineered, restyled Galaxie was again offered with the 427-ci

The big news from Ford for 1965 was, of course, the sporty 2+2 fastback and a high-winding 271-hp, 289-ci small-block V-8 backed with a 4-speed transmission. It was very popular with the performance-minded driver. Ford made the Mustang its performance flagship that year and for years to follow. (Photo Courtesy Jim Smart)

engine. *Car Life* tested a Galaxie 500XL with a 3.50 ratio and non-locking differential and recorded a quarter-mile time of 14.9 seconds at 97 mph.

Ford Galaxies had things pretty much all to themselves on the NASCAR circuit as Chrysler sat the year out after the sanctioning body declared that the 426 Hemi was not a production engine and thus was not legal for competition. While the big cars did not receive the full focus of the company when it came to drag racing there were several standout 1965 and many 1964 Galaxies on the dragstrips that were making performance headlines for the company.

Although the midsize Fairlane model, in the form of the 427 Thunderbolt, had been the top dragstrip performer for Ford in 1964, the focus shifted to the Mustang. The Fairlane had also been completely restyled for 1965, and the 271-hp 289 engine was still optionally available. Ford also added the new C-4 3-speed automatic transmission to the mix for 1965 and one of these cars, specially prepared by Les Ritchey's Performance Associates, dominated in both NHRA and AHRA class competition.

A one-off version of the Fairlane Thunderbolt was constructed by Dearborn Steel Tubing Company. This car, at first fitted with 427 High Riser power and later with the SOHC 427, proved to be a dominant performer in the NHRA B/FX class. The Falcon had pretty much been relegated to the role of compact economy car in 1965. While the Sprint model was still available and had received an increase in displacement through the addition of the Challenger 289 V-8, it included no actual performance parts and was rated at 210 hp with a 2-barrel carburetor.

But innovative thinker and factory drag racer Phil Bonner was not about to let the Falcon fade from the performance limelight, and he commissioned Holman-Moody to build him a 1965 model along the lines of the A/FX Mustangs and power it with the SOHC 427 engine. The result was one of the most successful match racers of the year, as Bonner and his *Daddy Warbucks* Falcon blazed a trail across America's dragstrips.

The main focus for performance at Ford in 1965 was directed at the Mustang, and rightfully so. A fastback Mustang, the 2+2, was introduced and when fitted with the optional 271-hp 289, it was quite a sporty performer. In an effort to prove that the Mustang could compete as a world class sports car, Ford contracted Shelby American to convert a series of the new fastbacks into super Mustangs.

Upgrades to the suspension and brakes, along with engine modifications to boost the horsepower from 271 to 306, put the Shelby-prepared Mustangs, labeled GT-350, into the winner's circle in short order. Four GT-350 Mustangs were shipped to Performance Associates, where Les Ritchey turned them into dragstrip terrors through the addition of Belanger Brothers exhaust headers, Gabriel drag shocks, an NHRA-approved bell-housing, a driveshaft safety loop, Casler cheater slicks, and 5.14 rear-axle gearing. Should the customer request, A/FX style traction bars and a drag race profile camshaft could be added. These cars proved to be the class of the field in the NHRA C/SP class.

To garner the most attention in drag racing, Ford went after the A/FX class with fervor. Dearborn Steel Tubing was contracted to develop a 1965 Mustang, powered by the SOHC 427 engine, in an effort to dominate the class. Working with drag racing coordinator Dick Brannan, Dearborn Steel constructed Ford's most serious drag car to date, and it was soon decided that an additional 10 of these cars would be constructed for members of the Ford Drag Council. Holman-Moody, best known for its preparation of stock cars, was contracted to build the additional A/FX Mustangs, along with any private contract or dealer cars that might be requested.

The Ford Drag Council cars made their competition debut at the NHRA Winternationals and received the publicity that Ford had hoped for. Bill Lawton, driving the John Healey–prepared Tasca Ford Mustang, claimed the Factory Stock Eliminator title. The Fords did better at this particular NHRA National event than they had done before, copping the class win in A/FX, B/FX, C/FX, AA/S, and AA/SA, as well.

But it wasn't long before a factory mandate led to a boycott of any direct competition between the factory Ford teams' legal A/FX Mustangs and the Chrysler teams' "funny cars" with their radically altered wheelbases. The apparent purpose for this was to slow the process of factory-backed race cars losing any resemblance to production models.

The 1965 Mustang could show its heels to many cars with more displacement when equipped with the optional 271-hp 289 engine. Benefiting from improved cylinder heads, a solid lifter camshaft, dual-point mechanical-advance distributor, free-flowing exhaust manifolds feeding dual exhausts, and a 4-barrel carburetor, the high-performance 289 was a potent, high-winding package. The high-performance 289 remained an option on the Mustang model until 1967. (Photo Courtesy Jim Smart)

After Dearborn Steel Tubing Company built a prototype car for Dick Brannan, Ford contracted Holman-Moody to build an additional 10 A/FX Mustangs for members of the Drag Council. Gas Ronda, the 1964 NHRA World Champion, was the recipient of this poppy-red Mustang powered by the SOHC 427 engine. Several of the Drag Council cars were delivered with 427 High Riser engines due to a shortage of "Cammers." The new Mustang scored its first big win at the NHRA Winternationals when Bill Lawton took home Mr. Factory Stock Eliminator honors.

This strategy did not last long, however, as Holman-Moody was contracted to build a Mustang that was far lighter and featured a stretched wheelbase for Drag Council captain Dick Brannan. The "Match Bash" Mustang, Bronco, was built specifically to run against the altered-wheelbase Chrysler team cars, which by this time had sprouted fuel injectors and were beginning to burn exotic fuels in place of gasoline. The NHRA was forced to scramble once again for a suitable classification for these factory funny cars and at first put them in the B/Altered or C/Fuel Dragster classes until the class rules could be worked out.

After catching wind of the fact that main rival Corvette would be receiving big-block power for 1965, Ford tapped Shelby American to design a new Cobra around the FE-series big-block V-8. The result was a good one, as the old snake charmer delivered a Cobra powered by Ford's 427 that packed enough venom to gain it the title of "the fastest accelerating production car in the world." A beast in every aspect, the 427 Cobra not only accelerated quickly, but it stopped and handled pretty darn well too.

To prove the point, Ford had factory driver Ken Miles put the new Cobra through its paces, and in a world where 0–100 times in 13.5 seconds were considered outstanding, Miles took the 427 Cobra from a standing start to 100 mph and back to a stop in just 13.8 seconds. With standard 3.54 rear-end gears, the Cobra could easily cover the quarter-mile in just over 12.5 seconds at 112 mph and top out at 165 mph. Renowned automotive writer Tom McCahill described the acceleration of the 427 Cobra as "feeling like you had been hit in the small of the back by a Louisville Slugger in the hands of Babe Ruth."

On the small-block Cobra side, while the Shelby team was tearing up the competition on the road courses, the team of Costilow and Larson was fielding the most successful of all the Dragon Snakes, which was a converted street model and not a true Dragon Snake as delivered from Shelby American. The team took home class victories at the NHRA Winternationals, Spring Nationals, and U.S. Nationals, only to be denied an NHRA Championship by virtue of running quicker than the class national record (which they held) during eliminations at the NHRA World Finals in Tulsa, Oklahoma.

This was the beginning of Bracket racing, where competitors were eliminated by posting a quicker elapsed time in eliminations than the established class record. In the case of the Costilow & Larson team, the NHRA points lost as a result of running quicker than its own national record cost them the championship that year and led Bruce to move to the Funny Car class, where cars were not handicapped by a class index.

Along with the cars built under contract for Ford's Drag Council members, Holman-Moody also secured permission to supply parts and build A/FX Mustangs for independent racers. Larson Ford from New York received this car, which was driven by Bob Hamilton. The car has been restored to its 1966 configuration when fuel injectors were added to the SOHC 427 powerplant. (Photo Courtesy Colin Date)

Considering the fact that they were all-out race cars, the A/FX Mustangs as delivered had very stock-appearing interiors. As the season progressed the cars became more modified to keep pace with modifications being performed by Chrysler's factory-supported drag teams.

Gas Ronda's A/FX Mustang was powered by the SOHC 427 engine that Ford had developed for NASCAR to counter Chrysler's 426 Hemi. Capable of producing well in excess of 600 hp, the engine quickly became the darling of Ford and Mercury drag racers.

The high-performance 289 in the Les Ritchey–prepared 1965 Fairlane proved to be both powerful and reliable. For AHRA competition the car was fitted with a 715-cfm Holley 4-barrel of the type found on the Shelby GT-350 and a ram air system that ducted cool air to the engine from the car's grille area. (Photo Courtesy Alan Pound)

While the Mustang received all the attention as Ford's performance car for 1965, other models made a splash of their own. Ford built two very special 1965 Fairlanes for drag racing that year, one of which was delivered into the capable hands of Drag Council member Les Ritchey. After being prepared at Ritchey's Performance Associates shop, this Fairlane, powered by the 271-hp high-performance 289 and backed with the all-new C-4 automatic transmission, went on a tear through the Stock/Automatic classes in both the NHRA and AHRA, setting records and claiming numerous wins. (Photo Courtesy Alan Pound)

The high-performance 289 engine was not a listed option for the Falcon in the United States, but six cars were built by Ford of Canada as B/FX drag cars. The Rankin Ford Wild Child is one of those cars. As was the case with many race cars of the era, the Rankin Falcon underwent numerous modifications, eventually having the small-block replaced with an SOHC 427 and the stock front suspension ditched for a straight-axle setup.

Ford's 425-hp 427 was available in all full-size models with the exception of the station wagon in 1965 and was Ford's choice to power cars in NASCAR stock car racing, as it had been since 1963. Two Ford Drag Council 427 Galaxies were fielded in the B/FX and AA/S classes in 1965. Several hundred production 427 Galaxies such as this 500XL model were produced that year.

The Fairlane was re-engineered to accommodate the 390-ci FE-series engine for 1966 in response to GM's popular GTO and Chevelle models. The top of the line were the sporty Fairlane GT (4-speed) and GTA (automatic). And 1966 was also the first year for the Select Shift C-6 automatic transmission, a great improvement over previous units.

In a move reminiscent of both the GTO and Chevelle, the GT and GTA 390 Fairlanes were fitted with simulated hood scoops with badging that indicated engine size.

Rated at an optimistic 335 hp, the 390 that powered the 1966 Fairlane, while an improvement over the standard 300-hp passenger car version, was not the deep breather required to put the Ford ahead of the competition. The engine's hydraulic lifter camshaft had a decent profile and the Holley 4-barrel carburetor with open-element air cleaner certainly helped, but the engine was handicapped by its restrictive intake and exhaust manifolds.

In an effort to stay on top in drag racing, Ford built 57 1966 Fairlanes with the new 427 Medium Riser engine. At 3,410 pounds, including a fiberglass hood with leading-edge air scoop, and with its improved 427 still rated at just 425 hp, these special cars proved to be just what Ford needed to bolster the Fairlane model's performance image. Factory-backed drag racers such as Ed Terry won their share of Super/Stock titles with the new Fairlanes in 1966. (Photo Courtesy Don Antilla)

The 427 Fairlanes for 1966 received engines that had carefully matched and fitted components from the factory, ensuring maximum horsepower and reliability. The new Medium Riser cylinder heads and intake manifold were a compromise to the High Riser setup, which required the use of a large hood scoop for clearance and an improvement over the Low Riser heads and intake, which did not perform as well. (Photo Courtesy Don Antilla)

Ford had tapped Shelby American to take its Mustang to a new level of performance in 1965, and this continued in 1966. With relocated and revamped suspension, better brakes, and other improvements, the Shelby GT-350 Mustang proved to be a world-class sports car, handing Ford a world championship in 1965. Four 1965 and four 1966 GT-350 Mustangs were converted into drag cars by Les Ritchey's Performance Associates, and these cars delivered drag racing titles to Ford and Shelby as well. (Photo Courtesy John Saia)

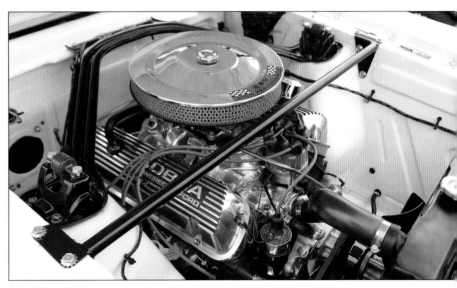

Shelby modified Ford's 271-hp 289 engine that was to power the GT-350 to produce an advertised 306 hp through the use of a high-rise aluminum intake manifold mounting a 715-cfm dual-feed, center pivot, Holley 4-barrel carburetor and tubular steel Tri-Y exhaust headers. The brace that ran from fender to fender across the top of the engine was added by Shelby to increase front-end stiffness for improved handling. (Photo Courtesy John Saia)

Shelby also fitted the GT-350 Mustang with racing-style seat belts, a wood steering wheel as used in the Cobra, and a dash-mounted tachometer. (Photo Courtesy John Saia)

Factory-backed Ford drag cars still relied on the SOHC 427 for power, but by 1966 the carburetors had been replaced by fuel injection and exotic fuel mixtures of methanol and nitromethane replaced gasoline in the fuel tanks.

Shelby American took the Cobra to new heights in 1965 when it redesigned the car from the original AC sports car to fit Ford's 427. The result was the quickest accelerating production car in history. Although Cobras continued to dominate the sports car racing circuit, Shelby followed up on his previous 289 Dragon Snake program with one amazing 427 version. Delivered to Harr Ford in New England and driven by Gus Zuidema, the 427 Dragon Snake set multiple NHRA national records, won class honors every time it raced, including the NHRA Winternationals and U.S. Nationals, and won 50 percent of the Eliminators entered. Zuidema set the NHRA A/SP class record at 10.38 seconds at 138 mph and later the A/MSP record at 10.02 seconds at 146 mph. (Photos Courtesy Carl Mentz)

The interior of the Holman-Moody–built 1966 stretched Mustang raced by Gas Ronda during the season bore no resemblance to that of the production line Mustang. One aluminum racing seat, a roll cage, and other safety equipment filled the passenger compartment. Also by this point modified C-6 automatic transmissions had replaced 4-speed manuals.

Ford, 1966

FORD REMAINS "FIRST ON RACE DAY."

With all its corporate support for racing in so many venues around the globe, Ford really seemed to miss the mark when it came to producing world-class muscle cars (with the exception of the Cobra, which was built in very small numbers and priced above the average buyer's budget) in 1966. To compete with the Chevelle SS 396, GTO, Olds 4-4-2, and Buick Skylark GS, Ford increased the overall size of the Fairlane and introduced two versions, the GT (4-speed) and GTA (which used the new C-6 automatic transmission), and fitted both cars with the 390 FE-series engine.

Unfortunately, the only departure from the same 390 that was found in station wagons that year was a better profile hydraulic lifter camshaft, Holley 4-barrel carburetor, and low-restriction air cleaner. Ford gave the engine an optimistic rating of 335 hp and, in spite of great styling and a clever advertising campaign, the 390 Fairlane failed to impress as a true muscle car in showroom form, running the quarter-mile in the 15-second range.

It should be noted that with proper tuning and dealer-available performance parts, the 390 Fairlane could easily compete with the competition on the street. The company did give the public a peek at what the following year had to offer when it built 57 Fairlanes powered by the 427 Medium Riser engine and stripped of most weight-adding amenities.

In the hands of drag racers with the proper factory connections, these cars proved to be winners in the Super Stock class. Ford continued to offer the 427 as an option on its Galaxie-based models, but the era of full-size muscle had pretty much come to an end.

Aside from NASCAR stock car tracks, where Ford took home 12 victories in spite of the fact that Chrysler Corporation cars were now legally running the 426 Hemi engine, 427 Galaxies were few and far between in 1966. Ford did find a use for the big Galaxies on the dragstrip with two unique factory-prepared entries. The 1964 NHRA World Champion, Mike Schmitt, took delivery of a Galaxie powered by the SOHC 427 for competition in the B/FX class. Ed Terry fielded a similar car motivated by a 289 Cobra powerplant for C/FX. Terry obliterated the class record, and the car ran so quick that many were inclined to think that it was 427 powered.

The model that had been tapped to be the performance flagship for the Ford line, the Mustang, continued with the 271-hp high-performance 289 small-block as its top option, because the car could not accommodate a big-block engine without major modifications. Shelby American toned down the GT-350 version of the Mustang, making it more user-friendly to a wider cross-section of drivers, and in doing so, greatly increased the production and sales numbers of the hottest version of the Mustang that year.

Car Life tested a GT-350 and reported that the car stopped the quarter-mile clocks in 14.0 seconds at 92 mph, making it more than a match for most dealer-available big-displacement muscle cars.

Car Craft had occasion to test a 1966 427 Cobra and found that even when hampered with rather tall 3.54 rear-end gearing, the car could still cover the quarter-mile in just 12.20 seconds at 118 mph. Shelby also built a 427 Cobra to Dragon Snake specifications in 1966. With the installation of a roll bar, Koni drag shocks, twin electric fuel pumps, a scatter shield, relocated battery, and 4.54 gearing in the rear, the car was shipped to Harr Ford in Worcester, Massachusetts. There, driver Gus Zuidema rolled up an enviable record in very short order, setting the NHRA A/SP class record at 10.86 seconds at 127 mph (later lowering it to 10.38 seconds), winning the 1966 NHRA Winternationals and NHRA Nationals, and finishing runner-up in the NHRA Division One Street Eliminator category. The Harr Ford Dragon Snake won its class every time it raced and took home half of the Street Eliminator titles that year as well.

The Drag Council Mustangs had been radically modified by 1966 to keep ahead of the competition. Now sporting extended wheelbases, fuel injectors, and running on exotic fuels, it was becoming more difficult to identify these racing versions from the Mustangs found in dealer showrooms. The line between racing victories on Sunday and dealer sales on Monday was becoming more blurred as the horsepower war being waged on the dragstrip escalated.

Mercury, 1965

CYCLONE CARRIES THE MERCURY PERFORMANCE BANNER INTO THE WINNER'S CIRCLE.

Although the 427 engine was still offered as an available option for 1965, the full-size Mercury line had grown to such huge dimensions and gained considerable bulk with luxury options, that performance-minded buyers more often looked to the midsize Comet Cyclone. Restyled for 1965, the Cyclone provided good street performance thanks to its standard 225-hp 289 small-block V-8 with available 4-speed transmission, bucket seats, dash-mounted tachometer, and other sporty features. To make customers aware that Mercury took performance seriously, the company tapped long-time West Coast subcontractor Bill Stroppe Engineering to prepare a series of Comet drag cars for factory drivers.

Two classes were targeted, A/FX and B/FX, the rules for which allowed fewer than the 50 units built that the NHRA placed on S/S class competition. The A/FX cars received either the 427 High Riser engine or the newly introduced SOHC 427. The 427 cars were delivered directly into the hands of the factory team drivers. The B/FX version, powered by a Stroppe-prepared 289-ci Cobra V-8 that delivered nearly 400 hp at 6,000 rpm, could be obtained through participating Lincoln-Mercury dealers. But because there were only 15 of them produced, it was the lucky racer, with the proper connections, who got his hands on one of those hot Comets that year.

Lincoln-Mercury advertising took full advantage of the immediate results delivered by the Stroppe-prepared cars through a campaign that depicted the factory racers and the slogan, "It was cold in February except where the Comets were running." The most recognized, and arguably the most successful A/FX Comet driver, was "Dyno Don" Nicholson, but it wasn't far into the 1965 season before he felt the need to radically alter the wheelbase and add fuel injectors to his Comet to keep pace with the Mopar funny cars.

While Mercury encouraged its team drivers to compete in NHRA legal events, it was the wildly popular world of match racing where professional racers such as Nicholson made their money. Even Arnie Beswick, who had been hired as a Mercury team member for 1965, continued to match race his GTO during the season. This caused some consternation with his sponsors at Mercury and led to his leaving the factory team early in the season.

The 1965 A/FX and B/FX Comets were full-on race cars that were stripped of normal production parts and fitted with lightweight components but still maintained a close appearance to their showroom cousins. This did not last, however. An interesting aside came when Eddie Schartman, who had yet to take delivery of his 65 A/FX Comet, brought out the former Don Nicholson Comet station wagon that he had been match racing so successfully and took home the Mr. Stock Eliminator title at the NASCAR Winter Drags in Daytona Beach, Florida.

The Mercury Comet received revised styling for 1965 with stacked headlamps and squared-off lines. The top performer was the Cyclone, which was powered by the proven 289-ci small-block V-8. Most were the 225-hp version, but a few received the 271-hp high-performance 289. (Photo Courtesy Ken Bennett)

The Super Cyclone 289 engine that powers Ken Bennett's 1965 Cyclone, fitted with a hydraulic lifter camshaft and 4-barrel carburetor, produces 225 rated horsepower. This combination made the Cyclone a spirited performer with manners.

Lincoln-Mercury contracted Holman-Moody-Stroppe to build 15 special lightweight Comet drag cars outfitted with high-performance 289 engines for the Factory Experimental classes.

These cars had fiberglass components, lightweight Plexiglas windows, and other modifications that made them race capable as delivered through participating dealers.

The interiors of 1965 Comet drag cars featured just two racing bucket seats. Radio, heater, sound deadener, seam sealer, rear window mechanisms, and back seat were deleted. The area that formerly contained the back seat was covered by a lightweight fiberglass insert.

Delivered with specially prepared high-performance 289 engines, the Comets relied on a single 4-barrel carburetor, four 2-throat Weber carbs of the type used on Cobras or (shown) variations thereof. This Factory Experimental Comet's engine has been fitted with a Mickey Thompson cross-ram intake manifold mounting two Holley 4-barrel carburetors.

Mercury drag team members were the recipients of 427 High Riser and SOHC 427 lightweight Comets prepared by Holman-Moody-Stroppe for competition in the A/FX class. "Dyno Don" Nicholson and other team members now found themselves in direct competition with the Chrysler factory drag teams and their counterparts at Ford. The Mercury team had great success in the A/FX classes, but most cars were eventually modified into match race vehicles before mid-season 1965 as the other factory teams cars were more radically altered.

Hayden Proffitt started the 1965 season at the wheel of a class-legal A/FX Comet powered by the SOHC 427 engine, but it wasn't long before he also altered his car's wheelbase, added fuel injectors, and used exotic fuels to match race against other factory teams.

Jack Chrisman, who made history by supercharging the 427 engine in his 1964 Comet and being the first full-body car to run over 150 mph in the quarter-mile, re-bodied the car as a 1965, powered by a supercharged, fuel-burning, SOHC 427 engine. The car's engine was set back into the driver's compartment and used direct drive–like fuel dragsters instead of a conventional transmission.

Mercury, 1966

THE L-M TEAM MAKES A GRAND DEPARTURE FROM PRODUCTION-BASED DRAG CARS.

In a move that set factory-supported drag racing on an entirely new path, the Mercury team quietly contracted the Logghe Stamping Company to construct chassis similar to those used in Top Fuel dragsters of the time; fit them with fuel-injected, 427 SOHC engines, backed by beefed-up C-6 automatic transmissions; and top them with a one-piece, fiberglass, lift-off body that replicated the 1966 Comet Cyclone.

In the hands of team drivers Don Nicholson, Ed Schartman, and Jack Chrisman, the new cars immediately took drag racing by storm, and there

was little that could match them. Other manufacturers scrambled to catch up, and in within a year, the factory wars on the dragstrips of America had spiraled dangerously out of control. Cars became more radical as superchargers and higher doses of exotic fuels were added, which created a situation where the horsepower being generated outpaced the tire and safety technology of the day.

SELLING PERFORMANCE

In July 1966, all Lincoln-Mercury dealers received a copy of the high-performance equipment catalog, along with a letter from T. G. Daniels, Sales Promotion and Training Department Manager, which encouraged dealers to take advantage of the purchasing power of the youth market and pointed out that there was additional profit potential in the sales and installation of performance parts, tuning, and general servicing of cars sold to customers interested in extra-high performance.

The astute owner of a 1966 Comet Cyclone could also take advantage of a Mercury-sponsored program where factory drag racing ace Ed Schartman could be contracted to prepare cars for competition. I saw one of these Comets by Ed Schartman run elapsed times in the high-12-second range, which was more than sufficient to defeat the numerous GTOs entered in his class on that day.

Mercury, which had gone winless in NASCAR competition in 1965 with the exception of one victory claimed by Darel Dieringer in a 1964 model, took advantage of a late ruling that allowed the midsize Comet body to compete in 1966 and managed to claim one checkered flag for the season.

Plymouth and Dodge, 1965

FUNNY CARS AND SUPER STOCKS.

Chrysler Corporation had followed a path similar to that of Ford in 1965, where selling performance cars off the dealer lots seemed to take a back seat to offerings fielded by factory-connected drag racers. Plymouth had introduced the Barracuda in 1964 to compete with the Mustang, and while the car provided decent street performance with its 235-hp 273-ci Commando V-8, there was still no substitute for cubic inches.

Dodge was a year away from fielding a Dart that received any attention from the performance-minded buyer. The 426 Street Wedge offered in the midsize line was a watered-down version of the previous Max Wedge engines, with just 365 hp to offer. Much more can be said about the A990

THE ONE AND ONLY GOLDFISH

When it comes to unique and rare race cars from Chrysler in 1965, none is rarer than the Goldfish. Plymouth dedicated a number of Barracudas to drag racing teams that year, but only one was equipped with the 235-hp 273 small-block V-8. That car passed into the hands of the factory Plymouth drag team of engineers known as the Golden Commandos, to be prepared for competition in the F/S class. The engine was blueprinted to factory specifications and the entire car was prepped for racing, as would be any other serious stock class competitor. NHRA class designations were based upon a formula of engine displacement and vehicle weight, thus F/S for this particular combination.

This is where the Goldfish's preparation departs from the spirit of the rules. It seemed that the Commandos, and other factory-backed teams, were not above bending the rules when it came to delivering victories to their factory benefactors. It is reported that in the neighborhood of 150 pounds were removed from the car through the removal of structure and perhaps some parts that were not readily visible to tech inspectors. The missing weight was replaced where it would do the most good, over the rear wheels. Reports are that weight was hidden between the rear seat and trunk area and the spare tire was filled with water. The Goldfish enjoyed considerable success in 1965, including a class win at the NHRA Nationals.

The factory designation for the lightweight Hemi Super/Stock package in 1965 was A990. These cars were true factory racers available with both automatic and 4-speed transmissions and replete with lightweight components, including special thinner side glass by Corning. Power came from the 426-ci race Hemi.

At least one of the A990 cars had a fiberglass instrument panel. Front sheet metal and doors, although no longer aluminum in 1965, were stamped from lighter gauge steel than standard production parts.

Super Stock and altered-wheelbase factory race cars from the Plymouth and Dodge camps, however, as they proved to be big winners for the company.

There were 101 Dodge Coronet–based and 100 Plymouth Belvedere–based A990 Super Stock cars built in 1965. They were offered with either the 4-speed manual "Hemi Box" or a modified TorqueFlite automatic that featured a reverse manual shift valve body and no Park setting. Power was provided by the 426 Hemi fitted with a solid lifter camshaft, aluminum cylinder heads, and two huge Holley 4-barrel carburetors mounted atop a magnesium cross-ram intake. To reduce the cars' weight and circumvent an NHRA rule against Super/Stock class cars using fiberglass body components, Chrysler resorted to chemical milling, which means acid-dipping the hood, fenders, radiator support, bumpers, doors, and deck lid.

The cars were also fitted with aluminum door hinges and thin side glass. A-100 van seats were mounted, and the back seat, along with sound deadener and seam sealer, heater, radio, carpet, and other creature comforts, were deleted. Unlike their altered-wheelbase cousins, the A990 cars closely resembled standard production cars, and in the hands of top drivers they proved to be formidable foes on the dragstrip.

Prior to the NHRA Winternationals drag races, the sanctioning body mandated that no cars would be able to compete in the A/FX class with a wheelbase alteration of more than 2 percent. The Chrysler teams were caught napping, having intended to debut their new radically altered "Funny cars" at Pomona.

A990 Super/Stock Dodges and Plymouths had their rear seats deleted and the factory bench seat replaced by lighter bucket seats used in Dodge vans.

The Making of a "Funny Car"

Chrysler Corporation began its altered-wheelbase drag car project with 13 examples, but this number soon dropped to 12 as one of the bodies succumbed to over-aggressive chemical milling (acid-dipping). The chemical milling, performed by an outside contractor, removed approximately 200 pounds from the bodies. The wheelbase alterations were performed by yet another subcontractor, Amblewagon of Troy, Michigan. The rear floorpans had a 15-inch section removed to move the rear wheels forward, and the rear quarter panels and wheel openings were modified to match. In the front, new frame rails were installed, which moved the front wheels forward 10 inches. Extended torsion bars, modified steering linkage, and a lightweight crossmember were installed to complete the modifications.

In a further effort to get the cars down to fighting weight, they received fiberglass fenders, hood, deck lid, doors, dashboard, bumpers, and Plexiglas side windows. Race ready with either an aluminum case 4-speed or modified TorqueFlite automatic transmission, the cars weighed less than the A/FX class 3,200-pound minimum, which allowed teams to add weight where it would do the most good.

At the AHRA Winter Championships, factory team driver Bud Faubel won the Mr. Stock Eliminator Crown. The altered-wheelbase Mopars were immediate crowd favorites. Thanks to capable drivers and teams such as Dave Strickler, Dick Landy, Ronnie Sox, Bob Harrop, The Golden Commandos, and The Ramchargers, Chrysler recouped its investment in spades, winning numerous match races and events that year, including the overall title at the Super Stock Nationals in York, Pennsylvania, considered by many to be the greatest drag racing event ever.

Circle Track Stars Go Straight

As a result of a 1965 NASCAR rules change that did not allow the Chrysler teams to compete with the 426 Hemi engine, the factory boycotted the series, leaving many top drivers without a series to race in. Two of the best, Richard Petty and David Pearson, used factory support to try their hand at drag racing during the 1965 season. Both had made promotional appearances behind the wheel of drag cars previously, as had some of the Ford team NASCAR stars, and were warmly received.

Pearson fielded a unique Hemi Dodge Dart station wagon that had been built in the shop of Cotton Owens, who was best known for his prowess with stock car construction. The Pearson effort got off to such a rocky start that Dodge called in Bud Faubel, one of its top drag racers, to sort things out and get Pearson going straight.

Petty Enterprises built a Barracuda powered by a fuel-injected Hemi for Richard. Not only did he and the car prove to be very much in demand for match race bookings, they made a formidable team on the dragstrip. Sadly, during a match race at a small southern dragstrip, Petty lost control of his car and went off the track. The crash resulted in injuries and one fatality among the spectators. The accident brought Richard's drag racing efforts to an end and he returned the wrecked Barracuda to his North Carolina shop, where it was buried.

The 426-ci Race Hemi with two Holley 4-barrel carburetors mounted on its special cross-ram intake manifold provided ample power to win in both the Super/Stock and Super/Stock automatic classes. Former Chevy racer Bill Jenkins and many others proved it in 1965.

Bill Bagshaw's Red Light Bandit proved that the A990 was not only remain competitive but also adaptable as he realized great success with his 4-speed car in NHRA's SS/B class. Ken Montgomery was still racing his #555 Plymouth A990 into the new millennium. (Photo Courtesy Bob Wenzelburger)

The term funny car arose from the radical wheelbase alterations performed on the Chrysler factory drag team cars designed to run in the NHRA A/FX class in 1965. A number of factory Dodges and Plymouths had their wheelbases slightly altered during the 1964 season and became known as 2-percent cars. The NHRA took the 2-percent wheelbase alteration and applied it to a rule, which precluded the funny cars from competing in the A/FX class. This rule did little to slow the escalation in the factory war being waged in drag racing, however. Bud Faubel, Dick Landy, and Dave Strickler were recipients of altered-wheelbase Dodges in 1965. (Photo Courtesy Bob Wenzelburger)

In response, four A990 cars were fitted with the lightweight parts package and rushed into battle against the A/FX Fords and Mercury team cars. Ace tuner and driver Tommy Grove fared the best of the Mopar team, taking his Plymouth into the final round before falling to Bill Lawton's Ford.

The "Funny cars" were left to debut at the AHRA Winter Championships and spent the majority of the season participating in match races. The A990 Plymouth of Bill Jenkins emerged victorious in the S/SA class and went on to claim Top Stock Eliminator honors.

Ronnie Sox, who had recently parted company with the Mercury Drag Team, and Lee Smith were two of the Factory Plymouth drivers at the wheel of altered-wheelbase cars during the 1965 season. The funny cars became more radically modified as the season progressed. (Photo Courtesy Bob Wenzelburger)

All of the Chrysler factory drag team cars were powered by the 426 race Hemi in 1965, some being equipped with the TorqueFlite automatic while others ran a 4-speed manual transmission. The 4-speed cars used short velocity stacks on the fuel injection, while the automatics ran long stacks. Testing had determined how to "tune" the stacks to take advantage of the RPM range, where the engine made the most torque when equipped with each type of transmission. (Photo Courtesy Bob Wenzelburger)

The interiors of the altered-wheelbase Dodges and Plymouths were even more sparse than those of the A990 cars. The addition of a roll bar provided safety and helped the structural integrity of the cars, which had been acid-dipped to the point where they were prone to bend under acceleration. Dave Strickler was known throughout the drag racing world as a master of the 4-speed shift, thus his Dodge was fitted with the manual transmission. The long, ungainly Hurst-designed shift lever was a challenge for those of lesser talents. (Photo Courtesy Greg Cook)

A look under the altered-wheelbase Dodge of Dave Strickler shows how the car's floorpan was cut and sectioned, allowing the rear axle and springs to be moved forward 14 inches. The purpose of this alteration was to gain additional weight transfer over the rear wheels, which aided traction off the starting line. (Photo Courtesy Greg Cook)

While not as radically altered as the rear, the front suspension mounting points on the Dodge and Plymouth "funny cars" were also moved forward to maintain the desired wheelbase. (Photo Courtesy Greg Cook)

The 426 Street Hemi was decidedly more docile than its race-only counterparts but no slouch in the horsepower department. Inline Carter 4-barrel carburetors on a cast-iron intake manifold in place of the cross-ram-mounted Holleys of the Race Hemi were the most obvious difference. Inside the engine less compression and a somewhat milder camshaft made the engine more suitable for street use.

The interior of Jere Stahl's Belvedere was sparse as was the fashion of base model Chrysler products of the 1960s, although it did have carpeting. Stahl replaced the long handle of the Hurst shifter that equipped the car with one more suitable for the quick shifts required to be a winner.

Plymouth and Dodge, 1966

INTRODUCING THE STREET HEMI!

Chrysler Corporation saw that in spite of the dragstrip successes by its Funny Cars in 1965, street cars that could back up its performance image were needed to bring young buyers into dealer showrooms. Enter the Street Hemi, a toned-down version of the engine that had won so many racing titles for Chrysler products over the previous two years.

The Street Hemi was based on the same cylinder block with cross-bolted main bearing caps, fitted with cast-iron cylinder heads, 10.25:1 compression, and a milder solid lifter camshaft. Fuel was fed to the beast by two Carter 3140 AFB 4-barrel carburetors on a cast-iron intake manifold. Ignition chores were handled by a dual-point distributor. Rated at 425 hp at 5,000 rpm and 490 ft-lbs of torque at 4,000 rpm, the street Hemi was available with either a 4-speed manual or TorqueFlite automatic transmission. In 1966 a total of 1,524 Plymouth and 1,168 Dodge models were ordered with the option.

Hot Rod tested a Dodge Coronet convertible equipped with the Street Hemi, TorqueFlite transmission, and 3.23 rear axle, posting a 14.60-second quarter-mile time bone-stock as delivered. After fitting the car with a set of Doug's headers, 4.56 axle ratio, Casler cheater slicks, and a dyno tune by Mopar ace Dick Landy, the car improved to 13.36 seconds, causing the writer to speculate that the car would be very competitive in the A/SA class.

Perhaps the most famous of all 1966 Street Hemi cars was the Plymouth Belvedere, fielded in NHRA's A/Stock class by longtime racer and header builder Jere Stahl, who was never bested in class competition during the season. Stahl's car, the Belvedere I model, was devoid of creature comforts but, aside from class legal modifications, was the same car that could be ordered through any Chrysler dealer that year. Stahl went on to wage numerous battles with Bill Jenkins and his small-block Chevy Nova during the 1966 season, a true David versus Goliath epic where Goliath (Stahl) emerged victorious.

Dodge produced a unique model of the compact Dart specifically designed for the drag racer on a budget. Called the D/Dart for the NHRA class requirement (D/Stock) that the car was built around, it was delivered nearly race ready from the factory with 4.86 ratio Sure Grip rear, heavy-duty 4-speed transmission, Weber racing clutch, 273-ci high-performance engine with Racer Brown camshaft, modified factory intake manifold with Holley 4-barrel carburetor, low-restriction air cleaner, Doug's headers, and a dual-point ignition system. The horsepower rating of 275, an improvement of 40 horses over the standard high-performance 273, and a shipping weight of 2,946 pounds made the car perfect for the class it was designed to dominate.

While the A990 cars continued to prove themselves more than competitive in 1966, the altered-wheelbase cars had become obsolete and the factory-backed race teams such as Sox & Martin were forced to build vehicles that were not based on passenger cars but were purpose-built, fiberglass-bodied race cars with tube chassis that bore less and less resemblance to anything available from a dealer as the season progressed.

Plymouth and Dodge had their best year yet on the NASCAR stock car tracks with Richard Petty claiming victory at the Daytona 500 with his Plymouth to start the year and David Pearson taking home the championship with his Dodge. Quite a few of Pearson's wins came at the wheel of a 1964 Dodge, which obviously didn't become too worn out from previous racing because the Chrysler teams sat out the 1965 season.

The introduction of the Street Hemi as a production option in Plymouth and Dodge models for 1966 resulted in NASCAR allowing it to be used in competition once again. This paid dividends for the Mopar teams, as Dodge recorded 19 wins and Plymouth brought home 15 for the year.

TIME TO ROLL OUT THE RINGERS

When *Car and Driver* conducted a comparison road test of Detroit's hottest midsize offerings for 1966, apparently some criteria were set down in advance. All the cars would have 3.55 rear-axle ratios and all would be driven by professional driver Masten Gregory during the official tests.

From that point forward, the entire show seems to have fallen apart as the representatives of the major car manufacturers involved, with the exception of Chevrolet, Buick, and Olds, apparently were under the misconception that this was to be a fair analysis of how each of these cars stacked up against another in various test criteria. Suffice it to say that the Pontiac, Mercury, and Ford teams came out loaded for bear with specially prepared "ringers" for the magazine to test.

Here is a list of the players:

- Pontiac GTO (prepared by Royal Pontiac with Bobcat kit) 389/360. Test weight: 3,620 pounds; quarter-mile performance: 14.05 at 105.15 mph.
- Chevelle SS 396/360. Test weight: 3,605 pounds; quarter-mile performance: 14.66 at 99.88 mph.
- Olds 442 400/350. Test weight: 3,490 pounds; quarter-mile performance: 14.59 at 100.55.
- Buick Skylark GS 401/340 (automatic transmission). Test weight: 3,550 pounds; quarter-mile performance: 14.92 at 95.11 mph.
- Fairlane GTA 390/335 (Holman-Moody prepared, 3.89 rear-axle ratio) Test weight: 3,640 pounds; quarter-mile performance: 14.26 at 99.00 mph.
- Comet Cyclone GT (prepared by Bud Moore Engineering) 390/335. Test weight: 3,474 pounds; quarter-mile performance: 13.98 at 103.8 mph.

Although this was hardly a fair comparison, it was a shining example of the ends to which auto manufacturers went to sell performance to the public. And as the decade progressed, things would get even wilder.

CHAPTER 6

1967–1969: THE FOCUS RETURNS TO STREET PERFORMANCE

These two years provided America with some of its most legendary muscle cars and refined a new breed of performance machine, the Pony car. High-performance engines from 302 to 427 ci in cars that rolled right out of the showroom equipped with many of the same speed parts that heretofore had only been available through the aftermarket. And as if that weren't sufficient, any number of enterprising high-performance-oriented dealers provided additional parts and tuning to bring the customer's car to an even higher level of performance.

While it took until 1967 for Chevrolet to respond to Ford's Mustang and Plymouth's Barracuda with a comparable model, the company got it right the first time with the new Camaro. Available in versions from a base 6-cylinder to the sporty RS, SS, and SCCA racing-circuit-inspired Z-28, the Camaro was an instant success. (Photo Courtesy CarTech Archive)

Chevrolet, 1967

ENTER THE CAMARO.

In September 1966, Chevrolet introduced its answer to the Mustang in the form of a new model called the Camaro. In similar fashion to the Mustang, the new Chevy came in various trim levels and with a base 6-cylinder engine and several V-8 engine options, including the 295-hp 350-ci L-30 small-block, which replaced the 327 partway through the year. At the top of the option list were three 396-ci big-blocks: the L-35 at 325 hp; the L-34 at 350 hp; and the king of them all, the L78, which boasted 375 hp. While there were just over 1,000 Camaros optioned with the L-78 engine in 1967, it was enough to announce that Chevrolet had jumped into the small car performance market with both feet.

While performance numbers of the L-78 cars are sketchy, *Motor Trend* tested an L-35, 4-speed Camaro with optional 4.11 gearing and posted a 0–60 time of 6.0 seconds and the quarter-mile in 14.50 at 95 mph. If 396 ci weren't enough to get the job done, you could contact Don Yenko Chevrolet who, with the blessing of the factory, would sell you one of his 104 dealer-upgraded Camaros, packed with the 427 engine and a host of aftermarket performance goodies.

Out in Chicagoland, Nickey Chevrolet was performing similar engine swaps, and those on the West Coast could call on Bill Thomas to upgrade their Chevy, as many did. In Long Island, New York, Joel Rosen had opened Motion Performance, and his business plan included converting some already hot new cars from Baldwin Chevrolet into super cars. He started things off right when he swapped not just any big-block into a 1967 Camaro, the L-88 427. Motion Performance went on to become associated with hot Chevys on the streets and dragstrips of the Northeast for years to come.

Another completely separate model of the Camaro was available in 1967, albeit in very limited numbers, the Z-28. Released in December 1966, it was designed around the rules set down by the SCCA for sports car competition; the Z-28 was as close to a dedicated race car as you could ever think of buying from your dealer showroom in 1967.

Power came from a 302-ci small-block V-8 with a rated 290 hp at 5,300 rpm. Taking into consideration that the high-revving small-block with its solid lifter cam, improved cylinder heads, and aluminum intake manifold with 780-cfm Holley 4-barrel carburetor easily revved closer to 6,800 rpm, the actual horsepower was estimated to be in the neighborhood of 360. Add to this the optional induction, which consisted of two Holley carburetors

Top-of-the-line performance for the new Camaro came in the form of the L-78 375-hp 396 big-block V-8. This combination proved to be more than a match for the 390-powered 1967 Mustang, and if it wasn't enough, there were several Chevrolet dealers who gladly upgraded a customer's car to 427 power. (Photo Courtesy CarTech Archive)

The bare-bones 427, 4-speed Biscayne two-door sedan was perhaps the ultimate sleeper you could buy from Chevrolet in 1967. The lightest full-size Chevrolet packing the biggest engine the company produced had become a favorite package for hot rodders since the mid-1950s. Baldwin Chevrolet offered a specially prepared 427 Biscayne called the "Street Racer Special" in 1968. (Photos Courtesy CarTech Archive)

on a cross-ram intake manifold and the horsepower was probably closer to 400. Another unique option available on the Z-28 was four-wheel disc brakes, at the time pretty much unheard of in a standard American production car outside of the Corvette.

Corvette for 1967 provided the ultimate in Chevy performance on three distinct levels. General Motors made four versions of the 427 engine as options in the new Corvette, from not so mild to scorching hot. First, the L-36, which sported a hydraulic lifter cam, 10.25:1 compression, and a single 4-barrel carburetor, was rated at 390 hp at 5,400 rpm with 460 ft-lbs of torque at 3600.

The next step up the ladder was the L-68, virtually the same as the L-36 with the exception of three 2-barrel carburetors in place of the single 4-barrel, rated at 400 hp.

Third, the L-71 made things really start to be serious as the compression jumped to 11.0:1, a solid lifter cam was added, and with the Tri-power carburetion, the 435 hp had 5,800 rpm and the same torque number of 460 but peaking at 4,000 rpm.

And fourth, you have the ultimate street beast, the "not really meant for the street" L-88.

At an additional cost of $1,500, discerning buyers received their Corvette with a number of mandatory deletions and options. Gone were the radio and heater, obviously dropped to discourage street driving; and in the no-choice category were heavy-duty suspension, power brakes, and M-22 4-speed transmission.

That brings us to the heart of it all, the L-88 engine. Conservatively rated at 430 hp, it included L-89 aluminum cylinder heads, an aggressive solid lifter cam, 12.5:1 compression, and an 850-cfm Holley 4-barrel carburetor that dumped copious amounts of only the highest octane fuel through an aluminum intake manifold. Just 20 examples of the L-88 Corvette were delivered that year, making them one of the most sought after of all performance Corvettes.

The L36 engine was also available in a stand-alone model of the Impala for 1967, the SS427. With a distinctive hood, special badging, and other trim differences to set it apart, the SS427 was available with the TH-400 automatic or a 4-speed manual transmission. It is interesting to note that although virtually identical, the L36 in the SS427 Impala was rated at 5 hp less (385) than when fitted to the Corvette.

The Chevelle received only minor changes, and there was a little shuffling of available engine options for 1967. The base big-block remained the 325-hp 396, while the L34 396 previously rated at 360 hp was downgraded to 350. The top of the heap was once again the 375-hp brute, which in a *Car and Driver* road test posted a 0–60 time of 6.5 seconds, with the quarter-mile coming up at 14.9 seconds. Considering the car's 3.73 rear-end gearing, it appears that these rather disappointing times spoke of either a poor driver or excessive wheel spin off the starting line.

Although the concept behind the Z-28 Camaro was based on SCCA Trans-Am series competition, the 302-ci cars with their underrated 290 hp made them an immediate favorite with drag racers. Bill Drevo ordered this car new in 1968, and when he did so his motives were slightly clouded. Although the car was ordered with the deluxe interior, which indicated that it was a street driver, Drevo had his dealer check the block for the optional 4.88 Posi-Traction rear on the order form and had the car painted a special silver available only on Cadillacs.

A NASCAR rules change for 1967 allowed the Chevelle body to be used, and legendary driver Bobby Allison took full advantage, putting his 1966 model in the winner's circle four times.

After Drevo took delivery, the car saw little to no street duty as Drevo found it was the perfect combination for the E/Pure Stock class. Turning elapsed times in the 13-second range, he won his class 18 weeks in a row. Drevo was so successful with his Z-28 that he received the attention of performance-minded people inside of General Motors, and some help in the form of special parts soon came his way. Since 1968 this car has rolled up just 1,900 miles, a quarter-mile at a time.

The 302-ci small-block V-8 that powered the Z-28 Camaros proved to be a perfect combination of cylinder bore, stroke, camshaft, cylinder heads, intake, and carburetion for the NHRA E/Stock class into which it fit, thanks to a conservative horsepower rating of just 290.

Aside from the aftermarket steering wheel, tachometer, and class-legal Hurst shifter, the interior of Bill Drevo's former Z-28 drag car looks exactly as ordered and raced in Pure/Stock, right down to the AM radio.

Part of the Z-28 high-performance package was this NASCAR-inspired ram air system, which ducted air from the cowling at the base of the windshield into the air-cleaner assembly. Interestingly, this system was not installed at the factory but rather placed in the trunk for dealer or owner installation.

BILL DREVO JR.
IHRA-AHRA NATIONAL & WORLD RECORD HOLDER
69 - 70 - 71 - 72 - 73 - 74 - 75 - 78 - 79 - 80 - 81

As can be seen by the lettering on the door of Bill Drevo's Z-28 Camaro, he accumulated an impressive list of wins and national records in two racing series while campaigning the car he named Quicksilver. And quick it was, running in the 13-second bracket.

Along with various stages of performance tuning and modifications, Yenko Super Cars were also fitted with special badges and other cosmetic enhancements to set them apart from the crowd at the local drive-in or drag-strip. This 427 Yenko Camaro sports a dealer-installed fiberglass hood, which is both functional and tasteful, while removing unwanted pounds from the front of the car. (Photo Courtesy CarTech Archive)

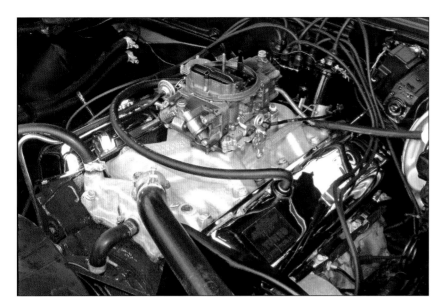

The decal on this big-block Chevy valvecover announces to the world that the team at Yenko Chevrolet in Cannonsburg, Pennsylvania, has worked its high-performance tuning magic under the hood. (Photo Courtesy CarTech Archive)

Don Yenko wasn't the only Chevy dealer turning out supercars in the late 1960s. Illinois dealer Fred Gibb teamed with legendary Chevy drag racer Dick Harrell, and under GM COPO #9738 he purchased 50 1969 Novas powered by the L-78 375-hp 396 big-block engine backed with a modified TH-400 automatic transmission and 4.10-geared 12-bolt rear axle.

The cars were stripped-down versions of the Nova, with the exception of SS emblems and bucket seats, and were delivered with a 90-day factory warranty due to their special nature. It is estimated that 12 to 18 of the 50 cars were shipped to the shop of Dick Harrell in Kansas City, where he tuned and/or performed further modifications to the cars as per customer request, including the installation of 450-hp 427 engines.

Aside from the exhaust note and these 396 fender emblems, there was little to outwardly indicate just how potent the Gibb-Harrell Nova actually was. And it was surely possible for the enterprising street racer to have the dealer remove the fender emblems.

The Gibb-Harrell Novas were all stripped models as delivered from the factory with the exception of bucket seats and console, which housed the shifter for the automatic transmission. The Sun tachometer mounted on the steering column was one of the Harrell add-on parts.

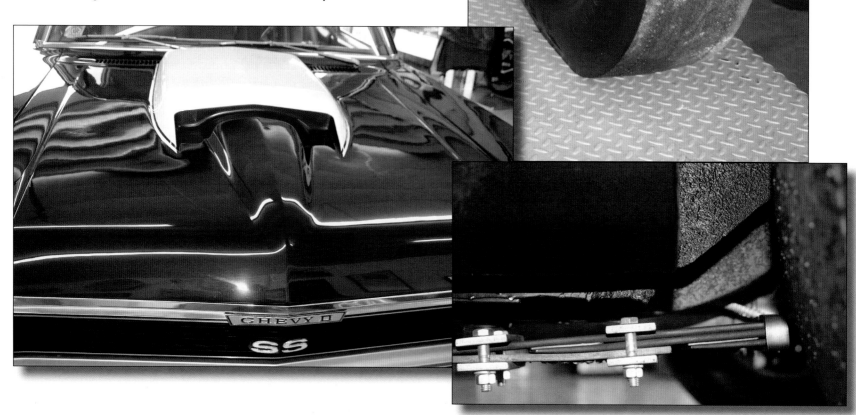

Some of the special modifications performed to customer order on Novas shipped to Dick Harrell's performance shop in Kansas City consisted of a fiberglass cowl-induction hood, Cragar S/S wheels, Racemaster drag slicks, and leaf spring clamps.

Part of the magic performed on this particular Gibb-Harrell Nova by legendary Chevy drag racer Dick Harrell was the installation of this aluminum intake manifold mounting three Holley 2-barrel carburetors as used to equip 427 Corvettes. Harrell added his own special air cleaner with accompanying decal. Also seen here are the aftermarket exhaust headers that were installed at the owner's request.

Even when ordered in the more upscale SS trim, the 1969 Nova was still somewhat understated when compared to what was rolling out of dealerships that year. But when optioned with the 375-hp 396 big-block engine, the compact Chevy's performance potential was anything but understated. (Photo Courtesy CarTech Archive)

The second year for this Corvette body style was 1969, and it once again carried the Stingray name on the fenders. The base engine that year was the 300-hp 350 with the LT-1 380-hp 350 optional. Two versions of the 427 big-block were available, with 400 and 435 hp, respectively, and the ultimate engine option for the Corvette in 1969 came in the form of the L-88 427, which was a race-only engine conservatively rated at 430 hp. The L-88 option was available in 1967, 1968, and 1969, with only 116 Corvettes being fitted with the option in 1969. Most of these cars went directly to those who intended to use them in serious competition.

The 427 emblems on the hood scoop of this Corvette informed the world that the car meant business. The bulge in the hood looked good and provided needed clearance for the big-block V-8.

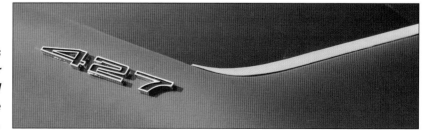

The most produced of the three versions of the 427 engine available in the 1969 Corvette was this one that delivered a rated 400 hp at 5,400 rpm with 460 ft-lbs of torque coming at 3,600 rpm. With three Holley 2-barrel carburetors resting under this special air cleaner, this version was just as visually impressive when the hood was opened but was also more forgiving toward everyday driving, thanks to a compression ratio of 10.25:1 and a hydraulic lifter camshaft.

The ultimate Camaro came in the form of the 1969 models fitted with the ZL-1 engine. The aluminum ZL-1 427 engine was designed for use in the Can Am racing series, but Chevrolet dealer Fred Gibb used his influence to have 50 Camaros built under the COPO program with this engine.

Along with being the quickest of all production Camaros, the ZL-1 cars have a couple of other interesting distinctions. In spite of the fact that the ZL-1 was a race-only engine, the cars came with the standard GM 5-year, 50,000-mile warranty. Also, these were the only series of cars ever to be purchased back from a dealer by the parent company. It seemed that no matter how much performance potential the cars displayed, the fact that the ZL-1 option cost more than the car itself made them hard to sell.

The interior of the ZL-1 Camaro is sparse, as would be expected in a factory race car. This particular vehicle is equipped with the TH-400 transmission, and the shift lever remains on the steering column. Aftermarket tachometer, gauges, and roll bar were owner added before racing the car. All ZL-1 cars came equipped with power front disc brakes, and the camshaft profile was so radical that there was very little vacuum available to operate the booster, making the cars hard to stop.

Other owner add-on parts to make the car more competitive on the dragstrip were Lakewood traction bars and Cure-Ride drag shocks. The exhaust system has been removed as it was not required for drag racing and only added weight to the car.

The heart and soul of this special Camaro owned by Jeff and Jake Murphy and restored to day-two (meaning with owner/racer added aftermarket parts) condition by Supercar Workshop in Latrobe, Pennsylvania, is the ZL-1 427 engine, which is fed by an 850-cfm Holley 4-barrel carburetor, the largest ever put on a Chevrolet production vehicle. Not only is the cylinder block cast from aluminum, which makes it lighter, it is also reinforced for strength and packed with all the best performance parts General Motors manufactured at the time.

Chevrolet, 1968

A COMPANY THAT PUBLICLY DOES NOT SUPPORT RACING.

While a mere $2,670 bought you a new Camaro in 1968, it was doubtful that many of the 6-cylinder plain-Jane versions were ordered that year. A car designed around Chevy's performance image and, with the youthful buyer in mind, a ton of more potent Camaros were destined to hit the streets and dragstrips that year. While the Z-28, with its high-winding 302, and the 350 cars were still strong performers, it was a proven fact that there was no substitute for cubic inches. That meant you could buy a new Camaro packing the potent 375-hp 396 big-block and a bunch of other goodies, for less than $4,300.

To show potential buyers what they could expect for the money, *Popular Hot Rodding* put the big-block Camaro through its paces, recording a quarter-mile elapsed time of 14.09 seconds at 99 mph. This was nearly .5 second quicker than a similarly equipped car tested the previous year.

Along with being the king of the hill in SCCA Trans Am series racing in 1968, the Z-28 Camaro made a big splash on the dragstrip as well. Longtime Chevy racer Dave Strickler was back in a Super Stock car in 1968 and he owned the NHRA SS/F class that year, turning elapsed times of 11.70 at 116 mph and winning the NHRA World Championship for his efforts.

Don Yenko Chevrolet continued the Yenko Super Car program, stuffing a total of 64 Camaros with the potent 427 and other modifications that truly turned the Camaro into a super car.

Another performance-minded Chevy dealer, Fred Gibb of LaHarpe, Illinois, saw the potential for an NHRA class-dominating combination if Chevrolet would just build a big-block (396) Nova. Gibb was able to use his influence with Vince Piggins at Chevrolet to cut a Corporate Office Production Option (COPO). This one was number 9738, which called for the construction of 50 (the minimum required to make the car legal for NHRA class competition) Novas equipped with the L-78 375-hp 396 engine backed with the TI I-400 automatic transmission. The only catch was that Gibb had to sell all 50 cars through his dealership.

The Novas were delivered late in the model year and each one was equipped with a 4.10 Posi-Traction rear, bucket seats, console, floor-mounted shifter, and radio delete. Gibb had no trouble selling these pocket rockets and even arranged for famous Chevy drag racer Dick Harrell to further modify some of the cars for customers (12 to 18 by most accounts) by installing 427 engines, or supertuning the L78 by installing Jardine headers, re-jetting the carburetor, re-curving the distributor advance, etc. Harrell also made available at extra cost special tri-power carburetion, an A&A fiberglass hood, tachometer, Cragar wheels, slicks, and suspension modifications.

Street Racer Special

Today you can only imagine picking up your local newspaper and finding among the auto ads the offering of a "Street Racer Special." But if you lived anywhere near Long Island, New York, in 1968, you found just such a deal offered for a mere $2,998.

Baldwin Chevrolet advertised a Baldwin-Motion Performance–modified Biscayne two-door sedan packing the 425-hp 427 with 11.0:1 compression, solid lifter camshaft, 785-cfm Holley 4-barrel carburetor, Muncie 4-speed transmission, heavy-duty suspension, radiator, and rear sway bar, along with "distinctive emblems" and called it the ultimate performance full-size sedan for serious street/strip use. I might ask that the "distinctive emblems" be deleted to make the car the ultimate "sleeper" for the street. And just in case you were thinking this might just be a sales ploy to move the less popular full-size muscle cars off the lot, *Super Stock* and *Drag Illustrated* tested just such a beast, fitted with 4.56 gears in the back, and recorded a most impressive 13.65-second quarter-mile time at 105 mph.

With the GM-wide complete A-Body makeover for 1968, the Chevelle grew 4 inches of wheelbase (116 inches up from 112) while the engine and transmission lineup remained unchanged. At the top of the option list once again was the 375-hp 396 (L-78). *Car Life* tested one equipped with a 4-speed transmission and 3.55 gearing. The results were a 14.8-second quarter-mile time at 99 mph.

Not to be overlooked was the still-potent 327 small-block V-8 option in the Chevelle. Developing 325 hp at 5,600 rpm and 355 ft-lbs of torque at 3,600 rpm, the lightweight, high-winding small-block made the Chevelle a top street performer that could surprise many big-block cars.

The Corvette received a new body style for 1968 as well, patterned after the mako shark concept of designer Larry Shinoda. Underpinnings of the car remained the same, but a number of new options made the Corvette better than ever before.

First was the 3-speed Turbo-Hydramatic automatic transmission to replace the dated 2-speed Powerglide, and second was the choice between two Muncie 4-speed transmissions, the standard M-21 or the M-22 "Rock Crusher" box. The engine lineup still included the 350-hp 327 as one of two available small-block V-8s and, of course, the 427, which once again came in four flavors: 390, 400, and 435 hp and the "more race than street" 430 horse L-88.

With its reputation as one of America's favorite performance cars, no shortage of magazine road tests were listed for the new Corvette, and the numbers were indeed impressive. With the 327/350 small-block and 3.70 gearing, a Corvette could cover the quarter-mile in 15 seconds flat at 92 mph. With the 435-hp 427 and 3.70 gearing, the end of the quarter-mile came up almost 2 seconds quicker at 13.30, with a trap speed of 108 mph. Almost no doubt exists that with proper gearing and a set of slicks, an L88 Corvette could easily get down into the 11-second range.

While a factory stock L-78 Nova as delivered to Fred Gibb could be expected to cover the quarter-mile in the low-14-second range at just over 100 mph, a Harrell-tuned version easily trimmed .5 second off that time. When track tested, a Gibb-Harrell prepared 427 Nova (estimated to produce 450 hp) equipped with headers and slicks posted a best quarter-mile elapsed time of 12.05 seconds at 115.78 mph.

Chevrolet, 1969

Big-block Novas grab major attention while COPO cars rule the roost.

If you were a savvy buyer in a Chevrolet dealership in 1969 (or had a savvy salesperson), with the check of a few boxes, you could special order one of the most legendary cars of all time. You didn't need Don Yenko's help; you could simply order your own COPO.

Super Novas

Not since the 1966 327/350-hp package of 1966 had anything even close to it been offered until the fall of 1968, when Chevrolet announced that the L-78 396 engine option would be available in the Nova. The 11.0:1 compression, solid lifter camshaft, big-valve cylinder heads, aluminum intake manifold, and a huge Holley 4-barrel carburetor added up to an advertised 375 hp at 5,600 rpm, along with 415 ft-lbs of torque at 3,600 rpm. Back all this up with a close-ratio 4-speed transmission, 3.55 rear axle, heavy-duty shocks and suspension, and stuff it in a 3,500-pound package and you have a great starting point for a super car.

Car Craft got its hands on an early production model to test and found out that all that torque had a tendency to shred the stock Polyglas tires instantly under hard acceleration, and the stock Muncie shifter balked at any effort to grab gears quickly. The best quarter-mile elapsed time with the stock Nova was 15.20 at 92 mph. Hardly impressive, but the potential lurking just beneath the surface was obvious. To unleash it, the car was treated to some common performance modifications and a tune by none other than Bill Thomas race cars to see what might happen. The addition of headers, a stronger clutch, traction bars, a Hurst shifter, 4.56 gears, and a set of slicks proved to be just what the Nova needed, as the next trip to the track resulted in a 12.85-second blast at 110.35 mph.

L-72 Camaro and Chevelle

During 1968, Don Yenko and others had lobbied long and hard for Chevrolet to build 427 Camaros and Chevelles as an RPO, and in November 1968 the idea won approval at the corporate level. Yenko received the first order of 50 Camaros and went to work turning them into Yenko Super Cars.

The L-72 option consisted of a 425-hp 427, four-bolt main bearing caps, forged-steel crankshaft, 11.1:1-compression forged pistons, aluminum intake manifold, and a 780-cfm Holley 4-barrel carburetor. Also part of the package was a special ducted hood that sealed to the air cleaner, heavy-duty radiator and suspension, and 12-bolt rear with 4.10 Posi-Traction. Yenko then added a Stewart Warner tachometer and gauges, Doug Thorley headers, Hurst dual-gate shifter on automatic transmission cars, special wheels, and YSC graphics. This brought the price of the Yenko 427 Camaro to just over $4,400.

After other performance-minded Chevy dealers caught wind of the 427 option for the Camaro and Chevelle and ordered some for sale, Yenko was by far the most prolific, selling 201 Camaros and 99 Chevelles in 1969. *Super Stock and Drag Illustrated* tested a Yenko-prepared L-72 Camaro and with a tune-up, open headers, and slicks, professional driver Ed Hedrick blasted through the traps in 11.94 seconds at 114.90 mph.

The Corvette underwent only minor changes for 1969, but good news could be found on the options list. The 327 small-block had grown to 350 ci, thanks to a .25-inch increase in stroke (the 4.00-inch bore remained) and the hotter of the two versions of the new small-block pumped out 350 hp at 5,600 rpm. A second 350, designated LT-1, was listed but did not make it into production until the 1970 model year.

The 390- and 400-hp 427 versions of the 427 engine were still on the list, along with the Tri-power 435 and laughably rated 430-horse L-88. The 435-hp version also received aluminum cylinder heads for 1969.

Rarest and most powerful of them all was the ZL-1 option. A race-only 427 used aluminum cylinder heads and an aluminum cylinder block. The engine had been designed for use in exotic racing sports cars, and the use of aluminum saved 100 pounds when compared to other versions of the 427. Again rated at a conservative 430 hp, the ZL1 was said to produce a far more realistic 585, and this rarest of all 427 engines only managed to find its way into two production Corvettes in 1969.

While it is understandable that no magazines got their hands on a ZL-1 Corvette for testing, it seems odd that the L-88 and 435-hp versions that were tested both had automatic transmissions and 3.36 and 3.70 gearing, respectively. The L-88's quarter-mile time of 13.36 seconds at 111.10 mph was only .3 quicker than that of the 435, indicating that the L-88 would have benefited greatly from better gearing.

ZL-1 Camaro

Many firsts are associated with the ZL-1 Camaro, including the highest horsepower engine Chevrolet ever sold, the smallest number RPO ever, the only use of an 850-cfm Holley double-pumper carburetor, a 5-year/50,000-mile warranty on what was essentially a factory race car, the

only cars that General Motors ever allowed to be returned by a dealer, and most of all, the fact that the engine option cost more than the suggested retail price of the car.

The ZL-1 engine was originally designed for use in the Can Am racing series Chaparrals and in 1969 was only supposed to be available in limited numbers for the Corvette. Fred Gibb used his influence to have 50 ZL-1 Camaros built under the COPO program. The cars were all optioned in a similar fashion with radio delete, 4.10 Posi-Traction rear, either M-21 or M-22 4-speed transmission or Special TH-400 automatic, transistor ignition system, and of course, the MK IV aluminum 427 engine rated at 430 hp.

Imagine Gibb's surprise when his cars began to arrive and he discovered the price for the engine option (COPO 9560) was $4,160. This meant that the cars would carry a cost to the buyer of $7,200 each. Realizing that there was no way he could sell the cars, Gibb convinced Chevrolet to take them back and 37 were returned to the manufacturer for resale to other dealers.

ZL-1 VERSUS CHEVROLET'S OTHER 427S

The ZL-1 began with an aluminum cylinder block featuring reinforced main bearing bulkheads with four-bolt caps and deeper bolt holes with steel Heli-coil thread inserts. The cylinder block was also drilled with two additional head-bolt holes on each bank for better gasket sealing. Beefier connecting rods with 7/16-inch bolts were added, along with a high-capacity oil pump. The camshaft profile was changed to increase lift from .560 to .600 inch and shorten duration from 364 degrees to 359.

The aluminum cylinder heads had larger exhaust valves (1.88 inches as compared to 1.84 on the L-88), open combustion chambers (another first for a big-block Chevy engine), round exhaust ports, and an 850-cfm Holley double-pumper 4-barrel carburetor. The overall weight savings compared to the iron 427 was 160 pounds.

Pontiac, 1967

ENTER THE FIREBIRD, BUT THE GTO STILL STEALS THE LIMELIGHT.

Pontiac released the Firebird, which was based on the same platform as the Camaro, to compete with Mustang and Cougar for 1967. The new model came with a wide variety of engine combinations, from the basic OHC 6-cylinder to the base 326 V-8, an H.O. version of the 326 that delivered 285 hp due to the addition of a 4-barrel carburetor, unique for a domestic car of the era. An OHC inline 6-cylinder engine called the Sprint mounted a huge Rochester Quadrajet 4-barrel carburetor. At the top of the heap was the 325-hp 400 shared with the GTO. Without the top version of

The Pontiac GTO received a few styling changes for 1967, but the big news came in the drivetrain. An increase in cylinder bore size to 4.12 inches brought the displacement from 389 to 400 ci. The Tri-Power induction was gone from the option list, replaced by a single Rochester Quadrajet 4-barrel carburetor. Also gone was the 2-speed automatic transmission. The GTO now sported the new 3-speed Turbo-Hydramatic. (Photo Courtesy Tony Gratt)

Motor Trend didn't do Firebird performance sales any favors when it outfitted a 400-powered test car with an automatic transmission and very tall 3.08 highway cruising gears. They managed a best of 15.4 seconds at 92 mph in the quarter-mile. *Car Life's* 4-speed, 3.36-geared example fared somewhat better at 14.7 seconds at 98 mph, but best of all was the 4-speed convertible tested by *Car and Driver*, as its 3.90 gearing delivered a very respectable 14.4 at 100 mph.

The GTO remained Pontiac's performance darling for 1967. The displacement was increased to 400, but gone was the tri-power carburetion, replaced instead with the H.O. 400 that, thanks to an improved camshaft, better exhaust manifolds, and an open element air cleaner, delivered the same 360 hp as the previous year's tri-carburetor model.

The big news came in the form of the Ram Air (R.A.) version, optional at an extra cost of $263. The R.A. 400 featured a longer duration camshaft, beefier valvesprings, and a functional hood scoop that ducted cold air to an open air cleaner that isolated the engine heat from the cooler, horsepower-producing outside air via a foam seal against the bottom of the hood. Pontiac wisely kept the horsepower rating for the R.A. engine the same at 360, and it didn't disappoint.

Car Life cleared the quarter-mile traps with a 4.33-geared version in 13.90 seconds at 102.80. The *Motor Trend* automatic example was just a click behind at 14.09 at 101 mph.

the 400, only offered in the GTO, the Firebird had to live in the shadow of its big brother for the first year.

It appears that the only difference in the Firebird's 400 engine when compared to the GTO version was the fact that Pontiac engineers had modified the secondary linkage on the carburetors of 400 Firebirds so the carburetors did not open completely, resulting in the lower-advertised horsepower rating. To aid the performance of customer Firebirds, dealer service departments were known to modify the linkage as an in-house fix.

The most notable difference between 1966 and 1967 GTOs came in the form of a new rear body panel, which presented a much cleaner look than that of the previous year. (Photo Courtesy Jeff LePine)

As had been the practice since its introduction in 1964, the GTO was available in a convertible model. While the added weight tended to hurt performance, there was no denying the cool factor of a GTO convertible on a summer day. Note that this GTO has the optional and very desirable Hurst mag wheels. (Photo Courtesy Jeff LePine)

Now displacing 400 ci, the GTO's engine was still rated at 360 hp at 5,100 rpm and produced 438 ft-lbs of torque at 3,600 rpm. The Rochester Quadrajet 4-barrel carburetor that replaced the Tri-Power made for a better driving experience overall and was easier to tune. (Photo Courtesy Jeff LePine)

The interior of the 1967 GTO remained sporty with front bucket seats, lots of imitation woodgrain on the dash, full instrumentation, and a console with Hurst shifter to control the 4-speed transmission. The grab bar, a GTO trademark from the beginning, allowed the passenger in the front seat to hold on during spirited driving. (Photo Courtesy Jeff LePine)

In 1967 the performance-oriented midsize cars from General Motors, including the GTO, were still civilized to the point that they carried four adults comfortably. (Photo Courtesy Jeff LePine)

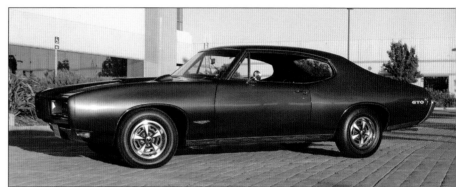

General Motors completely restyled its A-Body line for 1968 and the GTO took on a new look with a smooth-sided coke bottle shape, beaked nose, and other innovations, which included hideaway headlamps and a new front bumper constructed of a high-impact substance called Enduro that was painted body color. (Photo Courtesy Ken Skistimas)

The headlamps on the 1968 GTO were hidden behind the emblem on the grille. The headlamp doors were controlled by vacuum diaphragms. The new design grille was surrounded by the revolutionary Enduro bumper, which was designed to withstand impacts without damage to the car. (Photo Courtesy Ken Skistimas)

The 1968 GTO interior continued the sporty yet plush theme with bucket seats, console, and once again, a rear bench seat that allowed for adult passengers. When compared to the midsize performance offerings of some of its competitors, the GTO was downright plush. Woodgrain steering wheel with brushed stainless spokes and Pontiac Motor Division center cap was a nice touch. (Photo Courtesy Ken Skistimas)

The European flair introduced on the original GTO in 1964 carried over into 1968 with the 6.5-liter engine displacement designation displayed on emblems located low on each fender. (Photo Courtesy Ken Skistimas)

In 1967, Pontiac introduced the console-mounted Hurst Dual Gate shifter on GTOs equipped with an automatic transmission. Popularly known as the His/Hers shifter, the advertising for the Dual Gate spoke of how (when driven by a woman) the transmission shifted through the gears automatically, while moving the lever into the other gate allowed the gears to be selected manually for better performance. (Photo Courtesy Ken Skistimas)

A popular option on the GTO was this hood-mounted tachometer. Although it was unique in design and helped to set the car apart, the hood tach did not meet the needs of most GTO drag racers who often opted for the more conventional and easier-to-read steering-column-mounted aftermarket tachometer. The equally hard-to-read console-mounted tachometer was still available in 1968. (Photo Courtesy Ken Skistimas/Joseph Hake)

The standard 400-ci engine that had been introduced to power the GTO in 1967 remained for 1968, but available was the Ram Air II version, which featured improved cylinder heads with round exhaust ports and a #041 hot hydraulic lifter camshaft. Pontiac's crafty performance engineers underrated the horsepower at 360, the same as the previous year. (Photo Courtesy Ken Skistimas)

The Rochester Quadrajet 4-barrel carburetor that had been introduced on the GTO in 1967 carried over into 1968. The performance advantage of this design was its small primary throttle bores, which gave excellent low-end response until the huge secondaries took over. (Photo Courtesy Ken Skistimas)

Pontiac, 1968

THE FIREBIRD GAINS RESPECT, BUT THE GTO RECEIVES CAR OF THE YEAR HONORS.

The Firebird received new power for 1968 as the base 326-ci V-8 was replaced with a 350-cube version of the same engine. The big news came when the 400 Ram Air II (R.A. II) option became available mid-year.

The only contemporary road test, as reported by *Hot Rod* magazine, was with the H.O. 400 engine and not the much stouter R.A. II. This particular test car was likely to have passed through Royal Pontiac on its way to the test session, as it was reported that the 3.55-geared, 350-hp bird covered the quarter-mile in 13.79 seconds at 106 mph, which was far quicker than an R.A. II GTO tested that year.

The GTO received a redesign for 1968 and was selected *Motor Trend's* car of the year. The model also received a performance boost with the introduction of the R.A. II option, consisting of improved cylinder heads with round exhaust ports and an improved camshaft profile. Amazingly, in spite of these improvements the horsepower rating climbed just slightly over the previous year, to 366.

The same engine, when fitted to the Firebird, was rated at 340 hp, likely due to the carburetor linkage modification. Magazine tests of the GTO outfitted with the R.A. II indicated that it was capable of quarter-mile times in the mid-14-second range at 100-mph numbers that could have been affected by an increase in curb weight and/or lack of traction due to the additional horsepower.

But, as always, Royal Pontiac was available to any buyer who was serious about making his Pontiac perform and for a mere $650 over the sticker price of a new GTO, Royal outfitted the car with a blueprinted, performance-tuned, 428-ci engine rated at 390 hp. With fairly tall 3.55 gearing and an automatic transmission, this super GTO stopped the quarter-mile clocks in 13.8 seconds at 104 mph, while remaining a docile street driver.

Pontiac, 1969

PONTIAC REACHES THE PINACLE OF PERFORMANCE AND STYLING.

Not one to be left out in the ever-increasing competition of muscle car production and sales, Pontiac came up with a special package all on its own. Enter the GTO Judge.

Here Comes the Judge

The GTO received minor styling changes for 1969 with the big news coming in the form of the GTO Judge, which sported eye-catching colors, a rear deck spoiler, and special graphics. The 350-hp 400 remained the standard engine with the 360 hp R.A. II being upgraded to Ram Air III (R.A. III) status and receiving 6 more horsepower at 5,100 rpm in the process.

At the top of the heap was the Ram Air IV (R.A. IV), a dedicated muscle car engine in the finest sense of the word. While it shared the 10.75:1 compression ratio with the R.A. III, the R.A. IV received improved cylinder heads with 67-cc combustion chambers, round ports, and a matched high-rise aluminum intake manifold with larger Rochester Quadrajet 4-barrel carburetor. The camshaft numbers were .520-inch lift with 308/320 degrees of duration. The factory rated the R.A. IV at 370 hp at 5,000 rpm (well below where the engine actually made peak horsepower) and 445 ft-lbs of torque at 3,900 rpm.

Comparing the performance of the base 350-hp GTO with one equipped with the R.A. IV option, *Car Life* observed 14.9 seconds at 98 mph in the quarter-mile for the base-engine car and 14.4 seconds at 98 mph for the R.A. IV. This seemed to be a poor representation of the performance capabilities of such a potent package, and that was proven by yet another test performed on a R.A. IV GTO that had been tuned by Royal Pontiac, equipped with 4.30 gears and slicks. In this case the quarter-mile came up in just 12.8 seconds at more than 112 mph. There were just 271 GTOs equipped with the R.A. IV option in 1969, making it a very rare and desirable muscle car today.

Pontiac drag racing stalwart Arnie Beswick jumped on the Judge bandwagon in 1969 with a fiberglass replica body painted in Judge livery for his always popular funny car.

RAM AIR V

The July 1969 issue of *Super Stock* and *Drag Illustrated* featured a GTO Judge like none other. This particular car was outfitted with the Ram Air V (R.A. V) engine, an option that never made it into production.

The R.A. V, based on the same four-bolt main bearing reinforced cylinder block in the R.A. IV, departed radically from there. Internally, the block was fitted with a unique solid lifter camshaft to allow the engine to operate in the RPM range required by its unique cylinder heads. The heads had machined combustion chambers, as opposed to cast, and huge 2.19-inch intake valves.

But most unique was the tunnel port design on the intake side (large round ports that required dissecting tubes through their middles to accommodate the pushrods). Along with the tunnel port heads was a matching high-rise aluminum intake manifold on top of an 800-cfm Holley carburetor. Fitted with 4.88 gears, slicks, and a specially fabricated set of Doug Thorley headers, the R.A. V Super Judge easily clicked off the quarter-mile in 11.86 seconds at 116.65 mph.

Although a production run of 1,000 vehicles with R.A. V engines was initially planned, none were ever produced.

Firebird Trans Am

Pontiac performance guru John DeLorean wanted nothing more than to transform the Firebird into a world-class sports car. So in mid-1969 a new, limited edition Firebird featuring steering and suspension modifications to improve handling, along with the R.A. III 400 engine as standard equipment, was introduced. By this time factory-backed Mustangs, Camaros, and even AMC Javelins were doing battle in the SCCA Trans Am racing series, while Pontiac's participation was at first limited to Canadian-built Firebirds that were allowed to run the Chevrolet 302 engine. At the same time, the company was trying to work the bugs out of its own 303-ci powerplant.

This gave rise to the name Trans Am for the new model and recognition value from the obvious connection to performance. Pontiac built 697 Trans Am Firebirds in 1969 and the model became a big sales success. *Hot Rod* tested a new Trans Am equipped with an automatic transmission and 3.90 and recorded a quarter-mile time of 14.10 seconds at 100.78 mph, placing it right up there with big brother GTO's performance numbers that year.

Buick, 1967

A NEW ENGINE DESIGN MAKES THE GRAN SPORT A LEGITIMATE PLAYER.

GM's luxury midsize took a leap forward in the performance arena in 1967 when it dumped the 401 nailhead that had been the mainstay of Buick power for so many years and replaced it with a new 400-ci engine of more modern design. The new powerplant that became standard equipment on the Gran Sport model, now called the GS400, was rated at 340 hp and 448 ft-lbs of torque. A unique dual-inlet air cleaner of red plastic sat on a 750-cfm Rochester Quadrajet 4-barrel carburetor that fed fuel into the engine through a dual-plane intake manifold.

Motor Trend tested a 4-speed GS400 with 3.36 gearing and recorded a quarter-mile time of 15.20 seconds at 95 mph.

Buick, 1968

MAKING PERFORMANCE STRIDES.

The GS400 remained unchanged for the 1968 model year, with 340 hp being the most available. However, in its test of an automatic transmission GS400 with 3.91 rear-axle ratio, *Car Life* recorded a quarter-mile elapsed time of 14.4 seconds at 93.3 mph, nearly 1 second quicker than the 1967 model.

Buick, 1969

THE GENTLEMAN'S MUSCLE CAR COMES INTO ITS OWN.

GS400 equals luxury and performance. *Cars* noted that whatever the Buick Gran Sport lacked in "hairy, straight-line performance" it more than made up for in quality, class, and handling. While the standard 400-ci engine in the Gran Sport delivered 340 hp, the $199.05 Stage I option boosted it to 360.

The differences between the standard engine and the Stage I consisted of higher lift hydraulic camshaft, heavier valvesprings, lightweight pushrods, 3.64 rear-axle ratio, and a ram air system fed through two scoops mounted flat on the forward part of the hood. The 3,750-pound test car managed a 14.90-second elapsed time in the quarter-mile at 101 mph, which was slower than the previous year's test car. Although this wasn't considered world-class performance for a muscle car in 1969, those who were serious about racing a Buick GS could avail themselves of over-the-counter Stage II parts and steeper rear-end gears for all-out performance.

Olds, 1967

I'LL TAKE THE "YOUNGMOBILE" AND MAKE IT THE W-30, PLEASE.

After sneaking just over 50 examples of the tri-carburetor hot rod W-30 optioned cars out the door in 1966, Oldsmobile was hit by a GM corporate mandate that banned multiple carburetion in the midsize car line. So to stay in the performance game, the 1967 version of W-30 had to pick up in other areas. The 400-ci engine now carried the same 350 hp and 440 ft-lbs of torque rating as the standard 442 powerplant. Due to changes in the camshaft profile the maximum horsepower and maximum torque were achieved at 400 rpm higher than the previous year.

Also improved was the method of delivering cold air to the engine. Olds engineers ducted the intake hoses through the grille above and below the parking lights in an unobtrusive, yet effective, design. As had been the case in the 1966 W-30, the battery was moved to the trunk to allow for the ductwork that ran to the air cleaner. Also available for the first time in 1967 was the superior TH-400 transmission. When mounted behind the W-30 option, the transmission came with internal improvements, allowing for more positive shifts. Olds was able to increase the production of W-30 cars dramatically in 1967 as well, with 500 built.

Cars tested a W-30 442 with the dealer-installed 4.33 rear-axle ratio and took the otherwise stock car through the quarter-mile traps in 14.1 seconds at 103 mph. *Super Stock and Drag Illustrated* went one better as its simi-

In 1968, Oldsmobile continued its potent W-30 engine option and at the same time jumped into the midsize, smaller-ci performance car market with the high-performance Ram Rod 350. Outfitted with all the same performance goodies as the W-30, except the displacement, the Ram Rod provided the buyer with another choice and the drag racer with a car that could be competitive in a lower class. (Photo Courtesy Glen Morris)

The Ram Rod 350 engine was fed cooler outside air via dual ducts that opened under the front bumper of the car in the same manner as W-30 cars. Introducing cooler air into the carburetor increased horsepower. The Ram Rod easily developed 320 hp from its 350 ci.

larly equipped W-30 car stopped the clocks in 13.99 seconds at 102.40 mph. These respective elapsed times bettered the times of a standard non-W-30 442 by .5 second.

When compared with road test results for other muscle cars that year, the W-30 was quite impressive indeed.

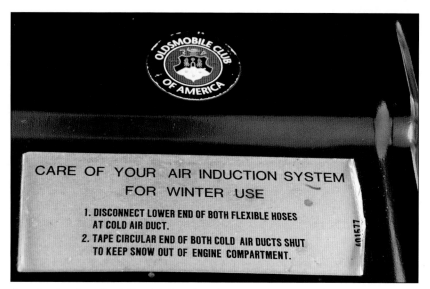

Due to the fact that the intakes for the ram air system on the Ram Rod and W-30 cars opened under the front bumper, Oldsmobile provided owners with instructions on how to prevent snow from entering the engine when cars were driven in winter weather.

In 1969, Olds dropped the crossed pistons Ram Rod 350 fender decals and replaced them with the designation W-31 in chrome on cars so equipped.

Oldsmobile continued its collaboration with the Hurst Corporation after the success realized with the limited production 1968 Hurst Olds and the follow-up cars really stood out in a crowd with dual snorkel scoops on the hood and gold graphics. (Photo Courtesy Bob Wenzelburger)

Olds, 1968

OLDSMOBILE'S TRIPLE THREAT PROVES THAT WHERE THERE IS A WILL, THERE IS A WAY AROUND CORPORATE RESTRICTIONS.

The performance line from Olds for 1968 continued the W-30 option, showed that where there is a will, there is a way around corporate regulations, and added yet another "W" car that was yet to be called one. Rolling out of Lansing, Michigan, for the first time was a new option for the F-85 and Cutlass line, known as the Ram Rod 350. Based on the 350-ci engine and rated at 320 hp, the Ram Rod was packed full of performance goodies such as a ram air induction system that was shared with the W-30, heavy-duty cooling system, a hot hydraulic lifter camshaft with .474 inch of lift and 308 degrees of duration, special cylinder heads with 455 valves, 11.5:1 compression, a performance-calibrated ignition system, and two choices of 4-speed transmissions.

Bone stock, the Ram Rod 350 with its lighter curb weight clicked off mid-14-second quarter-mile times at 100 mph, making it a force to be reckoned with both on the street and in the E/Stock class at the track. *Car Craft* prepared two W-31 cars for dragstrip testing, and the lighter of the two ran the quarter in 13.27 seconds at 104.76 mph. The Ram Rod's big brother, the W-30, was still available for those who needed those extra cubic inches and horses, and with the addition of headers and slicks, the *Car Craft* test car covered the quarter-mile in 13.33 seconds at 103.56 mph.

A little innovative thinking was all it took for the performance minds at Olds to get around the GM corporate ban on engines of more than 400 ci in midsize cars. Olds shipped some of them to a subcontractor that wasn't affected by the rule. Olds entered into an agreement with Hurst Corporation, a known manufacturer of aftermarket performance parts, to modify 515 442s into what became the first of a series of Hurst Oldsmobiles.

The cars were shipped from the Lansing, Michigan, assembly plant to Hurst affiliate Demmer Engineering where they were fitted with the 455-ci engine reserved for full-size Oldsmobiles upgraded with an improved camshaft profile and 10.5:1 compression. This resulted in 390 hp at 5,000 rpm and a stump-pulling 500 ft-lbs of torque at 3,600 rpm.

Suspensions were upgraded, a dual-inlet fiberglass hood ducted outside air to a specially designed air cleaner, a Hurst Dual Gate (also known as a His/Hers) shifter was installed in the TH-400 transmission, and each car was painted silver with black stripe accents and received special badging. The modifications added $683.94 to the car's price, bringing it to $4,700, but the limited production status and performance improvements certainly justified it.

When equipped with 3.42 rear-end gearing, the Hurst Olds could click off 14-second-flat quarter-mile times at 100.58 mph and with the optional 3.91 gearing, 13.98 seconds at 101.28 mph. With the addition of headers, slicks, and some simple transmission modifications, the folks at *Car Craft* received a 3,680-pound Hurst Olds to stop the clocks in 12.97 seconds at 108.17 mph.

Olds, 1969

NOT TOO MANY CHANGES, BUT WHY CHANGE A WINNING COMBINATION?

The Ram Rod 350 gained a new designation for 1969 as the W-31, so gone were the cool little crossed pistons and rods graphics that indicated a Cutlass so equipped in 1968. But the performance hadn't gone away, as tests of W-31 cars with 3.91 gearing and 4-speed transmissions recorded nearly identical quarter-mile times in the mid-14-second range at just under 100 mph as the previous year's Ram Rod had done. This proved that the W-31 Cutlass could run right with any of the other small-block performance cars of the day, including the Z-28 Camaro, Boss 302 Mustang, and 340 Dodge and Plymouth offerings.

The W-30 option remained unchanged, still conservatively rated at 360 hp and still capable of matching the best production muscle cars offered by any competing manufacturers, including those in the GM family.

The hot performer right out of the box for the Olds camp that year was once again the Hurst Olds, now wearing dual hood scoops, a rear spoiler, and a more noticeable white with gold stripes paint scheme. As luxurious as it was (which equates to heavy) and further hampered by 3.42 gearing, the slightly de-tuned 380-hp-rated 455 engine that motivated the Hurst Olds could still power it through the quarter-mile clocks in 14 seconds flat at 100 mph.

Ford, 1967

DESIGNING THE NEW MUSTANG TO FIT THE 390 BIG-BLOCK V-8 PROVED TO BE A BIG STEP IN THE RIGHT DIRECTION.

Having received word of the pending release of the 396 big-block Camaro, Ford responded by increasing the size of the Mustang to accommodate the 390 FE-series engine. Even though the advertised horsepower for the GT-390 used in the Mustang was dropped from 335 to 320, the package still seemed to have potential. That potential was proven by *Popular Hot*

While the Mustang grew in size to accommodate the 390-ci FE engine for 1967 and the Fairlane GT and GTA still had the 390 engine available, the big news from Ford performance was the availability of a production line 427 Fairlane. Having recognized the dragstrip advantage offered by a 427 Fairlane based on its 1966 factory drag team successes, Ford made the option available for 1967. (Photo Courtesy Don Antilla)

Rodding, which ran a series of articles on its 390 Mustang project car. By adding a series of readily available stock class legal performance parts, and without taking the engine apart, the project car recorded a best quarter-mile elapsed time of 13.29 seconds at 103 mph.

Most buyers, however, did not take such steps, and as a result, the basic 390 GT Mustang more often than not found itself an also-ran when compared to other muscle cars that year. *Motor Trend* tested one example with a 3.00 rear-axle ratio and only managed a best 0–60 time of 7.4 seconds and 15.6 seconds at 94.00 mph in the quarter-mile. The *Hot Rod* 3.25-geared Mustang performed somewhat better, posting a 15.31 at 93.45 mph.

While the 390 Mustang in stock livery may have been a disappointment, the company more than made up for it by offering a production 427 Fairlane.

Unlike the limited number of 1966 models that were only provided to drag team members, anyone with the knowledge and a big bankroll could order one of these rockets. Available with the 410-hp (single 4-barrel) or 425-hp (dual 4-barrel) versions, the 427 engine was available in all Fairlane models, except the station wagon. Taking advantage of the car's Stock and Super Stock class potential, most cars ordered ended up in the hands of serious drag racers. The 427 Fairlane was a true factory racer and in many cases, comfort options were deleted when the cars were ordered, but the only lightweight component came in the form of a fiberglass hood with a leading-edge scoop that directed cool air to the engine.

Powered by the 427 Medium Riser engine rated at 425 hp, which was the same rating that the original 427 Low Riser had in 1963, the 1967 427 Fairlane differed from others only through the addition of a lift-off fiberglass hood with a large leading-edge air intake scoop. Ford drivers set numerous drag racing records with the 427 Fairlane, and legendary driver Mario Andretti took one prepared for stock car racing to victory at the NASCAR Daytona 500. (Photo Courtesy Don Antilla)

Hot Rod tested a 427 Fairlane with 4.11 gearing and 4-speed transmission, and in spite of the open rear axle and pathetically skinny bias-ply tires, it managed to cover the quarter-mile in 14 seconds flat at 102 mph, which was proof of the potential on tap for Ford fans. Atlanta, Georgia's Hubert Platt and other Ford drivers wreaked havoc on the competition in NHRA's SS/B class in 1967.

Ford continued to actively support all forms of racing in 1967 and Ford-powered Top Fuel dragsters and Mustang-bodied funny cars continued to win on the dragstrips, while Shelby's Cobras and the GT-40 blistered the sports car tracks in America and Europe. Ford-powered cars also proved themselves to be dominant in the USAC Champ car (Indy) series and the brand took home 10 NASCAR Grand National victories in a year largely dominated by Richard Petty's Plymouth.

Arguably the best street performance car to ever roll out of Dearborn, the 1968½ Mustang Cobra Jet was a perfect combination of the 428-ci FE-series engine found in Thunderbirds and station wagons, fitted with a 390 GT hydraulic camshaft, late 406/early 427 cylinder heads, special cast-iron intake, Holley 735-cfm 4-barrel carburetor, and improved exhaust manifolds. Rated at a very conservative 335 hp, the 428 Cobra Jet produced closer to 400, and when made available in Mustangs and Fairlanes, it took the competition by surprise. Ford chose the 1968 NHRA Winternationals to introduce its new 428 Cobra Jet engine to the world. A number of 1968 Mustangs were prepared for Ford Drag Team members to enter in both Stock and Super/Stock classes. A longtime racer and member of the Ford Drag team, Al Joniec was one of those factory drivers. Competing in the SS/E class, Joniec eliminated fellow team driver Hubert Platt for the class win and then went on to hand Ford its first NHRA Super Stock Eliminator victory. Bill Lawton was also entered at the Winternationals in the SS/E Automatic class with a Mustang sponsored by Tasca Ford, the dealership credited with introducing the 428 Cobra Jet engine concept to Ford. (Photo Courtesy Bob Smith)

Ford built 50 special 428 Cobra Jet Mustangs to be made available to drag racers through dealers in 1968. Known as 135 cars due to their sequential serial numbering, the cars were an overnight sensation, putting Ford drivers in front at dragstrips from coast to coast. Vinny Lyons took delivery of his 135 car through Rye Ford in Rye, New York, and successfully campaigned the car in the northeastern United States.

As delivered, the 135-series 428 Cobra Jet Mustangs came in this plain white wrapper. And although they are often called factory lightweight cars, they actually had no lightweight components, although a few had sound deadener and sealer deleted. (Photo Courtesy Bob Smith)

Taking advantage of the larger Mustang body, Shelby American now offered two versions of the modified Mustang for 1967. The GT-350 continued to sport the 306-hp Cobra 289, while the new GT-500 received a 428-ci Police Interceptor engine with dual 4-barrel induction. At least one performance-minded Ford dealer, Mel Burns Ford of Long Beach, Cali-

fornia, offered an in-house built, Shelby-approved, 427-powered GT-500 called the Super Snake. This was a natural performance progression and probably a very good idea, since contemporary road tests of the GT-500 showed it to be only marginally quicker than the 289-powered GT-350 model. This was attributable to the increased weight on the nose of the car and lack of a limited slip rear axle.

Another Ford factory team driver who was the recipient of a Cobra Jet Mustang in 1968 was Phil Bonner. But being a racer who made his living through paid match races, Bonner chose not to compete in NHRA Stock or Super Stock classes. He fitted his Mustang with a 427 Tunnel Port engine and toured the match race circuit. (Photo Courtesy Bob Smith)

Within a very short time of the introduction of the 428 Cobra Jet engine, the NHRA factored the horsepower from 335 to 360. In spite of this and the fact that Ford stopped producing the engine in 1970, the combination continued to set records and win class and eliminator titles for not just years, but decades. This resulted in the NHRA factoring the engine several more times since 1968. (Photo Courtesy Bob Smith)

As with the previous GT-500, the GT-500 KR featured special options, badging, and a fiberglass ram air hood to set it apart from other Mustangs.

In mid-1968, Shelby introduced the GT-500 KR (for King of the Road) to replace the GT-500, which was now powered by the 428 Cobra Jet engine instead of the previous Police Interceptor. (Photo Courtesy Greg Kolasa)

To have the Boss 429 engine declared legal for NASCAR stock car competition, Ford had subcontractor Kar Kraft modify 1969 Mustangs to carry the huge engine. Sold alongside Mustangs powered by the 428 Cobra Jet engine, the Boss 429 models cost more and did not perform nearly as well on the street. (Reynald Belanger Photo)

Shelby introduced a 428 version of its special Mustang in 1967, calling the car the GT-500, and it served alongside the small-block GT-350. While the 1967 GT-500 was powered by a Police Interceptor version of the 428 with dual 4-barrel induction, it was not a great performer. (Photo Courtesy Henry Busch)

To have the Boss 302 racing engine declared legal for SCCA competition, Ford introduced a distinct model Mustang for 1969, called appropriately, the Boss 302. Specially equipped for performance and handling, the Boss 302 also stood out from the crowd, and other Mustangs, through the addition of special graphics, as well as race-inspired chin and rear deck spoilers. Because the engine made most of its power at higher RPM due to the size of the intake ports in its cylinder heads and the production car versions were fitted with a rev limiter, the Boss 302 did not live up to expectations when it came to street performance. (Reynald Belanger Photo)

Ford had taken full control of the production of the GT-350 and GT-500 Mustangs for 1969 models. The GT-350 received 351 Windsor power, while the GT-500 had the 428 Cobra Jet. Modifications to the cars were now little more than cosmetic when compared to earlier Shelby Mustangs.

Ford's advertising theme for 1969 was "The Going Thing" and a limited run of Going Thing promotional cars (Mustangs and Torinos) in red, white, and blue were offered regionally. This particular Going Thing Mustang is powered by the 428 Cobra Jet engine backed with a 4-speed transmission and is still in the hands of its original owner, Charles Crouch. (Photos Courtesy georgiashaker.com)

Following Chrysler's example, which had formed two teams of drag racers to travel to dealerships and hold performance clinics to promote its performance image, Ford formed two teams of its own. The West Coast team of Ed Terry and Dick Wood fielded a white Mustang and a Torino with blue accents; the East Coast team, Hubert Platt and Randy Payne, had similar cars painted blue with white accents. The concept was a huge success as clinic participants strived to mimic the success of the factory team drivers. The 1969 Mustang clinic cars were re-fitted as 1970 models by Holman-Moody-Stroppe and used through the 1970 season.

The year 1969 marked the beginning of a return to heads-up drag racing between stock-bodied production automobiles fitted with the manufacturer's most powerful production engine. This class, first called Pro/Super Stock or Heads-Up Super/Stock, became the Pro/Stock class that is still run today. Ford racer Al Joniec purchased a new Boss 429 Mustang from a local dealer and drove the car to his shop, where he commenced to turn it into a race car. Joniec purchased the more expensive Boss 429 model because he reasoned that the engine compartment had already been widened, which allowed for easy installation of the proven SOHC 427 engine he intended to use in the car. Joniec won his first Pro/Stock match race with this car over the Chevy of Bill Jenkins.

Another factory-supported drag racer, Sam Auxier Jr., built this 1969 Mustang for competition in NASCAR drag racing's Ultra/Stock class. Similar to earlier NHRA A/FX and match race cars, the Ultra/Stocks proved to be wildly popular because they resembled the production cars from which they were built.

NASCAR Ultra/Stock rules allowed for a minimum of interior accoutrements beyond the required safety equipment. Sam Auxier's "office" was quite austere but light, and that was the goal.

Sam Auxier selected the 427 Tunnel Port engine to power his 1969 Mustang. The engine got its name from the huge, round intake manifold runners and cylinder heads with matching round intake ports. Such was the size of the ports that the pushrods transected them via tubes down their middles. The Tunnel Port design had a very narrow, very high-RPM power band and worked well in drag race applications. It was never installed in a Ford production car.

Ford, 1968

DEARBORN'S BIGGEST STREET AND STRIP WINNER: THE 428 COBRA JET.

This year proved to be the biggest one yet for street performance cars in Ford's history. The company finally caught on to the fact that the secret to showroom supremacy could be found in easily maintained, reasonably priced, high-performance cars built in sufficient numbers to make them readily available to the general public. The year 1968 gave birth to the now-legendary 428 Cobra Jet engine. The Cobra Jet was based on an idea born within the East Providence, Rhode Island, dealership of Robert F. Tasca Sr., a longtime proponent of racing cars for the purpose of selling cars.

Tasca stuffed a 428 Police Interceptor FE engine, which was optional in the full-size Ford line, into a 1967 Mustang. The combination proved to be tractable to a fault, easily built with existing parts, and best of all, it turned the Mustang into a rocket. In his pitch to the Ford brass, with whom he shared a close relationship, Tasca called his Mustang the KR, for King of the road. While the company didn't buy the name (until later) it was sufficiently impressed with the performance potential and decided to build

THE 428 COBRA JET

Based on the FE-series engine, which was first introduced in 1958, the Cobra Jet was a marvel in simplicity when compared to other Ford performance engines of the day such as the 427. The 428 proved itself to be far easier to maintain and much more forgiving in daily driving situations than the 427. The Cobra Jet's displacement was a result of the 4.13-inch bore of the earlier 406, combined with a 3.98-inch stroke, cast-iron crankshaft.

The hydraulic lifter cam sported a rather mild profile borrowed from the 390GT engine. Pistons were cast and, when combined with cylinder heads very similar to early 427 Low Riser castings, a compression ratio of 10.6:1 was achieved. Improved cast-iron exhaust manifolds helped the big engine breathe and a 735-cfm Holley 4-barrel carburetor fed fuel through a cast-iron intake manifold specially designed for the engine. Horsepower was rated at 335 (the same as the 1966 GT-390) at 5,600 rpm and it achieved 445 ft-lbs of torque at 3,400 rpm. The actual horsepower was estimated to be close to 400 and the NHRA almost immediately factored the rating to 360 for competition purposes.

On December 26, 1967, Ford announced the availability of the 428 Cobra Jet to its dealers under DSO 84-5660 and 84-5661.

the 428 Cobra Jet engine, to be optional in the performance car line, which included the Mustang, Cougar, Torino, and Mercury Cyclone.

Ford decided to unleash the 428 Cobra Jet upon the public and also some unsuspecting competitors at the NHRA Winternational drag races in Pomona, California. The company shipped six Mustangs to the shop of Bill Stroppe in Long Beach, California, for preparation. The cars were prepared to compete in the Super Stock and Stock classes (five SS/E and one C/SA) and would be handled by Ford Drag Team members Gas Ronda, Don Nicholson, Hubert Platt, Jerry Harvey, and Al Joniec.

At the Winternationals, the cars did not disappoint as the SS/E class runoff came down to the team cars of Al Joniec and Hubert Platt, with Joniec taking the win. Both cars were then eligible to compete in Super Stock Eliminator, where Joniec again defeated Platt in one round of competition on his way to a huge victory for the Ford camp. Unfortunately, Hubert Platt, tasked with driving the Tasca Ford Mustang in C/SA, missed the call for the class final and was disqualified. In the SS/EA class runoff, Gas Ronda lost a close one to Dick Landy's 440-powered Dart 12.01 to 12.02.

Another big boost to Ford's performance prestige came when *Hot Rod* tested a 428 Cobra Jet Mustang and, after recording low-13-second quarter-mile elapsed times on street tires, declared it the quickest stock production car it had ever tested. When the option became available in April 1968 Ford dealers were hard pressed to keep Cobra Jets in stock, and they quickly proved to be one of the best street and dragstrip performers to roll out of Dearborn.

Super Stock and Drag Illustrated received a 1968 Torino powered by the 428 Cobra Jet for testing and begged the question, "Will this be 1968's supercar king?" The test car was equipped with the C-6 automatic transmission, and Ford's new Traction-Loc differential fitted with 3.89 gears.

135-SERIES COBRA JET MUSTANG

The 50 non-GT Mustang fastbacks equipped with the 428 Cobra Jet engine scheduled for assembly at the Dearborn plant on December 30, 1967, came to be known as the 135-series cars due to their sequential vehicle identification numbers (VINs) beginning with 135. All the cars were painted Wimbledon white with black vinyl interior and fitted with manual drum brakes. These cars have mistakenly become known as lightweight Cobra Jets, even though they actually featured no lightweight components and only the first 20 produced had body sealer and sound deadener deleted. Sold through participating dealers, the majority of the cars went directly to drag racers who wasted no time putting Ford performance on the map at dragstrips from coast to coast.

Despite the fact that the car tipped the scales at nearly 4,000 pounds and the automatic transmission was allowed to shift on its own, the Torino cleared the quarter-mile traps in 13.85 seconds at 99 mph. Manually shifting the automatic, removing the air cleaner, and loosening the engine drive belts reduced the elapsed time to 13.52 at 105.05 mph, leaving the magazine scribes duly impressed.

The Shelby version of Ford's Mustang also received Cobra Jet power mid-year in 1968 in the form of the GT-500KR for King of the Road. Bob Tasca's original name for his pet project had finally found a home, as the CJ became optional to the 428 Police Interceptor engine in the GT-500, which, while still rated at 360 hp, had lost its dual 4-barrel induction system to a single 715-cfm Holley carburetor. The Cobra Jet had proved itself to be a better performer than the other versions of the 428 that carried higher horsepower ratings, so it went a long way to bolster the Shelby's image. The Cobra was gone from the lineup by this time and 1968 marked the beginning of Ford's prolific use of the name and Cobra badging on a series of vehicles over the next several years.

Thanks to the aerodynamic shape of the new Torino body style and the introduction of tunnel port cylinder heads for the 427 engine, Ford teams brought home 20 checkered flags on the NASCAR stock car circuit in 1968, and former Dodge driver David Pearson copped the series championship for Ford.

Ford, 1969

THE GOING THING.

While 428 CJ Ford products continued to make a name for themselves on the nation's dragstrips and back roads, the car magazines continued their love affair with Ford's hot new offerings. *Super Stock and Drag Illustrated* tested a top-of-the-line Mustang Mach I. Outfitted with the C-6 Automatic, and 3.91 Traction-Loc rear, writers stated that the car was "packed with a whole raft of extra goodies" and weighed a "fat 3,610 pounds" and were amazed that the car ran the quarter-mile in 13.94 seconds at 115 mph.

The magazine also had occasion to test the Torino-based Fairlane Cobra, which it described as "Ford's economy performer" and was somewhat disappointed when the C-6 automatic, 3.50-geared test car could manage no better than 14.82 seconds at 101 mph in the quarter-mile, while the *Car and Driver* test car, equipped exactly the same, stopped the clocks in 14.04 seconds at 100.61 mph, and a 4-speed model in the hands of *Motor Trend* recorded a 14.5-second elapsed time at 100 mph.

Boss 302

To take full advantage of the Trans Am series rules in 1969, after realizing poor results from 302-ci engines equipped with tunnel port cylinder heads during the 1968 season, Ford developed a new engine based on the 302 Windsor (4.00-inch bore and 3.00-inch stroke) for 1969. The Boss 302, as it was called, used canted valve, large port cylinder heads from the Cleveland foundry that was eventually used on the 351 Cleveland (335 engine series) released in 1970. These heads had huge 2.23-inch intake and 1.72-inch exhaust valves. The cylinder block also sported four-bolt main bearing caps, 10.5:1 compression, a 290-degree mechanical lifter camshaft, and a 780-cfm Holley 4-barrel carburetor on an aluminum intake manifold. The factory rated the horsepower at 290 at 5,800 rpm with 290 ft-lbs of torque at 4,300 rpm.

The special Mustang that carried the Boss 302 engine and name was designed by Larry Shinoda and, aside from unique styling, the Boss 302 featured handling modifications that set it apart from all other Mustangs of the time, so much so that when *Car and Driver* tested a preproduction model, they gave it an "A" and exclaimed that it was "easily the best Mustang yet."

But while the Boss 302 Mustang had great styling and may have out-handled and out-braked other Mustangs of the time, when it came to the straight-line performance, most performance enthusiasts thought it came up short. With quarter-mile elapsed times in the mid-14-second range at 98 mph, the Boss 302 paled when compared against many of the top muscle cars available at the time.

The blame might very well be placed on the fact that, as in the case of the Boss 429, an engine with huge cylinder head ports and valves was fitted with too mild a camshaft and further hindered by a factory-installed rev limiter that shut off the power (6,100 rpm) well in advance of the point where the engine developed maximum horsepower. Understandably the factory engineers had to consider the number of warranty claims that could potentially roll in for blown engines due to missed shifts in the RPM range this engine was capable of.

Boss 429

In an effort to gain dominance on the NASCAR circuit, Ford engineers developed a new performance engine called the Boss 429. Based on the 385-series 429/460-ci engines used to power T-Birds and Lincolns, the Boss version's most obvious difference came in the form of its huge aluminum cylinder heads, which sported semi-hemi, crescent-shaped combustion chambers filled with 2.28-inch intake and 1.90-inch exhaust valves. The Boss 429 cylinder block also enjoyed strengthened main bearing webbing, four-bolt main caps, and an improved oiling system over the standard 385-series blocks.

But there were more contradictions in the Boss 429 than any other factory high-performance engine in recent memory. Starting at the top, the Boss 429 received a single 735-cfm Holley 4-barrel carburetor (by comparison the Boss 302 received a 780-cfm version of the same carburetor). Next up was the camshaft, an anemic hydraulic lifter grind, and compres-

sion ratio of 10.25:1. Combine these factors with a set of cylinder heads that sported intake ports the size of tennis balls and a factory-installed RPM limiter that shut off the engine at 6,100 revs and you have a recipe for dismal street performance.

In another bizarre twist, instead of installing the Boss 429 into the aerodynamically modified Torino Talladega, the car that Ford actually raced in the NASCAR series, subcontractor Kar Kraft of Brighton, Michigan, radically modified a series of Mustangs to accept the Boss 429. (NASCAR rules required that a minimum production available run of an engine or body style be produced to be declared legal for competition. So, in essence, had Ford built the Torino Talladega equipped with the Boss 429 engine instead of the 428 Cobra Jet, there would have been no need for a Boss 429 Mustang). With a horsepower rating of 375 hp at 5,200 rpm and 450 ft-lbs of torque at 4,500 rpm, the unique, limited production Boss 429 Mustang sadly provided buyers with little bang for their performance buck. It soon became common knowledge that the Boss 429 was no match for even a fair-performing 428 Cobra Jet Mustang.

However, Ford factory driver Dave Lyall proved that with the proper attention, the Boss 429 could be a top dragstrip performer, as he put his Mustang right in the thick of things in the newly formed Pro/Stock class. Another top Ford man, Al Joniec, bought one of the new Boss 429 Mustangs and promptly installed his tried-and-proven SOHC 427 engine. In Joniec's first match race after completing the car, he dropped Bill Jenkins's Camaro, which was considered one of the top competitors in the class at the time.

On the NASCAR circuit, things were starting to become as bizarre as they had on the dragstrips, as Dodge came to the party with the Daytona, sporting a wedge-shaped nose and a huge wing on its trunk lid. All of these modifications were, of course, designed to give Chrysler an aerodynamic advantage, and Ford was required to respond if it intended to remain

THE DRAG TEAM/ PERFORMANCE CLINIC PROGRAM

Following Chrysler's lead, Ford established a Performance Clinic Program in 1969. Two teams, consisting of Ed Terry and Dick Wood on the West Coast and Hubert Platt and Randy Payne east of the Mississippi, hit the road to share performance parts combinations and tuning information at Ford dealerships across America. At the same time both teams were actively competing with respective Torino and Mustang drag cars in Super Stock and Pro/Stock class competition. Not only did the teams provide much appreciated information to the Ford faithful, they were also setting records and winning races with Ford products, which directly equated to sales at the dealer showrooms.

competitive. Although still a departure from the standard production model Torino, the Torino Talladega took a far less radical approach to defeating the air than did its competition at Dodge.

The most obvious change to the Talladega was the extended front-end sheet metal and its sloping lines. Available in just three colors, the 749 Torino Talladegas were all optioned the same with the 428 Cobra Jet engine and automatic transmission. Oddly enough, while the production number on these cars satisfied the NASCAR rules, Ford chose to install the engine intended to run in competition, the Boss 429, in a completely different model, the Boss 429 Mustang.

Big news for Ford in NASCAR came with the addition of Richard Petty to the factory team. Petty decided to switch camps when Chrysler Corporation, his benefactor of many years, decided to throw all of its support behind Dodge teams running the new Daytona for 1969, effectively leaving Petty and other Plymouth teams out in the cold. With help from Petty, Ford teams won 26 NASCAR races in 1969.

Mercury, 1967

COUGAR COMES ON BOARD AND COMET GETS THE LEGENDARY 427 ENGINE.

Although factory-supported racers continued to shatter quarter-mile records with fuel-burning, SOHC 427 race vehicles that appeared similar to the dealer-available Cyclone, the real performance car from Mercury that was available to the public, albeit in very limited numbers, came in the form of those Comets and Cyclones equipped with the now legendary 427 side-oiler engine. While the Cyclone's styling screamed muscle car, the most formidable 427 Comets to hit the streets and dragstrips that year came in the form of the base-model 202, which for all intents and purposes had the appearance of a car that Grandma would drive to church on Sunday.

Canadian John Elliott was the youngest of his countrymen to win an NHRA title when he took his 427 Comet 202 to victory in the A/SA class at the NHRA Nationals. His teammate, Barrie Poole, took advantage of the existing rules to fit a 427 into a Comet station wagon for competition in the SS/C class. Poole proved the potential of the combination when he posted the quickest elapsed time in his class at the NHRA Springnationals

Mercury, not to be outdone by its cousins at Ford, made the 427 Medium Riser engine an option in its midsize Comet line for 1967. The rarer Comets proved to be no less potent than the 427 Fairlanes. The engine code designation for the single 4-barrel 427 engine changed to W for 1967 and this version was the rarest of them all. George Aberts's Cyclone is one of these cars and when other options on the car are taken into consideration, it is one of a kind. (Photo Courtesy George Aberts)

Mercury opened the 1968 model year offering a milder version of the famed 427 engine as an option on the Cougar. Now featuring a cast-iron intake manifold and hydraulic valve lifters and only available with an automatic transmission, the 427 was now rated at 390 hp and a special model of the Cougar, the GT-E was built around it. The option didn't last long, however, as it was soon replaced by the 428 Cobra Jet engine.

before losing in a close runoff against the Camaro of Bill Jenkins for the class championship.

To compete with the Mustang, Ford's Lincoln Mercury Division introduced a new model for 1967 called the Cougar. Sharing a platform with its Mustang cousin, the Cougar was also available with the 390-ci FE engine as an option. But with a higher curb weight than the Mustang, the 390 Cougar did not immediately reach supercar status. That had to wait until 1968.

Mercury performance had a great year in 1969 as it matched in-house rival Ford model for model, engine for engine. Mercury also fielded an aero warrior on the NASCAR circuit in the form of the Cyclone Spoiler. As required, the manufacturer made production versions of the car available to the public with the Cale Yarborough and Dan Gurney editions, named for two of the Mercury factory team's top drivers at the time.

No bucket seats, just a standard vinyl-covered bench. No fancy console, just a lever on the steering column to select the gears in the C-6 automatic transmission. As a matter of fact, there is very little in the way of obvious options that might reveal the performance potential of this mighty Montego. (Photo Courtesy Kimberley Nelson)

When it came to Mercury muscle cars/sleepers for 1969, nothing could top Daryl Nelson's plain-Jane Montego hardtop. This stealth-black Montego didn't sport the sexy aerodynamic roofline of the Cyclone, but it did pack a big surprise between those squared-off front fenders. (Photo Courtesy Kimberley Nelson)

If the ram air scoop should be overlooked, one peek under the Montego's hood revealed its secret weapon, the 428 Cobra Jet. Backed up by a C-6 automatic and putting power to the ground via a Traction-Loc differential, this unassuming cruiser could easily click off quarter-mile times in the 13-second range, making it a match for almost any other street muscle car of its day. (Photo Courtesy Kimberley Nelson)

The Mercury muscle car that made a proud statement in 1969 was the Cougar Eliminator. Bold colors, strong graphics, and a spoiler on the deck lid were in keeping with the trend of the time without being over the top. It was a beautifully styled, well-balanced muscle car and it could have the Boss 302, the 351-4v, the 390, or the mighty 428 Cobra Jet engine. (Photo Courtesy Harry Unruh)

Considered a step up in luxury from its cousin the Mustang, the Cougar usually had a higher trim level, making it the choice of those who wanted a more gentlemanly muscle machine. In this case the C-6 automatic transmission is controlled through a console-mounted shift lever with simulated leather-grain T- handle. (Photo Courtesy Harry Unruh)

Mercury, 1968

A DE-TUNED VERSION OF THE 427 QUICKLY GIVES WAY TO THE MIGHTY 428 COBRA JET.

The big news for 1968 was the introduction of a toned down, more tractable version of the famous 427 engine to power Cougars. With a cast-iron intake manifold, lower compression (10.9 to 1), and machined to use hydraulic valve lifters, the still beefy 427 was rated at 390 hp. Produced in limited numbers prior to being replaced by the 428 Cobra Jet engine option, the 427 GTE Cougars, even when fully loaded with accessories and excessively tall rear-end gearing, could still cover the quarter-mile a full second quicker than its 390-powered predecessor.

Once the 428 Cobra Jet engine option became available in the Montego and Cougar, a whole new era of street performance began for Mercury. Similar to the midsize Ford Cobra model (based on the midsize Fairlane), Mercury introduced the Montego-based Cyclone that offered performance and visual appeal while retaining the capability to carry four people in comfort.

Mercury, 1969

TOP CATS AND CYCLONES CHALLENGE THE COMPETITION.

Like many of its competitiors in 1969, Mercury stepped up to the plate and created a couple of popular packages of its own.

Cylcone

Mercury's top performers for 1969, the Cyclone and Cougar, were stuffed full of the 428 Cobra Jet engine and neither model disappointed. *Car Craft* tested a 428 CJ Cyclone equipped with a C-6 automatic transmission, 3.90 Traction-Loc rear axle, and a host of style and comfort amenities. Even in boulevard cruiser form, the Cyclone covered the quarter-mile in 14.00 seconds flat at over 100 mph.

Super Stock and Drag Illustrated had a Cyclone, referred to as "The Strong Wind from Dearborn," optioned with the 4.30 Detroit Locker rear. It stopped the quarter-mile clocks in 13.99 seconds at 103.92 mph. Optioning a Cougar in similar fashion provided the aspiring drag racer an opportunity to fit into a lower stock or super stock class than a similarly equipped Mustang due to the additional weight carried by the Mercury. Not to mention the "sleeper" factor that accompanied the Cougar to any stoplight encounters against more commonly found muscle cars.

Eliminator

The sportiest model in the Cougar line for 1969 was the Eliminator, and it packed a punch. Along with Ford, Mercury had also set its sights on the SCCA Trans Am racing series in 1967, finishing second to the Ford Mustang team before taking up the challenge to compete in the NASCAR Grand American series in 1968, where it took home the championship.

If a manufacturer realizes racing successes, it makes perfectly good marketing sense to build a street-legal production model that encompasses the visual excitement of the racing version. The Cougar Eliminator was set apart from other models with racing mirrors, chin and deck spoilers, a hood scoop, and special graphics and colors. The base engine for the model was the 290-hp 351 Windsor. Also included in the option list was the 320-hp 390, the Boss 302, and two versions of the 428 Cobra Jet, with and without ram air.

Mercury commissioned subcontractor Kar Kraft to construct two lightweight Boss 429 Cougar drag cars for factory drivers Don Nicholson and Ed Schartman for competition in the new Pro/Stock class in 1969. While Nicholson swapped out the Boss 429 for his more familiar SOHC 427 very early on, Schartman campaigned his car with Boss 429 power, but it soon became obvious that the Cougar was still too heavy to be a winner and a new body style was needed in 1970. Both cars did, however, manage to serve a useful purpose as Mercury performance clinic cars before being sold at the end of the season.

The Cyclone Spoiler II was Mercury's counterpart to the Ford Torino Talladega, a specially built model with an aerodynamic nose package for NASCAR competition. While the NASCAR racing versions ran with 427 and later Boss 429 power, the base engine for the production Spoiler II was the 351 Windsor with the 390 and 428 Cobra Jet being optionally available. In the capable hands of drivers Cale and Lee Roy Yarborough, Spoilers visited victory lane four times during the 1969 NASCAR season.

Plymouth and Dodge, 1967

THE 440S AND THE HEMI RULE THE ROOST.

Perhaps the biggest thing to happen off the track for Chrysler's performance in 1967 was the introduction of the Supercar Clinic Program at the NHRA Winternationals. Ronnie Sox and Buddy Martin embarked on a nationwide tour of Plymouth dealerships, where they displayed their factory-supported race cars and explained to attendees the performance parts that Chrysler had to offer and how to best set up their cars for maximum performance.

The grueling clinic schedule kept the Sox and Martin team on the road constantly during the season, yet they still found time to race, with Sox taking home the Super Stock Eliminator win at the NHRA Springnationals with his Hemi Plymouth GTX. The Supercar Clinic proved to be wildly successful, even leading to production of a Plymouth drag racing board game and a slot car set.

Not only did the Plymouth and Dodge teams do well on the nation's dragstrips in 1967, the year proved to be their best yet in NASCAR stock car competition, with Dodge scoring 5 victories while Plymouth brought home an unprecedented 31 checkered flags and Richard Petty claimed yet another series championship.

Plymouth GTX and Dodge RT

Plymouth and Dodge introduced new models powered by a new high-performance engine based on the Belvedere and Coronet midsize models. They became known as the GTX and Coronet R/T, respectively. Power was provided by a high-performance version of the 440-ci big-block. With its 4.32-inch bore and 3.75-inch stroke, 10.0:1 compression, a healthy hydraulic lifter camshaft, and improved cylinder heads, the 440 was rated at 375 hp and delivered 480 ft-lbs of torque. And if the 440 didn't get the job done, you could always opt for the 426 street Hemi engine at extra cost. But more expensive didn't always mean quicker in the realm of street performance, as evidenced by the road test results from that year.

The 426-ci Street Hemi engine, first introduced in 1966, continued for 1967 and was available in Dodge Coronet and Plymouth Belvedere models. Dodge and Plymouth also introduced the Coronet R/T and Plymouth GTX performance models, respectively, and these cars received a 375-hp 440 engine standard with the Street Hemi optional.

Popular Hot Rodding found that a Coronet R/T Hemi with automatic transmission and 3.54 gearing could muster a quarter-mile time of only 14.60 seconds at 98 mph. The *Car Life* Hemi Charger with automatic and 3.23 gears cranked off a better, but not world-class time of 14.2 seconds at

With the introduction of the Plymouth Road Runner and its counterpart from Dodge, the Super Bee, Chrysler took a step back and a leap forward at the same time. Based around a bare-bones version of the midsize Belvedere and Coronet models, the Road Runner and Super Bee combined a light body style with a high-performance driveline à la the 413 and 426 Max Wedge cars that put the company at the forefront of Super/Stock drag racing and street performance earlier in the decade. The new models, with the high-performance 383 engine as standard, provided the consumer with an affordable high-performance car and appealed to the youth market through the clever use of inexpensive cartoonish graphics. The result was a car that could be had with either a 4-speed manual transmission or Chrysler's superior 727 TorqueFlite automatic, capable of stopping the quarter-mile clocks in just over 14 seconds in stock trim for less than $3,500. Both the Road Runner and Super Bee were offered with the 426 Hemi engine backed with either the TorqueFlite or 4-speed manual gearbox and the standard transmission cars received the beefier 9-3/4-inch Dana rear-axle assembly to handle the Hemi's awesome torque. (Photo Courtesy Patrick O'Leary)

96 mph. The Car and Driver tests of a Hemi Belvedere with automatic and 3.23 as compared to a similarly equipped but heavier GTX 440 showed the best the Hemi car could muster was a 14.50 elapsed time at 95 mph, while the GTX crossed the traps .1 second quicker. These tests went a long way to prove that when it came to street performance as delivered from the factory, the 440 wedge was the way to go for Mopar fans in 1967.

Big-Block Barracudas and Darts

Having caught wind of the fact that both Ford and General Motors planned to upsize their pony cars to accommodate big-block V-8s, prolific supporter of Chrysler performance and Dodge dealer Norm Kraus of Mr. Norm's Grand Spaulding Dodge fame pressed the company to build a 383 big-block Dart for 1967. After being told by the factory engineers that it was impossible to stuff the 383 in a space designed for the small-block 273, Mr. Norm set out to prove them wrong. Kraus had his dealership parts and service team perform the modifications necessary to accomplish this impossible feat in short order, and with his considerable influence within the Dodge Division when it came to matters of high performance, the factory eventually rolled out 458 Dart GTS models powered by the Charger 383 V-8.

The downside to the swap came in the need for more restrictive exhaust manifolds to clear the steering components and the fact that someone decided to fit the engine with a smaller carburetor. The result was a horsepower rating of 280, down from the 320 when the same engine was optioned in other Dodge models and a car that had trouble with the 390 Mustang, 400 Firebird, and particularly, the 396 Camaro. Plymouth had followed Dodge's lead by making the 383 optional in the newly restyled Barracuda Formula S model, but once again there were factors relating to exhaust manifold clearance that led to a reduction in power from the other Super Commando from 330 to 280.

The best quarter-mile time *Car and Driver* could manage with its test car was 15.4 seconds at 92 mph. *The High Performance Cars* Barracuda test car showed a little more promise by recording a 14.98 second at 91.50.

Dodge's answer to the Road Runner was a stripped Coronet, again 383 powered, called the Super Bee. The Coronet R/T continued alongside the Super Bee to compete with the GTX and both models also offered the 426 Hemi engine as an option.

Chrysler Corporation took a step back from the Funny cars in 1968 and like the competition at Ford turned its attention toward production-based race cars that the average buyer could better relate to. The biggest news for MOPAR racers in 1968 came in the form of the LO23 and BO29 Hemi Super/Stock factory lightweight Dart and Barracuda. Chrysler contracted with the Hurst Corporation to build a limited series of race-only, radically lightened, Hemi-powered Darts and Barracudas that would be sold through participating dealerships for just over $5,000. Many of the cars were delivered to the racer as shown here, race ready, but with the fiberglass front fenders and hood still in the gel coat and the body in primer. (Bob Wenzelburger Photo)

Chrysler wasn't shy about advertising the 426 Hemi engine on its vehicles from the mid-1960s into the early 1970s, and the company also took full advantage of advertising race wins delivered by the Hemi.

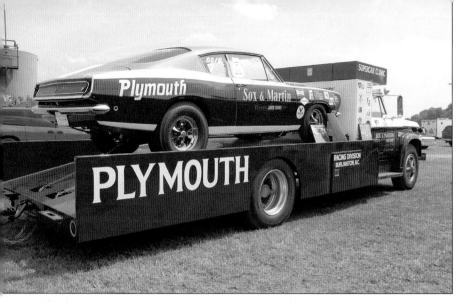

Perhaps the most famous and successful factory race team of the era was composed of Ronnie Sox, Buddy Martin, and engine-builder Jake King. The Sox & Martin 1968 Hemi Barracuda was a dominant force in Super/Stock racing through 1969, when the car became one of the pioneering vehicles for what became the Pro/Stock class.

The Sox & Martin Hemicuda and GTX were also used as part of the Supercar Clinic Program and were on display at Chrysler dealerships during seminars put on by the team. (Photo Courtesy Bob Wenzelburger)

Plymouth and Dodge both fielded limited-production factory lightweight Super Stock Hemi cars in 1967. The designations WO23 (Dodge Coronet two-door hardtop) and RO23 (Plymouth Belvedere two-door hardtop) delivered to a select few racers a car devoid of sealers and sound deadener, rubber floor mat in place of carpet, deleted radio, heater, and a trunk-mounted battery. A scooped hood directed cool air to the engine and was one of the only external clues to the special purpose of these cars. Vehicles equipped with automatic transmission received a Chrysler 8-3/4-inch heavy-duty rear with 4.86 ratio gears, and those ordered with the 4-speed transmission were upgraded to the 9-3/4-inch Dana rear with 4.89 ratio gearing.

The engine, although listed as the 425-hp 426 Hemi, was not the tamed-down version of the Street Hemi available in regular production models that year. Instead the Super Stock Hemi was replete with two

This LO23 Hemi Dart has been meticulously restored as an example of one of the most successful factory race cars of the era. Considering that these vehicles were meant for drag racing competition only and quickly became obsolete after being run hard, it is amazing that any of them still survive. (Photo Courtesy CarTech Archive)

Holley 4-barrel carburetors sitting astride an aluminum cross-ram intake manifold designed with much input from legendary drag racer "Akron Arlen" Vanke, a recipient of one of the factory-supported RO23 Plymouths. By Arlen's own account, the cars, which fell into NHRA's SS/B class, performed well but when equipped with the 4-speed transmission could not overcome the 427 Fairlanes of Ford's factory drivers.

Differing slightly from the previous Race Hemi, the 426 in the factory Darts and Barracudas was fitted with a mild camshaft when delivered, allowing the racer to select a grind to replace it prior to competing with the car. The magnesium cross-ram intake manifold mounted two 735-cfm Holley 4-barrel carburetors, and while the factory horsepower rating was the same as the Street Hemi at 425, these engines produced at least 550. These cars were built with the NHRA SS/A and SS/AA class in mind, and they proved to be so successful and dominant that NHRA later created the SS/AH class designed specifically for the Hemi Darts and Barracudas to compete against one another. (Photo Courtesy CarTech Archive)

The interiors of the Factory Super Stock Hemi Darts and Barracudas were all business. Devoid of all creature comforts and options, the cars were fitted with lightweight Bostrum seats, the backseat was removed, and even the window mechanisms were deleted, leaving a simple strap and snap arrangement to raise and lower the side windows. Roll bars were required by sanctioning agencies for safety. (Photo Courtesy CarTech Archive)

Chrysler continued the Road Runner, Super Bee, GTX, and Coronet R/T into 1969, again with great success both in sales and racing. The Supercar Clinic Program continued to grow and Mopar's A-Body cars with their 340-ci engines claimed a large share of the market with those seeking high performance at a discount price. The Road Runner and Super Bee had the 440-6-ci high-performance engine added as an option between the standard 383 and the 426 Hemi. This Road Runner has the functional Air Grabber system (available for the first time in 1969) evidenced by the red inserts in the vertical scoops on the hood. The Air Grabber system was manually controlled by a cable to keep out unwanted weather. (Photo Courtesy Wes Eisenschenk)

Two things that street racers across America learned to look out for in the late 1960s was a Mopar with this emblem on its ram air hood and a Dodge bearing a fiberglass, lift-off hood with lettering that read "440 6-BBL" on its scoop. The first, of course, warned that a 426 Hemi lurked within and the second indicated one of the most potent engines of the era, the 390-hp 440 equipped with three 2-barrel carburetors. On many occasions the 440 6-barrel car proved to be the quicker of the two in street trim.

Plymouth and Dodge, 1968

INTRODUCING THE ECONOMY MUSCLE CAR.

Road Runners and Super Bees provided performance on a budget while Charger R/T, Coronet RT, and GTX appealed to the more luxurious but still performance-minded crowd. And the good news was that they were all available with the Hemi.

Mopar's New Small-Block

Chrysler introduced an all-new small-block high-performance engine based on the LA series in 1968. At 340 ci and with an advertised horsepower of 275 the new engine proved to be a potent performer on both the street and dragstrip when mated with the lightweight Dart and Barracuda body styles. The NHRA factored the horsepower rating to 295 almost immediately. *A 340 Dart GTS* magazine test car optioned with an automatic transmission and 3.23 gearing turned in a quarter-mile time of 14.68 seconds at 96.2 mph, proving to be considerably quicker than the previous year's 383 big-block Dart GTS.

Perhaps the biggest street muscle car news to come out of Chrysler in 1968 was the introduction of two models that embodied the spirit of the taxicab-like Max Wedge cars of 1962 and 1963: the Road Runner and the Super Bee. Capitalizing on some more-than-clever marketing ideas, Plymouth introduced the Road Runner, based on the popular cartoon character of the time that always seemed to outrun and outsmart his competition, the car was a bare-bones model Plymouth Belvedere midsize. This made it a light car, just 3,400 pounds, and when combined with a 383-ci big-block V-8 that had received the cylinder heads, camshaft, exhaust manifolds, and oil pan windage tray from the high-performance 440 and a price tag of $2,896, Plymouth had a winner on its hands. For the most serious buyer, the Road Runner could have the 426 Hemi engine for an additional $714.

Dodge followed suit with a similar car that was based on the Coronet model, the Super Bee. Dodge's version was adorned with bumblebee stripes, badging, and optioned in a similar fashion to the Road Runner, yet the base price came in slightly higher at $3,027.

Super Stock and Drag Illustrated received a new Road Runner with the standard 4-speed transmission and 3.54 Sure-Grip differential for testing and invited two of Plymouth's best, Ronnie Sox and Buddy Martin, to handle the driving chores and check the factory tune, respectively.

After adjusting his seating position, removing the factory air cleaner, and experimenting with air pressure in the Polyglas tires, Sox got the car down to a very respectable 14.27-second quarter-mile time. Suffice it to say, a performance tune, along with the addition of slicks and steeper gearing, could put the Road Runner into the mid-13-second range easily.

The magazines were all over the new Road Runners and Super Bees, and the factory released upscale 440-ci 375-hp versions of each, the Plymouth GTX and Coronet R/T, respectively. And, of course, few could wait to get their hands on the 426 Hemi.

The *Motor Trend* quarter-mile time of 14.9 seconds at 95 mph with a 440, 4-speed, 3.23-geared Charger R/T proved that more cubic inches isn't always better when the car is considerably heavier. For example, they stopped the clocks with the 383 4-speed 3.23-geared Super Bee in 14.87 seconds at 96.25 mph.

But *Super Stock and Drag Illustrated* found that a 4.10 gear ratio woke up the 440, as its 4-speed Coronet R/T cleared the traps in 13.83 seconds at 102.27 mph.

Both *Car and Driver* and *Popular Hot Rodding* tested the Charger R/T optioned with the 426 Hemi. The automatic 3.23-geared model ran the quarter-mile in 13.50 seconds at 105 mph, while the 4-speed, 3.54-geared car managed only 13.90 at 104.96 mph.

LO23 Hemi Dart and BO29 Hemi Barracuda

On February 20, 1968, Chrysler announced to dealers the availability of two 426 Hemi-powered cars for "use in supervised acceleration trials." The cars, based on the Dodge Dart and Plymouth Barracuda, were prepared by the Hurst Corporation, a performance subcontractor with a proven record. The description of components is as follows: 426-ci 8-cylinder engine with dual 4-barrel carburetors, 12.5:1 compression ratio, cross-ram intake manifold, 1-11/16 x 1-11/16–inch Holley carburetors, and Competition Hooker headers, exhaust pipes, and mufflers. (While they did not have to be connected, NHRA rules for the Super/Stock classes required that cars in competition have a full exhaust system. Thus rudimentary single pipe and muffler systems were hung under the cars to meet this rule.)

Also included were a high-capacity oil pump, roller timing chain (reduced stretch for more consistent engine performance), mechanical valve gear, dual-breaker distributor, transistor ignition, metal core ignition wires, and unsilenced air cleaners. Also, deep-groove fan-drive pulleys, a heavy-duty radiator, an aluminum seven-blade fan equipped with viscous

drive, special offset 15-inch rear wheels, and a Chrysler-built 8-3/4-inch large-stem pinion gear set. Also included was a heavy-duty axle shaft with automatic transmission (4.86 axle ratio), Dana-built 9-3/4-inch heavy-duty

FACTORY WARS

The 1968 Super Stock Nationals is perhaps one of the best examples of how each of the major auto manufacturers, Chrysler, Ford, and General Motors (although they still claimed not to support racing) did battle on the dragstrip in the mid- to late 1960s and into the early 1970s. Each brand seemed to have found its niche in a particular class or classes of competition by this point and the all-deciding factor of which reigned supreme very often came down to the running of the Stock and Super Stock Eliminators.

The Super Stock Nationals was a three-day affair and many of the biggest names in factory drag racing were in competition. The following is a breakdown of class and eliminator titles at that event, showcasing a cross-section of how the major auto manufacturers available high-performance cars were represented. Winning elapsed times and speeds are not included, nor are all classes run. Also, Funny Car classes are not included due to the fact that by this time (1968) the cars bore only a passing resemblance to their production counterparts and while factory supported, they used very few production components that had not been extensively modified.

July 19, 1968

Top Stock Class Winners
A/S Terry Clark, 396 Chevelle
B/S Bill Izykowski, 427 Biscayne

Top Super Stock Class Winners
SS/B Ronnie Sox, Hemi Barracuda
SS/C Downing and Ryan, 427 Fairlane
SS/E Bob Brown, 428 CJ Mustang

SS/F Dave Strickler, Z-28 Camaro
SS/BA Dave Oldfield, Hemi Dart
SS/EA Bill Lawton, 428 CJ Mustang
SS/FA Dick Landy, 440 Dodge R/T (Landy was also entered in SS/B with his Dart)

July 20, 1968

Top Stock Class Winners
A/S Mike Radish, 396 Chevelle
B/S Bill Izykowski, 427 Biscayne
D/S Brejik, Olds W-31 Cutlass
D/SA Stasky Katsounis, W-31 Cutlass

Top Super Stock Class Winners
SS/B Ed Miller, Hemi Barracuda
SS/C Roger Cook, 427 Camaro
SS/E Bob Coble, 428 CJ Mustang
SS/F Hubert Platt, 428 CJ Torino
SS/BA Shirley Shahan, Hemi Barracuda
SS/EA Bill Lawton, 428 CJ Mustang
SS/FA Dick Landy, 440 Dodge R/T

On July 21, the Experimental Super/Stock Eliminator title was won by Ronnie Sox in his Hemi Barracuda in a close race with Dick Landy's Dart. Landy later claimed the overall Super Stock Eliminator title with his 440 Dodge R/T.

On the NASCAR circuit, the drivers of Hemi Plymouth Road Runners fared very well, taking home 15 checkered flags while the Dodge Charger teams won just 5.

axle with manual transmission (4.89 axle ratio), Sure Grip differential, 135-amp-hour battery located in the rear compartment, front disc brakes, 4-1/2-inch bolt circle, fiberglass front fenders, fiberglass hood with scoop, lightweight steel doors, lightweight front bumper, lightweight side window glass, and high-capacity fuel lines. All this with a business coupe interior (two bucket seats, no rear seat).

For manual transmission only: Special heavy-duty 10-1/2-inch clutch and flywheel, safety steel clutch housing, and a competition "slick shift" 4-speed transmission.

For automatic transmission only: High-stall speed torque converter (large drive lugs and 7/16-inch-diameter attaching screws, and a heavy-duty manual shift TorqueFlite transmission.

The following items were deleted from this body type: heater, body sealer and sound deadeners, silence pads, outside mirrors, right-side seat belt, and body color paint. No optional equipment of any kind could be ordered.

For the sum of $5,146 plus destination fees, serious racers could get their hands on the quickest production Plymouth or Dodge vehicle on the planet and compete at the top of NHRA's SS/B class. Production numbers for these cars are generally listed as 70 Barracudas and 75 Darts, while the number of class championships and eliminator titles claimed by them beginning in 1968 made it seem as if they were everywhere.

Almost all of the top-name Plymouth and Dodge drag racers of the era were at one time associated with either a Hemi Dart or a Hemi Barracuda. In class competition it always boiled down to either a Hemi Dart or a Hemi Barracuda taking home the win, as no other manufacturer fielded a car that could compete in SS/B. The Hemi cars were later reclassified as SS/A (4-speed) and SS/AA (automatic) by the NHRA and more recently have been assigned their own class SS/AH, where they are content to do battle with one another for the glory.

In 1968 the Hemi Barracudas and Darts may have had their way in SS/B, but when it came time to run for Super/Stock Eliminator, a runoff pitting all the class winners against one another and handicapped based on the class national elapsed time record, the Hemis showed their stuff against the factory Fords and GMs, and more often than not, they claimed the win there as well.

Plymouth and Dodge, 1969

THE ULTIMATE STREET PERFORMERS FROM CHRYSLER MAKE THEIR DEBUT.

Although Chrysler hit a home run with the creation of the affordably packaged Road Runner in 1968, the company was not content to rest on its laurels.

Road Runner and 440 Six-Packs

The Plymouth Road Runner, along with the Dodge Super Bee, not only gained more optional cubic inches, 440 up from 383, for 1969 they were also the recipients of possibly the meanest Mopar powerplant since the 426 Stage III Max Wedge, the 440 Six-Pack. The most distinctive visual clue that something special lurked beneath was the lift-off fiberglass hood with the huge open scoop and the graphic "440 Six-Pack."

Found therein was a 440-ci (4.32-inch bore 3.75-inch stroke) cylinder block stuffed with carefully matched and Magnaflux-checked connecting rods, 10.1:1 compression pistons, and an aggressive hydraulic lifter camshaft. On top were high-performance cylinder heads and a high-rise Edelbrock aluminum intake manifold with three Holley 2-barrel carburetors flowing a massive 1,375 cfm. A specially designed open-element air cleaner mated the carburetors to the hood scoop. The package was rated at 390 hp at 4,700 rpm and 490 ft-lbs of torque at 3,200. While this package carried a lower horsepower rating than the 426 Hemi (also optional that year) the 440 Six-Pack often proved itself to be the superior performer on the street.

Calling the 440 Six-Pack "a happy medium between the 335-hp Road Runner and the 426 Hemi," *Drag Racing* tested a 4-speed equipped with 4.10 rear-end gears with the aid of Ronnie Sox. Buddy Martin was on hand to check the car's state of tune, and on a cold day at Cecil County Dragway in Maryland, Sox tripped the quarter-mile clocks in 12.98 seconds at 111.66 on stock Polyglas tires.

Hot Rod tested a Dodge Charger 500 with the 426 Hemi, 4-speed, 4.10 gears, and recorded a best elapsed time of 13.48 seconds at 109 mph. *Car Life* managed only a 13.8 at 104.2 mph with an automatic transmission, 4.10 geared 440 Six-Pack Super Bee. *Car and Driver* recorded a 14.0 in the quarter-mile at 99.55 in a standard 383/335 Super Bee with automatic transmission and 3.55 gearing. *The Speed and Super Car* Hemi Road Runner test car with 4.10 gears and an automatic transmission clicked off a 13.32 at 107.65 mph and *Motor Trend's* test of the 440 GTX, the Road Runner's more generously appointed big brother, recorded a 13.7 at 102.8 when optioned with the automatic transmission and 4.10 gearing.

These test results make it obvious that Chrysler had much to offer in the way of performance in its midsize cars in 1969.

'Cuda and Dart Get the 440

Taking a cue from some performance-minded dealers who had been applying the pressure for a big-engine, small-car offering, Chrysler made the 375-hp version of the 440 optional in the Dodge Dart GTS and Plymouth 'Cuda for 1969.

Super Stock and Drag Illustrated put a 'Cuda with automatic transmission and 4.10 gears through its paces, and in spite of traction problems created by the nose heavy car with stock tires, they managed a best of 13.89 seconds at 103.21 in the quarter-mile.

Drag Racing was more serious with its 440 Dart GTS test car and enlisted the assistance of Dodge Funny Car driver Charlie Allen to wring it out. After pronouncing that the stock tires were useless, Allen had larger G-70 street rubber installed. With no other tweaks, the 3.55-geared, automatic-equipped Dart ripped off a quarter-mile time of 12.70 at 112 mph. Allen's personal GTS 440 Dart, with an engine blueprinted to Super Stock specifications and a few other drag racing modifications, ran 11.98.

In July 1969, *Cars* tested a prototype 440 Six-Pack Dart GTS, which lacked the hotter cam used in other Six-Pack applications. With 3.91 gearing and automatic transmission, the test car ran the quarter-mile in 13.00 at 107 mph, but the scribes at *Cars* had little good to say about the package, aside from its straight-line performance.

For the Mopar small-block enthusiast, the 340 was still optional in both the Dart GTS and 'Cuda. *Car Life* reported that an automatic-equipped 340 Dart with 3.23 gearing was good for a quarter-mile time of 14.82 seconds at 96 mph, while the *Motor Trend* 4-speed 'Cuda test car with the same gearing was much quicker at 14.22 seconds at 99.10 mph. Both cars remained a potent package for a reasonable price.

While continuing to dominate in NHRA class and Super Stock Eliminator in 1969, Ronnie Sox, Dick Landy, and other Mopar drag racing stars were dabbling in a new racing class and match racing series called Pro/Super Stock with the Hemi Darts and Barracudas. Here they faced Boss 429 and 427 SOHC Mustangs and 427 Camaros in heads-up competition as in the early days of factory drag racing, and the fans loved it. Before the end of the season, the concept morphed into one of the most popular classes ever to hit drag racing, Pro/Stock. It was a venue where fans could see cars similar to those they drove in head-to-head competition.

Dodge Daytona

The years 1969 and 1970 saw the "Aero warriors" on the NASCAR stock car racing circuit. Always eager to stay in front, the engineers at Dodge devised an ingenious plan to outsmart the air and allow their cars to go faster than those of the competition. Considering the theory of less aerodynamic drag, which in turn requires less horsepower to move the vehicle, engineers gave birth to the Dodge Daytona.

Along came a Dodge Charger–based, limited production, radically modified performance car featuring a pointy nose, humps at the top of the front fenders for tire clearance and suspension travel, and a huge wing mounted on the deck lid. NASCAR rules required that 500 examples of any vehicle be produced before being allowed to compete, so Dodge went about making the Daytona available and completely street legal with either the 440 or 426 Hemi engine. Although the outrageous styling did little to help Dodge's performance image on the street (plenty of other models upheld that end), it served them well in the NASCAR series, where the brand scored 21 victories.

American Motors, 1968

RAMBLER IS BACK IN THE PERFORMANCE GAME.

The Rambler was back with a vengeance. In 1966, American Motors had introduced a new short-deck series V-8 engines in 290- and 343-ci versions. The new design was a vast improvement over the previously used V-8 that had been around since the 1950s and, although powerful, was very heavy. In 1968, the company introduced two new models that soon proved that the Rambler guys were finally back in the performance game for the first time since 1957.

First up was the Javelin, a four-seat sporty model that *Road & Track* raved over and *Motor Trend* put at the top of its list of Sports/Personal cars. *Car Life* tested a Javelin optioned with the 343-ci 4-barrel engine (the 390 became optional later in the year) and reported a quarter-mile time of 15.4 seconds at 93 mph. Showing just how serious the company was about performance, it hired former Corvette team guru Jim Jeffords to take the Javelin SCCA Trans Am series racing. While the first-year effort did not result in a winning record, the AMCs proved that they were capable of running with the Z-28 Camaro and Mustangs on the circuit.

The folks from Kenosha really stunned the automotive world when World Land Speed record holder Craig Breedlove, his wife, Lee, and Ron Dykes used two specially prepared versions of a new model called AMX (for

American Motors stepped up its performance game in a big way in 1969 with one of its hottest offerings, the SC/Rambler built with cooperation from the Hurst Corporation. A combination of a lightweight body, AMC's potent 390 ram air engine, standout styling, and a reasonable price made the economy compact SC/Rambler a potent package for street and strip.

American Motors Experimental after a concept car) to set 106 world speed and endurance records at the Goodyear Test Track in Texas. On February 15, 1968, at Daytona International Speedway, American Motors introduced the AMX to the American public. The car was a two-seat GT-style sports car with a 97-inch wheelbase, 1 inch shorter than America's other two-seat sweetheart, the Corvette.

Available with an optional 390-ci 315-hp engine that produced 425 ft-lbs of torque, backed up by a BorgWarner 3- or 4-speed automatic trans-

mission, dual exhausts, and special traction bars at the rear, the AMX was a potent powerhouse. Add the optional Go-Package and you had beefier suspension, power disc brakes at the front, and a Twin-Grip differential. For the serious enthusiast, AMC made its Group 19 performance parts available through the dealer parts network.

Car and Driver magazine's 390 AMX test car stopped the quarter-mile clocks in 14.8 seconds at 95 mph; proof that AMC could field a strong street performer.

The 315-hp 390-ci powerplant that had been introduced by AMC in 1968 fit nicely between the fenders of the SC/ Rambler. With stock times in the mid- to low-14-second range, the engine design lent itself well to modifications that allowed the hot little compact to stop the quarter-mile clocks along with the best muscle cars that Detroit had to offer.

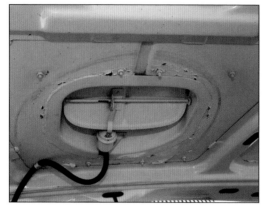

While somewhat crude in its execution, the vacuum-operated ram air system atop the SC/Rambler engine was a solid design that proved itself on the street and in competition. The open-element air cleaner was sealed to the hood via a rubber ring.

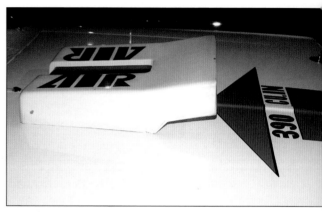

The SC/Rambler's hood featured a snorkel-style scoop to feed fresh air into the engine and cool graphics that cleverly pointed out the direction the air traveled across the hood and into the scoop.

Sitting on top of the Super Stock AMX's 390 engine, specially assembled at Hurst and packed with some of the best performance parts available at the time (including cylinder heads by Crane), was this aluminum cross-ram intake manifold mounting two Holley 4-barrel carburetors. The velocity stacks on top of the carburetors sealed to the scoop opening in the car's hood.

The interior of the SC/Rambler was somewhat bare bones as, after all, the model was based on AMC's compact economy car. The car came equipped with a Hurst shifter to control the 4-speed transmission, a steering-column-mounted Sun Tachometer, and a carryover of the red, white, and blue outside graphics on the headrests.

American Motors collaborated with Hurst in the development and construction of 50 specially equipped AMX-based cars for competition in NHRA Super/Stock. With touches by such racing legends as H. L. Shahan and Howard Maselles, the Super Stock AMX package made an immediate impression in drag racing. So potent were the cars that the NHRA immediately factored them into a higher class. In spite of this, the Ramblers dominated, setting numerous class records and winning Super Stock Eliminator titles at numerous NHRA and AHRA events well into the 1970s. (Photo Courtesy Doug Boyce)

American Motors, 1969

PUTTING THE BIG THREE ON NOTICE.

The introduction of the Javelin and the AMX in 1968 proved to be a tremendous hit, both in sales and credibility in the muscle car market. Not content to stand pat, AMC created two new offerings in 1969 that cemented its place in the muscle car arena.

Giant Killers from Kenosha

The Javelin and AMX were joined by AMC's most unique offering yet, the Hurst SC/Rambler, or Scrambler, as it was often called. AMC collaborated with Hurst to modify a series of its base economy model Ramblers into eye-catching, lightweight, low-priced powerhouses. And to call the idea a success is an understatement.

The cars were stuffed with the 315-hp 390 engine that powered the AMX and Javelin, which was then backed with a close-ratio 4-speed transmission and Hurst shifter with T-Handle. A Sun tachometer was mounted on the steering column and a dual exhaust with special-tone mufflers and chrome tips was added. A 10½-inch clutch and Twin-Grip differential with 3.54 gearing were standard, as were power front disc brakes and rear axle torque links that aided traction off the starting line.

Also in the package were a heavy-duty cooling system with power flex fan and shroud, increased ratio non-power steering, and heavy-duty front sway bar, springs, and shock absorbers. This was topped off with a functional hood scoop for cold-air induction to the engine, custom grille Hurst SC/Rambler badging, sports steering wheel, racing mirrors, hood pins, special interior treatments, mag-style wheels mounting Goodyear Polyglas tires, and two patriotic red, white, and blue paint schemes that made the boxy little car stand out from the crowd.

Advertised as "a Rambler that does the quarter-mile in 14.3 seconds" (*Popular Hot Rodding* put this claim to the test and ran the quarter-mile in 14.1 seconds) and the promise that "with this car you could make life miserable for any GTO, Road Runner, Cobra Jet, or Mach I." In 1969, you could own this special, limited production giant killer for just $2,998.

Javelin was back on the Trans-Am series circuit in 1969 with an eye toward greater things. With Bob Tullius, Jerry Grant, and Ron Grable driving for the factory team, AMC hoped for an even better year than it had in 1968. Unfortunately this was not the case, as AMC came up far short of winning the championship it desired.

AMX was again the top street performer with the 390 virtually unchanged from the previous year. *Motor Trend* noted a big jump in performance with its 1969 test car, however, posting a quarter-mile time of 14.1 seconds right smack in the realm of the hot street cars of the day.

Super Stock AMX

The big news of the year for AMC involved another special car developed with the assistance of the Hurst Corporation. With an eye toward making a big splash in the NHRA/AHRA Super/Stock classes, AMC commissioned Hurst to build the required 50 units of a factory race car based on the AMX. The cars were shipped to Hurst with all the weight-saving deletes completed, where they were further modified and fitted with 390-ci engines assembled by longtime drag racing great H. L. Shahan with 12.4:1 compression JE forged pistons, a Crane roller camshaft, Crane modified cylinder heads, and an Edelbrock cross-ram intake manifold with two 615-cfm Holley carburetors. A Mallory ignition system and Doug's headers completed the package.

Modifications were done to the rear suspension to maximize traction off the starting line. Henry's axles and 4.44 gears completed the rear end. The hoods were cut for a scoop that pumped cool air to the Holley carburetors, sealed by foam rings on velocity stacks. BorgWarner T-10 4-speed transmissions and Hurst Super Shifters were used in all of the cars. Cost to the racer in 1969 was $5,994, and many former Mopar and Chevy racers came on board with the American Motors racing team and began making their presence known in the NHRA SS/D class immediately, with elapsed times in the high-10-second range. This led to the sanctioning body re-factoring the cars into a class higher (SS/C) where they continued to win and set records for several years, long after AMC was absent from factory participation in racing.

CHAPTER 7

1970–1971: BEFORE THE CURTAIN COMES DOWN

A decade that began with some of the mightiest machines ever to roll off a Detroit assembly line would bear witness to big-block V-8 engines that struggled to produce 350 hp within three short years.

When it came to potent performance from Chevrolet in a midsize package, nothing could beat a 1970 Chevelle equipped with the 454-ci, 450-hp LS-6 engine option, and drag racers took full advantage. Ray Allen was a national champion with his convertible version sponsored by Briggs Chevrolet. (Photo Courtesy CarTech Archive)

Chevrolet, 1970

LS-6: THE RULING CLASS FROM CHEVROLET.

In 1970, Chevrolet, in an effort to stay ahead of the competition, created one of the best muscle car engines in history.

A Big Year with a Big Engine

The Chevy big-block V-8 grew from 427 to 454 ci in 1970 with a 4.25-inch bore and 4.00-inch stroke. The top two performance offerings were listed as LS-5 and LS-6. The LS-5 delivered 360 hp at 5,400 rpm and a stump-pulling 500 ft-lbs of torque at 3,200 rpm. The compression ratio was listed at 11.25 to 1. A Rochester Quadrajet 4-barrel carburetor, cast-iron intake manifold, and hydraulic lifter camshaft completed the package. When installed in the Corvette, the LS-5 was rated at 390 hp.

The LS-6 shared bore, stroke, and compression ratio with the LS-5, but thanks to a solid lifter camshaft, aluminum intake manifold, and Holley 4-barrel carburetor, it pounded out 450 hp at 5,600 rpm and again 500 ft-lbs of torque at 3,200 rpm.

The good news for Chevy performance fans was the fact that both versions of the 454 were available in the Chevelle, Camaro, and Corvette.

An LS-7 version, with 465 rated horsepower, never made it into a production car due to increasingly stringent emissions regulations, but it was made available through the parts network to select Chevy racers.

One of the most successful Chevy drag racers in 1970 was Ray Allen. Carefully selecting his mount and the NHRA class he wanted to dominate, Allen went with an LS-6 Chevelle convertible and automatic transmission. The additional weight of the convertible body when factored with the rated horsepower dropped the car one class lower than a similarly equipped hardtop and, by doing so, provided the competitive advantage of being at the "top" of the chosen class. In magazine tests the big-block Chevys were a popular choice in 1970, with the LS-6 models receiving the most attention.

Speed and Super Car tested an LS-6 Chevelle with a 4-speed and 3.31 gearing, which posted a quarter-mile elapsed time of 13.55 seconds at 104 mph. The *Car and Driver* automatic transmission, 3.70-geared LS-6 cleared the clocks in 13.81 seconds at 103.80 mph, while *Hot Rod* achieved the best results with 4.11 gears and a 4-speed with an elapsed time of 13.44 seconds at 108.17 mph.

The Camaro underwent a styling change for 1970, and the Z-28 was the recipient of the 350-ci LT-1 small-block that powered the Corvette. While there was no real difference between the LT-1 engines in the two models, the Z-28 was rated at 360 hp while the Corvette was rated at 370. The LT-1 engines were assembled with carefully selected internal parts, 11.0:1 compression, aggressive, solid lifter camshaft profile, aluminum intake manifold, and 780-cfm Holley 4-barrel carburetor.

The package proved to be a very potent street and strip performer, as shown by *High Performance Cars* magazine's 4.10-geared test car that

The LS-6 454 engine featured a steel crankshaft, four-bolt main bearing caps, 11.25:1 compression, forged pistons, solid lifter camshaft, and an 800-cfm Holley 4-barrel carburetor on an aluminum intake manifold. The engine's 450 rated horsepower came at 5,600 rpm, while it developed 500 ft-lbs of torque at 3,600 rpm.

Don Yenko Chevrolet ordered the best production performance cars that the factory had to offer and then set about performing in-house modifications that turned them into Yenko Super Cars. One of several Chevrolet dealership owners who took cars to the next level of performance, Yenko performed his magic on 175 Novas in 1970. Given the designation YS-90, they were known as the Yenko Deuce cars.

clicked off a 13.88-second quarter-mile at 101 mph and *Car Craft's* similar car, which delivered a time of 14.11 seconds at 102.73 mph. An LT-1 Corvette with 4.11 gearing tested by *Car Life* cleared the quarter-mile traps in 14.17 seconds at 102.17 mph.

COPO Novas and the Yenko Deuce

The last year for the big-block Nova was 1970 because insurance costs for the 375-hp cars had already begun to climb, which impacted showroom sales proportionately. Small-block cars were not yet impacted as much, and reading the market like the professional he was, Don Yenko convinced Chevrolet to build 177 Novas powered by the LT-1 small-block under the COPO program. Of those, 175 non-SS Novas with rubber floor mats, standard bench-seat interiors, heavy-duty suspension, 12-bolt Posi-Traction rear axle, and either M-21 4-speed or TH-400 automatic transmission were earmarked to Yenko for transformation into the Yenko Deuce.

At Yenko's direction, the conversion of 50 cars was performed by the Hurst Corporation. All Yenko cars received special identifying trim, a hood-mounted tachometer, and an underdash gauge cluster. Wheel upgrades were also made available. With headers and slicks, the LT-1 allowed a Yenko Deuce to cover the quarter-mile in the 13-second range at more than 100 mph.

During the late 1960s and early 1970s, the Yenko emblem was synonymous with Chevrolet performance. A racer himself, Don Yenko saw the potential for taking production line high-performance cars to the next level for his customers and, as a result, rode a wave of success for several years.

The Yenko Deuce cars featured a special identifying stripe package in a contrasting color to the body paint, and because Hurst shifters were used as part of the dealer modifications, a Hurst emblem was also included. Yenko offered different levels of modification, including performance tuning of stock engines.

The hood graphics on the Yenko Deuce indicated that a LT-1 was lurking beneath. Another Yenko option was the hood-mounted tachometer, popular on the Pontiac GTO and Firebird.

The 1970 Yenko Deuce was powered by the same 350-ci LT-1 high-performance small-block engine in the Z-28 Camaro. Using COPO #9010 for the engine and #9737 for the suspension package when ordering the Novas, Yenko started his conversion with the 370-hp engine and sport suspension.

Yenko cars received their own special center caps when ordered with mag-style wheels. This was just one more way to show that the car was indeed something special as compared to the average Chevy of the day.

Yenko kept the car's overall weight down by not adding unnecessary creature comforts to the interior of the Deuce. The standard vinyl-covered bench seat got the job done just fine. The Hurst shifter was one of his must-have additions, along with a set of analog gauges mounted under the dash to monitor engine oil pressure, coolant temperature, and electrical system voltage. Special Yenko appliques on the door panels set the car apart from the standard Nova.

The Wallace Chevrolet decal on Tom Kusmiesz's unrestored 1970 Yenko Deuce has a story to tell beyond the fact that the car was prepared by Yenko and sold through that dealership. As the story goes, Wallace Chevrolet was located in a not-so-nice part of town, so vehicles parked on its lot oftentimes had certain accessories stolen. As a result, Wallace started ordering cars from Yenko with standard equipment normally found on its cars omitted, such as the sport mirrors and certain exterior emblems._ Another non-stock feature found on Yenko cars sold through Wallace Chevrolet is the addition of hood locks, which were installed for obvious reasons.

Taking a cue from its high-performance-oriented dealers, Chevrolet introduced COPO Camaros and Novas in 1969. This Hugger Orange 427 COPO Camaro screams performance. Throw in the fact that the car was ordered through Nickey Chevrolet, one of America's largest and most performance-oriented dealers, and then treated to the ultimate Stage III treatment by Bill Thomas, and it doesn't get much better.

Chevrolet, 1971

CHANGES IN THE WIND.

As was the case across the car industry, 1971 marked the end of performance cars for Chevy fans as well. Obviously there would be no corporate mandate against racing from a company that had denied it was supporting racing since 1963. Rather, the line began to lose certain options, such as the big-block in the Nova, and horsepower ratings, although not plummeting just yet, began to fall. Some explained that the lower horsepower numbers were only a reflection of a change in how the numbers were arrived at, but a closer look at the specifications of even the top engine options showed a marked reduction in compression ratios. Combine this with both retarded camshaft and ignition timing, and the decline in performance is understandable.

Here are two prime examples: A 1971 454 Corvette posting a quarter-mile elapsed time of 14.70 seconds, as opposed to the previous year's LT-1 small-block, which was .6 second quicker. A 71 Z-28, now rated at 330 hp, .7 second slower than the 1970 model.

Dark days were ahead for GM performance.

Later versions of the Pontiac GTO and Trans Am equipped with ram air were unique in their design, with yards of foam being required to seal the air cleaner to the widely separated air-intake scoops on the hood.

Pontiac, 1970

PONTIAC PERFORMANCE REMAINS STRONG, BUT SALES NUMBERS BEGIN TO FALL.

You could have your GTO any one of three ways in 1970. The 400 R.A. III engine was standard, the 400 R.A. IV was optional, and new on the scene was the 455 H.O. torque monster. The 455 used the R.A. III camshaft for a little more punch and delivered a rated 360 hp at 4,300 rpm with 500 ft-lbs of torque at 2,700 rpm.

Eager to test a GTO powered by the new engine, *Car and Driver* found that its 3.31-geared, 4-speed test car could only manage 15 seconds flat in the quarter-mile at 96.5 mph, while *Car Life* did slightly better with its automatic-equipped test car at 14.76 seconds at 95.94 mph. By comparison the *High Performance Cars* 400 R.A. III, 3.90-geared GTO ran a 14.45 at 100 mph, and the 400 R.A. IV car tested by *Car Craft* blasted out a 14.02 at 98.90 mph.

At the beginning of the 1970 model year, the only engines available for the GTO Judge were the 400 R.A. III and R.A. IV, but later in the production run the 455 H.O. also became available. Sales of the GTO and GTO Judge declined rapidly in 1970, as insurance costs skyrocketed.

The Firebird and Trans Am underwent styling changes for 1970, with the latter receiving wheel spats, a front air dam, and the rear-facing shaker scoop that became its trademark. The Trans Am was

The 1970 and 1971 GTOs maintained great appeal through styling and performance, but the end was fast approaching. At the end of the performance era in Detroit, Pontiac was the last to fall. Super Duty 455 engines remained on the list of available options until 1974. With compression ratios in the low 8:1 range, along with retarded ignition and camshaft timing, and ridiculously lean jetting in its carburetors, the SD 455 still managed 310 rated horsepower, which by comparison to earlier models sounds low but it was actually higher than any other GM offerings at the time. (Photo Courtesy Justin Focus imaging/Mimi Siracusa [70] Gary Atkins [71])

powered by the 400 R.A. III engine, rated at 335 hp. A Trans Am with 3.91 gearing and 4-speed was tested by *Hot Rod*, which reported a quarter-mile time of 13.90 seconds at 102 mph. Many call the 1970 Trans Am the last true high-performance car of the muscle car generation.

Pontiac, 1971

TRANS AM WAS THE LAST ONE TO LEAVE THE PERFORMANCE PARTY.

There were no Ram Air engine offerings for the GTO in 1971, and with the standard 400 engine's compression ratio dropped to 8.2:1, the rated horsepower was now 300. The optional 455 H.O., which had 8.4:1 compression and 345 rated horsepower, was available with automatic transmission only. This was also the last year for the GTO Judge, as the Trans Am took the limelight away from its big brother.

Feeling the heat of declining sales due to insurance costs and emissions regulations, Pontiac attempted a reasonably successful but short-lived end run by introducing a stripped-down model called the LeMans GT-37. Even when equipped with the 300-hp 400 GTO engine, the car could be listed as a V-8 Tempest when being insured, and as a result did not throw up the red flags that the GTO did. *Hot Rod* magazine appreciated the concept and found that a LeMans GT-37 with 3.55 gearing and a 4-speed outran the GTO in the quarter-mile thanks to its reduced weight. The test car posted a 14.40 elapsed time at 97.50 mph.

The Firebird and Trans Am, while stealing much of the limelight from the GTO in 1971, suffered the same woes when it came to an actual high-performance engine. The top option was the 455 H.O., rated at 325 hp. Even when equipped with the 455 H.O., the Trans Am and Firebird could manage no better than high-14-second quarter-mile times.

Pontiac fired the last shots of the muscle car era when in 1973–1974 [Author: which year?] it announced the availability of the 455 Super Duty engine. Fewer than 500 of these engines were produced, but they harkened back to the Super Duty engines of the 1960s with a reinforced cylinder block, four-bolt main bearing caps, Magnafluxed and shot peened forged-steel connecting rods, a special crankshaft, and redesigned cylinder heads that reportedly flowed 20 percent more air than the R.A. IV with 2.11-inch intake, and 1.77-inch exhaust valves.

Reportedly capable of sustained 6,000-rpm use, the engine was red-lined at 5,800. When *Hot Rod* tested a 455 Super Duty Trans Am in 1973, it appeared that performance was not dead in America as the car clicked off a 13.54-second quarter-mile at 104.29 mph. Sadly it later came to light that the car was a "ringer" specially prepared for the test with an improved camshaft and higher-ratio rocker arms. The 455 SD cars actually ran in the high-14-second range; and the test turned out to be a false flag.

Buick, 1970

GSX: THE GENTLEMAN'S MUSCLE CAR; OVERLOOKED AND UNDERRATED.

How underrated you ask? How about the *Motor Trend* test car that weighed 3,810 pounds and blasted through the quarter-mile traps in 13.38 seconds at 105.5 mph with a 3.64 rear-axle ratio. Suffice it to say a deeper gear in the rear would have put this behemoth down in the high-12-second range. As it stood, the Buick ranked right at the top of the muscle cars tested during that era.

Stage I

For 1970, Buick upped the available cubic inches in its top V-8 option to 455. The Stage I option consisted of an improved oiling system, improved cylinder heads with 2.13-inch intake, and 1.75-inch exhaust valves, in addition to a hot hydraulic lifter camshaft, quicker ignition timing, and a specially tuned carburetor. Rated horsepower was 360 and the torque number was an impressive 500 ft-lbs. To properly showcase all this muscle, Buick added the GSX model, which stood out from the crowd thanks to tastefully applied graphics and a rear deck spoiler.

Here it is, the car that was arguably one of the best muscle cars, and certainly the most underrated muscle machine of the late 1960s and early 1970s, the Buick GS Stage 1. Often referred to as the gentleman's muscle car, the GS Stage 1 combined crisp GM midsize styling with luxury and brute power. Not your grandfather's Buick by any stretch of the imagination.

The heart of the Buick GS Stage 1 came in this 455-ci package, conservatively rated at 360 hp and developing a massive 510 ft-lbs of torque. Improvements in the camshaft, cylinder heads, and ram air made this the most powerful engine Buick ever built.

The only outward indication that this Buick was anything more than the average GM A-Body of the era was this obscure emblem that advertised the Stage 1 engine option. The GSX model offered that year provided more of a performance car appearance with special colors, graphics, and a specific deck spoiler.

Stage II

Buick had big plans for the future when it developed the Stage II package in 1970. It included reworked high-flow cylinder heads, TRW forged pistons, MK IV 7,000-rpm camshaft and valvetrain assembly, Edelbrock B4B intake manifold, Carter Thermoquad carburetor, and Kustom Equipment headers. This little-known option was available through the Buick parts system and several dealer-connected drag racers took full advantage.

The Stage II package was reported to add 50 hp over the already pow-erful Stage I, and this was evidenced by the performance of a race-prepared car sponsored by Reynold's Buick in West Covina, California, that posted elapsed times in the 10.70s at 123 mph. The Stage II was slated to become a production option for 1971 but was canceled when the compression ratios for all Buick engines were lowered to meet federal regulations.

The Stage I remained an option for 1971, but the compression ratio was reduced to 8.5:1 and the horsepower rating dropped to 345. The entire Buick line reflected the emasculation of the once mighty and unchallenged American big-block V-8 through the remainder of the decade, and the company did not produce a hint of performance again until the 1980s with the introduction of the Turbocharged V-6 midsize Grand National model.

MAGAZINE TESTS REVIEW

Car Craft undertook the task of drag testing eight muscle cars with the results published in the November 1969 issue. With the exception of the Mercury Cougar, which was a Boss 429 prototype that never went into production, all the cars were stock production models with no apparent factory "ringers," as had been the case with many magazine road tests in the past.

That is perhaps with the exception of the Chevelle, which inexplicably realized an improvement in quarter-mile times of nearly 1.5 seconds from the baseline runs, attributed to "cooling off the engine" and "the driver having a pause for meditation over power shifting." Comparing this test to others done at the time on the same model cars indicated that any number of factors, particularly rear-axle ratio, had a direct impact on a car's quarter-mile performance.

- LS-6 450-hp 454 Chevelle 4-speed and 3.55 rear-axle ratio. Best elapsed time: 13.12 at 107.01 mph.
- Dodge Challenger 440 Six-Pack, 390-hp TorqueFlite automatic, and 3.23 rear-axle ratio. Best elapsed time: 13.62 at 104.28 mph.
- Ford Torino 375-hp 429 Super Cobra Jet, C-6 automatic, and 3.91 rear-axle ratio. Best elapsed time: 13.85 at 104.06 mph.
- Mercury Cougar Boss 429 prototype 375 hp, 4-speed, and 3.91 rear-axle ratio. Best elapsed time: 13.83 at 102.10.
- W-30 Olds 442, 370-hp 455, TH-400 automatic, and 3.42 rear-axle ratio. Best elapsed time: 13.88 at 95.84 mph.
- Plymouth Hemi Cuda, 425-hp, 4-speed, and 3.54 rear-axle ratio. Best elapsed time: 13.10 at 107.12 mph.
- Ram Air IV GTO, 370-hp 400, 4-speed, and 3.90 rear-axle ratio. Best elapsed time: 14.02 at 98.90.
- And inexplicably, instead of choosing the AMX, *Car Craft* decided on, the AMC Rebel with 325-hp 390, 4-speed, and 3.54 rear-axle ratio. Best elapsed time: 14.50 at 98.37 mph.

Oldsmobile, 1970

THE EVIL DR. OLDS HAS BEEN VERY BUSY AND THE RESULTS SHOW IT.

It seemed that Olds engineers were saving the best for last, even if they didn't realize that their 1970 performance cars would be some of the last. Now sporting 455 ci from the factory, without having to involve the Hurst Corporation, thanks to a 4.12-inch bore and 4.25-inch stroke, the engines destined for the W-30 optioned cars included the following: factory blue-printing, a radical hydraulic camshaft (.475-inch lift, 328-degree duration), heavy-duty valvetrain, 10.5:1 compression, improved cylinder heads with 2.07-inch intake and 1.63-inch exhaust valves, aluminum intake manifold, special Rochester Quadra-Jet carburetor with 1.375-inch primary and 2.25-inch secondary bores, and low-restriction exhaust manifolds.

Cold air was now ducted to the engine via a fiberglass hood with two leading-edge scoops and the front of the car was relieved of more weight thanks to plastic inner fenders. Horsepower was rated at 370 at 5,200 rpm and torque was 500 ft-lbs at 3,600 rpm. A 442 so equipped and backed with a TH-400 automatic and standard 3.42 gearing tipped the scales at 3,880 pounds. Magazines called it the "ultimate Olds supercar" and the *Hot Rod* test car covered the quarter-mile in 13.98 seconds at 100.78 mph: a true heavyweight contender.

Olds also fielded the 350-ci W-31–optioned Cutlass models in 1970 with many of the same improvements seen on the W-30. The smaller engine

Olds mounted a fiberglass hood with dual air inlets that connected to an open air cleaner sealed to the underside of the hood with foam and operated with a vacuum diaphragm on its W-30 and W-31 cars in 1970. Standard steel inner fender panels were replaced by lighter plastic versions in a distinctive red color.

got by with slightly smaller intake and exhaust valves (2.00 and 1.63 inches), a camshaft profile that closely matched the 455, and an aluminum intake manifold. Weighing 200 pounds less, the W-31 Cutlass could cover the quarter-mile in the mid-14-second range at 100 mph, making it a top competitor in its class.

Oldsmobile enjoyed one of its best years in decades on the streets and dragstrips of America, with many dealerships and even the comedy team of Tom and Dick Smothers getting on board. With back-door factory support being provided, Olds racers scored numerous class records, victories, and Eliminator titles.

Oldsmobile, 1971

THE DROP IN HORSEPOWER SPELLS THE END FOR ONE OF GM'S BEST MUSCLE MACHINES.

The mighty W-30 suffered the same fate as all other GM performance engines in 1971. Compression dropped to 8.5:1, the horsepower was rated at 20 fewer, and sales began to go into a free fall. The Hurst Olds, which had been dropped after 1969, was brought back in 1972, but by that time the model was little more than a special trim and paint package that paled when compared to the earlier models.

Ford and Mercury, 1970

COULD THIS BE THE LAST PERFORMANCE YEAR?

Ford continued to invest huge sums of money supporting various forms of motorsports and getting great returns for its investment. However, the writing was on the wall that the performance years were waning fast and 1970 could well be the last.

Torino and Cyclone

While the 428 Cobra Jet engine (based on the FE series) was enjoying its last year in the Mustang for 1970, it had already been replaced in other Ford performance cars. Since Shelby was no longer involved with Ford, the Cobra name found itself adorning the flanks of yet another Torino model.

The Torino had undergone a complete redesign for 1970, more stream-lined in shape but larger in dimension and heavier in weight. The engine that carried the Cobra Jet name forward was the 429-ci (385 series) power-house that had previously been developed to motivate Lincolns and Thunderbirds in 1968. In its transformation to Cobra Jet, the 429's already beefy cylinder block received four-bolt main bearing caps, improved forged-steel connecting rods with spot-faced 3/8-inch bolts, forged-aluminum pistons that squeezed 11.3:1 compression out of cast-iron, and canted valve cylinder heads featuring huge round intake ports with 2.25-inch intake and 1.72-inch exhaust valves.

One version of the 429 Cobra Jet used a hydraulic lifter camshaft, cast-iron intake manifold with a 715-cfm Rochester spread-bore 4-barrel carburetor, and was rated at 370 hp. The other version, the Super Cobra Jet, could only be obtained by checking the option block for the Drag Pac, which indicated either a 3.91 Traction Loc or 4.30 Detroit Locker differential.

The Drag Pac, or Super Cobra Jet, differed from the Cobra Jet in that it sported a solid lifter camshaft, an engine oil cooler, and a square-bore cast-iron intake manifold mounting a 780-cfm Holley 4-barrel carburetor. The advertised horsepower rose by just five (375) through the addition of the Drag Pac option.

Both the Cobra Torino and Mercury Cyclones, when equipped with the 429 Cobra Jet and Super Cobra Jet 429, proved themselves capable of quarter-mile performances in the high-13-second range at more than 100 mph, in spite of being encumbered with more weight than the 1969 models.

Although the shape of the new Torino and Cyclone models made them appear more aerodynamic than the previous models, this was not born out on the NASCAR circuit as Ford took home just seven wins and Mercury three for 1970.

1970½ Falcon

Ford inexplicably introduced a stripped down, two-door sedan version of the Torino midyear in 1970, hanging the name Falcon on it right after pulling the pin on the original Falcon, the compact car that Ford had first introduced in 1960. The original Falcon had lost much of its shine, particularly when it came to performance, with the introduction of the Mustang, and by December 1969 had been replaced by the Maverick.

Enter the 1970½ Falcon, based on the Torino body style. Total production of 26,000 units showed that this new version of the Falcon was not well received by the probably confused motoring public, but there was good news to be found among the options listed for the performance-minded buyer.

As it turned out, along with the base 250-ci 6-cylinder engine, the option list also contained the 370-hp 429 Super Cobra Jet engine found in the heavier Torino models. Weighing considerably less than similarly equipped Torinos, drag racers choosing the Falcon body gained an immediate advantage. Fewer than 100 429 Cobra Jet or Super Cobra Jet 1970½ Falcons were ordered before the model met an early demise.

Boss 302 Mustang, Boss 429 Mustang and Cougar

The Boss 302 Mustang and Cougar, along with the Boss 429 Mustang, were back for 1970 and apparently the engineers at Ford got the hint that the Boss 429 did not live up to expectations as a street

Ford's Torino was radically restyled for 1970 by designer Bill Shenk. The model took on the Coke bottle shape that became very popular in the early 1970s. This vehicle is a Torino GT. The GT model was available with V-8 engines from 302 to 429 ci that year, and this particular car is equipped with the 429 CJ (Cobra Jet) backed by a Toploader transmission. (Photo Courtesy Lee Lundberg)

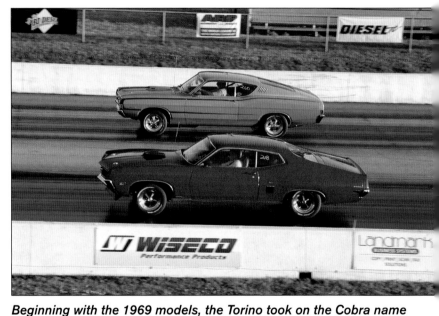

Beginning with the 1969 models, the Torino took on the Cobra name and the restyle of the model is obvious in this photo of a 1969 Torino versus a 1970 Torino GT. The Cobra was available with three versions of the 429-ci (385, or Lima, series) V-8: N-code 360 hp, 10.5:1 compression with hydraulic valve lifters and Rochester carburetor; C-code 370 hp, 11.3:1 compression, solid lifters, Holley carburetor (non-ram air); and the ram air version C-code, which produced 375 hp. (Photo Courtesy Lee Lundberg)

The 385, or Lima, series engines were wider and heavier than the FE, and even though the Torino had been upsized for 1970, it was still a tight fit under the hood. The factory ram air setup featured a shaker scoop affixed to the top of the open air-cleaner assembly, which it pro-truded through a hole in the car's hood. (Photo Courtesy Lee Lundberg)

The Mercury Cougar and Ford Mustang remained largely unchanged for 1970, which meant that the 385 series 429 engine did not fit the engine bay. As a result, the top option for both was the 428-ci Cobra Jet FE engine as it had been the previous year. This was, however, the last year for the FE-series engine in these models as they underwent a redesign for 1971. (Photo Courtesy Diego Rosenberg)

performer in 1969. They attempted to rectify the situation with a solid lifter camshaft and lighter connecting rods that allowed the engine to rev quicker, helping to offset the loss of bottom-end power due to the engine's huge intake ports.

A Boss 429 Mustang tested by *Super Stock and Drag Illustrated* clicked off a respectable 13.64-second quarter-mile at 104.65, but this improvement over the previous model year was too little too late as Ford only built 499 Boss 429 Mustangs in 1970, less than half the number built in 1969.

Aside from a cylinder head revision, the Boss 302 was mechanically unchanged for 1970 and while the SCCA Trans Am Mustangs were scoring win after win on the track, the street version as tested by *Car Life* could only manage a 14.85-second quarter-mile time at 96.10 mph. *Car Craft* tested a Mustang Mach I optioned with the 300-hp 351 Cleveland, automatic transmission, and 3.50 axle and found that it ran the quarter-mile only .25 second and 2 mph slower than the Boss 302.

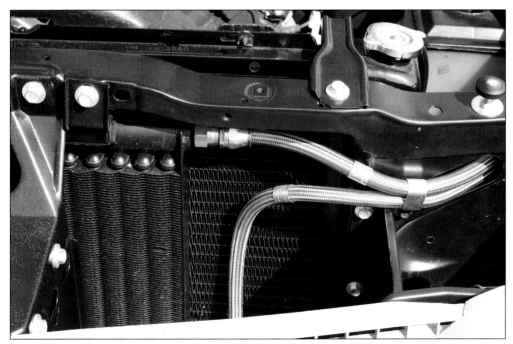

An easy way to identify cars equipped with the 429 Super Cobra Jet engine (and the 428 version as well) is by the external oil cooler fitted to the front driver's side of the radiator support.

The FE-series 428 Cobra Jet V-8 engine was already a very tight fit for the engine compartment of either a Cougar or a Mustang. While production numbers for cars so equipped were down from 1969, it was not for lack of performance. Still underrated at 335 hp, the 428 Cobra Jet was one of the top performance engines of its time and remained popular with drag racers for the next four decades. (Photo Courtesy Diego Rosenberg)

One improvement made at the factory across the Ford line for 1970 was the installation of a Hurst shifter on those equipped with the 4-speed transmission. (Photo Courtesy Diego Rosenberg)

As it had been all along, Cougar remained the high-end model in 1970 when compared to the Mustang and that was most obvious from the interior view. Cougars optioned with the 428 Cobra Jet, and particularly those equipped with a 4-speed transmission, were far less numerous than similarly equipped Mustangs. (Photo Courtesy Diego Rosenberg)

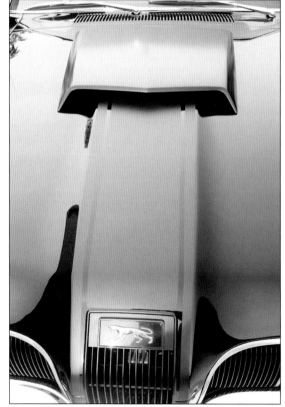

The 1970 Cougars equipped with the Ram Air 428 Cobra Jet engine used this factory hood scoop that blended nicely with the car's lines while remaining functional. The Eliminator model was continued into 1970 but the graphics, particularly on black cars, were understated when compared to the previous model year. (Photo Courtesy Diego Rosenberg)

The Boss 302 Mustang was back for its final year in 1970 with slight restyling and a more understated and cleaner overall look. The model's underpinnings remained the same, allowing it to handle and brake better than any other model in the Mustang line. The Boss 302 was available with and without the shaker hood scoop in 1970. (Photo Courtesy Chase Van Dyne)

A number of Ford drag racing stalwarts entered the Pro/Stock ranks early in 1970 with specially prepared Boss 429 Mustangs with some success. Sam Auxier Jr. was one longtime Ford racer who began the season with a Boss 429 Mustang sponsored by Henry Woodfield Ford. However, it wasn't long before the evolution of the class showed the Boss 429 Mustang to be too heavy a platform and most Ford teams switched to the lighter Maverick body using either the Boss 429 or proven SOHC 427 engine for power. The Auxier car was refitted with a 351 Cleveland engine, which proved to be a winning combination for Sam's brother Rick Auxier.

The engine that gave the Boss 302 its name remained mostly unchanged, with the exception of a modification to the cylinder heads for 1970 and as a result suffered from similar street performance limitations that had plagued the 1969 models. On the racetrack, which was the purpose for introducing this model from the beginning, it was a completely different story. The Ford factory team Boss 302 Mustangs swept the 1970 SCCA Trans-Am racing series.

By the end of the 1970 season, Ford had dropped out of the SCCA Trans-Am racing series and had pretty much pulled the pin on any support of motorsports. So while the Boss 302 Mustang was gone from the lineup and the redesigned Mustang had gained both dimensional size and 100 pounds, there was one last gasp from Dearborn when it came to performance. The Boss 351 Mustang was a standalone model as the Boss 302 had been, and although it was built in limited numbers and hardly advertised by a company bent on distancing itself from performance, the Boss 351 proved to be one of the best overall street performance cars Ford built.

Both the graphics and the overall look of the Boss 351 Mustang was understated. Even the functional ram air hood that fed the hungry Boss 351 Cleveland engine beneath it was hard to spot at first glance.

Along with the exterior, the 1971 Mustang line received a new interior design. The 4-speed cars received a Hurst shifter, a practice begun with the 1970 models that improved the overall driving experience.

The Boss 351 engine was based on the 351-ci Cleveland (335 series) engine that had been introduced in 1970. Often confused with the 351 Windsor V-8, which was based on the 302 small-block, the Cleveland was a different design. The Boss 351's internals showed a racing pedigree with 11.0:1 compression, four-bolt main bearing caps, and a solid lifter camshaft. The engine's splayed-valve cylinder heads with its huge intake ports were fed by a 750-cfm Motorcraft 4-barrel carburetor, on top of which sat an open-element air cleaner that sealed to the hood scoop.

Even more rare and less publicized than the Boss 351 Mustang in 1971 was the fact that the same 429 Super Cobra Jet engine that powered the much larger and heavier Torino and Torino Cobra models was also available in the Mustang. Sam Hand's 1971 Mustang Sports Roof is one of 56 Mustangs equipped with the 429 CJ Ram Air engine, one of 38 with a 4-speed transmission, and one of 29 that were Drag Pac Super Cobra Jets. (Photo Courtesy Taylor Kirkpatick)

The 429-ci, 375-hp engine takes up every inch of the Mustang's engine bay. And with that much weight over the front wheels, the car was not a standout in the handling department. But when it came to straight-line performance, few stock production cars could match this Mustang in 1971. (Photo Courtesy Taylor Kirkpatick)

The handful of 1971 Mustangs optioned with the 429 Ram Air engine were even more understated in their appearance than the Boss 351 model, with the only indication of this car's performance potential being the small lettering on each side of the air-intake scoops on the hood. (Photo Courtesy Taylor Kirkpatick)

Had it not been for the two-tone color treatment, the interior in Sam Hand's 1971 Mustang received no notice at all. But optioned the way it was, creature comforts were not an immediate concern when this car was ordered. The only obvious concession was the tilt steering wheel, which may indicate that the original owner was a large person as this option allowed easier entry and exit. (Photo Courtesy Taylor Kirkpatick)

Ford, 1971

THE BOSS 351 AND 429 SCJ MUSTANGS: TOO LATE TO SHARE THE LIMELIGHT.

With skyrocketing insurance costs and congressional hearings into how the funds spent by auto manufacturers on performance impacted highway safety, Ford was almost out of the racing business entirely before the end of 1971. Even when it came to the last two of Ford's best street performers, there was very little corporate advertising of their existence. The Boss 302 and Boss 429 were gone from the lineup. As a matter of fact, some dealers still had Boss 429 Mustangs gathering dust in their showrooms.

For the 1971 model year, the Mustang received a redesign and grew substantially over previous models. The Boss 302 was replaced with a high-performance version of the canted-valve 351 Cleveland (335 series) engine that had been introduced in 1970, and Ford put it in a stand-apart performance model of the Mustang, the Boss 351. Although its understated graphics did little to attract attention to a Mustang that was longer, wider, and 100 pounds heavier for 1971, the Boss 351 was a true performance engine and the last from Ford for many years.

It wouldn't be hard to describe the manner in which the Boss 351 came assembled from the factory as blueprinted; the connecting rods were Magnafluxed and shot peened and the 11.0:1 pistons were fitted in the block to exact specifications. An aggressive solid lifter camshaft bumped the valves in the cylinder heads with huge round intake ports. A hood-mounted ram air system fed a 750-cfm Motorcraft carburetor and helped give the Boss 351 an honest 330 hp.

Also included in the package was a 4-speed transmission, 3.91 Traction-Loc differential, and heavy-duty suspension. The folks at *Super Stock and Drag Illustrated* reported that a Boss 351 test car ran the quarter-mile in 13.64 seconds at 104.65 mph, better than many big-block cars were capable of at the time.

Only 1,806 Boss 351 Mustangs rolled off the assembly line in 1971. Sadly, they were mostly lost to history during the dark days of Detroit performance to follow.

With the Boss 429 gone from the scene, Ford engineers took advantage of the increased dimensions of the new Mustang, which allowed them to shoehorn the 429 Super Cobra Jet (385 series), as found in the Torino since 1970, between the fenders of the Mustang. The newly gained weight, particularly when equipped with the 700-plus-pound 429, won it few friends from members of the automotive press, who had occasion to test it because brute torque and horsepower alone did not add up to what they had come to expect from previous Mustang models. Negative comments about handling, etc., aside, *Car and Driver* proved that the new Mustang with the 370-hp 429 Cobra Jet engine with automatic transmission and 3.50 gear-

ing had plenty of "grunt" as they recorded a 13.97-second quarter-mile at 100.22 mph.

Before the cessation of factory support, Ford and Mercury teams scored 16 NASCAR racing victories that year with the majority by the 1969 Mercury Cyclones fielded by the Wood Brothers with drivers David Pearson, A. J. Foyt, and Donnie and Bobby Allison. Pearson recorded one win (Bristol, Tennessee) with a 1971 Torino, and Benny Parsons did likewise with a 1970 Torino at Macon, Georgia. Without the Wood Brothers and their two-year-old Mercurys, the 1971 NASCAR season would have been a total romp for the Plymouth teams.

The lack of support from the Detroit auto manufacturers, and the money it brought to the series, was immediately evident in the NASCAR series through a reduced number of entries. In an effort to offset the deficiency, NASCAR ruled that the lighter, small-block Grand American series cars (Mustangs, Camaros, and Javelins) would be included in the field at six Grand National races that season with a proviso that championship points would be recorded separately for each series.

Bobbie Allison saw a potential advantage against the super-speedway cars on the flat, short track at Bowman-Gray stadium in Winston-Salem, North Carolina, and entered a 1969 Mustang owned by Melvin Johnson. Richard Petty set the lap record and put his Plymouth on the pole, but Allison was able to get around him for the win at the end.

A corporate mandate from Ford Motor Company pulled the plug on all corporate support of racing activities before the end of the 1971 model year, leaving many racing teams out in the cold. A dark cloud, similar to the one experienced in 1957 with the AMA ban on factory participation in racing, descended over Dearborn, where it remained for years.

Plymouth and Dodge, 1970

THE RAPID TRANSIT SYSTEM AND THE SCAT PACK KEEP RIGHT ON ROLLING OUT TOP PERFORMERS.

Both Plymouth and Dodge added new low-priced performers packing 340 power for 1970. The Valiant-based Plymouth Duster and Dart-based Swinger models allowed the performance enthusiast on a budget to own a sporty little car that ran a mid- to low-14-second quarter-mile elapsed time for less than $3,000. Both cars were an immediate sales success and their power-to-weight ratio made them very popular in NHRA Stock and Super Stock class drag racing.

The Road Runner and Super Bee took on a slightly more luxurious feel for 1970, but all the same engine options returned, including the 426 Hemi. The same held true for the Coronet R/T, GTX, and Charger R/T line.

Having allowed stablemate Dodge's bizarre winged Daytona to grab most of the stock car glory in 1969, Plymouth came back in 1970 with a winged warrior of its own. Called the Superbird, Plymouth had to build at least 500 production cars to be declared legal for NASCAR competition. The 375-hp 440 engine was standard equipment on the production Superbird, with the 426 Hemi available. While the extended front sheet metal and huge trunk-mounted wing may have proved to be a great advantage on the high-banked stock car tracks, it did little to ingratiate the cars to buyers, with many sitting unsold for months.

Dodge Challenger and AAR 'Cuda

Dodge introduced a new model called Challenger, which was in direct competition with the Plymouth 'Cuda, but it seemed that there were enough buyers to keep both brands from suffering. The Challenger shared its engine option lineup with the 'Cuda, with the Challenger R/T being the performance car.

While the Superbird concept was designed around a desire to attain higher speeds on stock car oval tracks through aerodynamics, some of the cars found their way onto the dragstrip also. Taking advantage of the fact that the car's increased weight dropped it into a lower class than a standard Road Runner, drag racers, including factory-backed teams such as Sox & Martin and Jack Werst, took full advantage.

Plymouth and Dodge decided to get on board against Ford and Chevrolet on the SCCA Trans-Am racing circuit for 1970, and to legitimize their effort, production versions of their race cars were built for sale to the public. The Dodge Challenger and AAR 'Cuda Trans-Am models set themselves apart visually from other models through the generous use of graphics, ground-effects spats, exhaust that exited just in front of the rear wheels, and a scooped fiberglass hood.

Carrying the Road Runner cartoon theme to the engine compartment, Plymouth dubbed its elaborate ram air setup the Coyote Duster. This version is fitted to a 440 engine with a single 4-barrel carburetor. The flap that opened on the hood to allow outside air into the engine was controlled by a diaphragm. Under full throttle, the diaphragm opened when engine vacuum dropped off.

The Coyote Duster ram air setup on Road Runners equipped with the 440 Six-Pack engines for 1970 was of similar design but with a different air cleaner to accommodate the three Holley 2-barrel carburetors. One drawback to this setup was the fact that the throttle linkage on the carburetors was vacuum operated, causing maintenance and tuning problems.

Plymouth 'Cudas equipped with the 440 Six-Pack and 426 Hemi engines in 1970 and 1971 featured this unique fiberglass shaker-style hood scoop with the engine callout affixed to its sides in chrome. The cooler outside air was isolated from the engine compartment heat by a large rubber sealing ring around the scoop.

The dramatically redesigned 1970–1971 Plymouth 'Cudas had vinyl-tape side trim called hockey sticks that included engine size callouts just in case the casual observer didn't notice the emblems on the shaker hood.

Under that hood lurked the potent 340 with three 2-barrel Holley carburetors à la the Six-Pack on top. Rated at 290 hp, the same as the Z-28 and Boss 302, the street versions fared better than the de-stroked racing models that, while running in the top five at a number of races, did not deliver the winning season hoped for by Chrysler.

Car Life tested an AAR 'Cuda and reported mid-14-second quarter-mile elapsed times, which were comparable to an automatic transmission, 4.10-geared 'Cuda with the standard 340. One of the factors that hampered the AAR and Trans Am street performance was the vacuum-operated linkage that operated the three carburetors and often did not function properly.

Chrysler offered its largest number of performance models in 1970 and the automotive magazines clamored to test as many as possible, particularly the new Challenger and 'Cuda, which showed great promise. *Car Craft* put a 440 Six-Pack Challenger R/T with automatic transmission and 3.23 gearing through its paces and reported that the car could cover the quarter-mile in 13.62 seconds at 104.28 mph. *Car Craft* found that its Hemi Challenger with a 4-speed and 4.10 gearing could manage a best of 13.10 seconds at 103.20 mph.

The Popular Hot Rodding Six-Pack, 4-speed, 4.10 geared 'Cuda stopped the clocks in 13.97 seconds at 104 mph. *Car Craft* found that a Hemicuda with automatic and 4.10 gearing was good for 13.69-second elapsed times at 105.63 mph, while the 4-speed, 4.10 geared test car clicked off a 13.10 at 107 mph. The Hemi Road Runner once again received the attention of *Super Stock and Drag Illustrated* and its 4.10 geared, automatic transmission Beeper recorded a quarter-mile time of 13.34 seconds at 107.50 mph.

Plymouth Superbird

Not satisfied to depend entirely on the Dodge Daytona to deliver NASCAR glory, Chrysler introduced the Plymouth Superbird for 1970.

Chrysler's Dodge Division countered the Plymouth 'Cuda with the Challenger R/T in 1970, and offered the same engine and transmission options as the Plymouth. The Challenger was subtler than the 'Cuda in the manner in which outside air was introduced to the engine. No shaker scoop here, just two horizontal intake scoops molded into the hood.

The emblems on either side of this Challenger's vinyl top indicate that not only is it an R/T model but also an SE, which was the top of the line for this model and usually more highly optioned with creature comforts than other Challengers.

The top engine option offered in the 1970–1971 Dodge Challenger was the 426-ci, 425-hp Hemi engine. Two inline Carter AVS 4-barrel carburetors and a mild hydraulic lifter camshaft made the Hemi easier to maintain and drive under normal conditions while retaining more than ample torque and horsepower to shred the Polyglas rear tires on command.

Similar to the Daytona in appearance, the winged Road Runner with the pointy nose received the 375-hp 440 as its standard powerplant, with the

In typical 1970s Chrysler product fashion, this Challenger's interior is mostly plastic with imitation woodgrain, in spite of the fact that it is the higher SE model. The cool factor is greatly enhanced by the Hurst shifter with Pistol Grip handle connected to the car's 4-speed transmission that protrudes from the console. With 426 Hemi power under the hood, the 150-mph speedometer is no joke.

As if the visual impact provided by opening the hood and seeing the 426 Hemi engine with its distinctive black crackle finish valvecovers was not enough, the lid of the open-element air cleaner that sealed to the hood scoops had a decal to inform the world that this was indeed a Hemi.

440 Six-Pack and 426 Hemi listed as options. Just 135 Six-Pack Superbirds are reported to have been produced that year.

Sales of the street version of the new model could hardly be described as brisk, but there was some very good news that helped offset the negative. The introduction of the Superbird brought Richard Petty back to Plymouth for the 1970 season. And the Plymouths and Dodges had a grand year in NASCAR as a result, winning 21 and 17 races, respectively.

Fear for the safety of drivers and fans due to the increasing track speeds brought about by the more aerodynamic cars led NASCAR to institute rules changes mid-1970 in an effort to slow things down.

Plymouth's highly successful drag racing team, Sox & Martin, received a new Hemicuda with which to do battle against the Fords and Chevrolets in the NHRA Pro/Stock class. It turned out that the team may have been too successful. Due to lobbying by other teams, the dominant Hemicudas, along with the SOHC 427 Maverick of Don Nicholson, had weight penalties added due to the hemi-headed engines, and by the close of the 1971 NHRA season, changes were in the wind that eventually took Pro/Stock down the same slippery slope as A/FX before it and the cars became further removed from production-based models.

The Sox & Martin team and "Mr. 5 and 50" Jack Werst also received Hemi Superbird drag cars for NHRA Super/Stock competition in 1970. With Sox & Martin going the 4-speed route in SS/E, Werst fielded his automatic car in SS/EA. As was usually the case, Sox was a winner with his mount, while Werst scored no wins at all during the 1970 season with his Superbird.

Years later Werst revealed the reason for his lack of wins. The factories were so dedicated to winning races that they often played fast and loose with the class rules to gain an advantage. Of course, any class or eliminator win required that the sanctioning body thoroughly examine the winning car to determine its legality. In the case of the Werst Superbird, the car was outfitted with a 500-ci Hemi engine and a rear wing that had considerable weight added to aid traction.

As explained by Werst, the only purpose for the existence of his car was to eliminate the Chevy of Ray Allen, who was dominating in S/S Eliminator. Once Allen was defeated, Werst was to purposely jump the start in the next round of competition, thus eliminating himself. He would then load up his car and leave the remaining legal Mopar cars in competition with a greater chance of victory and the resulting showroom sales that went with it.

Chrysler was enjoying one of its best years of racing and high-performance sales, yet the dark cloud of outside regulation was creeping into the halls at Chrysler. Although many attractive performance options were still offered in 1971, horsepower ratings began to slide, and sales took a nosedive.

Plymouth and Dodge, 1971

BRIGHT COLORS AND GRAPHICS PROVE TO BE NO SUBSTITUTE FOR HORSEPOWER.

Chrysler was feeling the external pressures that demanded less emissions and increased fuel mileage, and while many of the same models with the same optional engines returned for 1971, lower horsepower ratings and the higher cost of automobile insurance associated with performance cars resulted in the sales of such cars dropping dramatically.

For example, sales for the Dodge Super Bee dropped from 15,506 in 1970 to a mere 5,054 in 1971, and for the first time the Super Bee and Road Runner listed a small-block engine, the 340.

The 440 Magnum's rated horsepower dropped from 375 to 370, the 440 Six-Pack dropped from 390 to 380 hp, and while the 426 Hemi remained rated at 425, magazine road tests reflected the effects of the de-tuning.

The hot 340 small-block saw the addition of a huge and uniquely designed Carter Thermo-Quad 4-barrel carburetor, but the horsepower rating in this case remained at the conservative 275 it carried since introduction. The pony cars seemed to be under less scrutiny when it came to insurance premiums at this point and the performance numbers remained consistent for at least one more year.

Due to significant rules changes in NASCAR, the winged Dodges and Plymouths had disappeared. Just the same, Plymouth and Dodge teams scored 29 wins for the season, with the majority of the checkered flags going to Richard Petty's Plymouth.

By the end of the 1971 drag racing season, even the top Chrysler teams had begun to scale back their efforts as the factory once again distanced itself from overt support of competitive motorsports, and by 1973 it was pretty much over.

AMC, 1970

AMX HOLDS ON TO THE TOP SPOT FOR AMC PERFORMANCE, AND JAVELIN GOES AFTER TRANS-AM GLORY.

The AMX was back as the top performer from AMC in 1970. The SC/Rambler was gone, but the AMX gained a new performance sidekick, the Rebel Machine. Powered by the same 390 as the AMX but rated at 340 hp due to a different intake manifold design, The Machine stood out with its red, white, and blue paint scheme, graphics, and a slick hood scoop. The AMX gained a 290-hp 360-ci base engine, with the 390, now rated at 325 hp due to an improved cylinder head that flowed 20 percent better than the previous casting, the top option. A Hurst shifter and an aggressive hood scoop, along with other cosmetic changes, completed the package.

Motor Trend was duly impressed with the new AMX and clicked off a 14.68 quarter-mile time at 92 mph with its 3.54-geared test car. The scribes at *Hot Rod* wrung out a new Rebel Machine, which, although heavier than the AMX, had 15 more horsepower and a 3.91 gear. The Machine stopped the clocks in 14.49 seconds at 93 mph.

AMC mounted an effort to continue its factory Super/Stock AMX program in 1970 and in an effort to save the costs involved in building 50 additional 1970 versions of the Super Stocker, they shipped the required cosmetic pieces, along with the improved cylinder head, to retrofit the existing cars.

At some point the NHRA learned of the cylinder head change and declared that the cars could no longer compete in the SS/C class. The AMC

American Motors was still in the performance game in 1970 but sadly the lack of funds, coupled with increased fuel and insurance costs, spelled doom for the underfunded company's efforts. The year 1970 was to be the last that the AMX was a true two-seat sports car, but many argue that the final model was indeed the best.

The AMX for 1970 received this aggressive air scoop positioned on the leading edge of its hood and the underside-mounted vacuum-operated ram air setup that fed the 390-ci high-performance V-8.

The last American Motors car to carry the AMX name was a sub-model of the Javelin. While still a sporty vehicle with a functional ram air hood feeding its engine, the car was a mere shadow of the factory muscle cars produced by the company just a few years earlier.

The cockpit of the Javelin AMX stayed true to its performance roots with a full array of gauges in an engine-turned cluster. The Hurst shift linkage also remained, adding to the car's drivability.

In keeping with the trend of the time, the AMX's interior received a liberal dose of faux wood graining. But the Hurst shifter and lack of a back seat kept things real for the performance-minded buyer.

teams had started out with intentions to run in the SS/E class, and even before entering competition they had been factored into SS/D. Then, as some believe due to their dominance, they were factored yet again into SS/C. This effectively ended AMC's Super Stock AMX program, although the cars remained competitive in SS/C for some time.

AMC's Trans-Am racing program received a huge shot in the arm in 1970 when the company partnered with successful team owner Roger Penske to field the new Javelin in the series. The Penske/AMC team had top drivers Mark Donohue and Peter Revson wheeling their cars, and although the series championship eluded them once again, they more than proved that the Javelin was a force to be reckoned with.

AMC, 1971

THE END IS NEAR FOR A SUCCESSFUL PERFORMANCE CAR LINEUP.

In an effort to offset some of the performance-robbing legislation coming to the auto industry, the AMX, which was no longer a sporty two-seater but merely a sub-model of the Javelin, received a 401-ci engine rated at 330 hp. With 3.90 gearing and a 4-speed, *High Performance Cars* managed a respectable 14.80 quarter-mile time at 94 mph. The 360-ci engine had found a new home in a new performance model, the Hornet SC/360, and *Hot Rod* reported that with 3.54 gearing, the car could match the AMX's times with ease.

American Motors continued supporting several racers who ran the Pro/ Stock class in the early to mid-1970s, until the NHRA made a rules change that effectively ended the struggling company's efforts for good.

On a brighter note, with factory support for Trans-Am waning for the Ford and Chevrolet teams, Penske and Donahue brought a championship home to AMC in dominating fashion.

CHAPTER 8

DETROIT MAKES A COMEBACK IN A BIG WAY

T he technology required to make the modern V-8 perform as it once did finally caught up with clean-air and fuel-mileage regulations.

In 1995, Ford's Special Vehicle Team (SVT) designed and developed the first race-only car to roll out of Dearborn in decades. Based on the SN95 Mustang, the Cobra R was available only to those holders of competition racing series licenses. And with a mere 250 units built, serious Mustang racers got in line early. You could get the Cobra R in any color you desired as long as it was white. Lighter than the standard production Mustang, and packing a bigger punch under the hood, the R was primarily designed for SCCA-style racing but could easily tackle the dragstrip with a few modifications.

Ford

THE DEARBORN CONTINGENT COMES BACK EARLY AND STRONG.

In 1995, Ford did something it had not done since 1968. It built a limited series of Mustangs specifically for racing.

Cobra R

The 250 SVT Cobra R Mustangs had many body-lightening deleted creature comforts and were pretty much track-ready as delivered. The cars had no back seat, radio, heater, power windows, sound deadeners, and even the factory fuel tank was replaced by a lightweight foam-filled fuel cell.

Powered by a 351-ci version of the 302 Windsor engine, the Cobra R was rated at 300 hp and due to a higher intake plenum, a fiberglass hood with a bulge for clearance was required. The engine was backed up by a heavy-duty clutch and Tremec 5-speed manual transmission with short-throw shifter. The suspension was stiffened with different spring rates, shocks, and sway bars, which were all geared toward improving handling.

A proviso included with the announcement of the availability of these special Mustangs stated that potential buyers must possess a valid competition license from a motorsports sanctioning body. The 250 car production run was sold out in just five days. While the Cobra R was certainly drag-strip capable, with a little work most found their way onto sports car racing circuits.

Cobra Jet

Wishing to capitalize on the dragstrip successes that sportsmen racers were enjoying in the ever popular Mustang, Ford decided to support Stock and Super Stock drag racing for the first time in 40 years. The company announced plans to build 50 specially equipped, non-street-legal Mustang drag cars and call them, of course, Cobra Jets.

They were powered by a fuel-injected 5.4-liter (329.5 ci) overhead cam, four valves per cylinder, aluminum V-8 with specially ground camshafts, Manley H-beam connecting rods, Mahle forged pistons, and a 65-mm throttle body with a Ford supercharger and racing air intake. The rated horsepower was 420.

The cars were stripped of any creature comforts or government-required safety features. Each had a 9-inch rear-axle housing with a Strange aluminum center section carrying 4.88 gears. The suspension was also drag race modified with adjustable shock absorbers and Panhard and three-link rear bars. The brakes were race prepped and the steering was non-power-assisted. Transmission choices were 6-speed manual or optional automatic.

The 50 cars were immediately spoken for by Hajek Motorsports of Ames, Oklahoma, buying the first 10 sequentially numbered cars. Brent

With its plain white wrapper, the Cobra R Mustang might be easy to overlook, but closer examination revealed the understated Cobra and SVT badging that told the true story of what lurked within. The special badging was also carried over to the center caps on the wider wheels that were part of the package.

Although the Cobra R had been stripped of as much weight as possible through the deletion of highway use safety equipment and unnecessary creature comfort options, the only true lightweight component was the specially molded fiberglass hood with its large bulge to accommodate the high-intake plenum mounted on the engine. So there was no confusion with sanctioning bodies regarding the legality of the special hood, Ford molded its production part number in a prominent position.

THEIR OWN CLASSES

So great were the successes and performances of the new factory-prepared cars that the NHRA soon figured out that they would need their own class to keep things fair for the Stock and Super/Stock class competitors with earlier model cars. As a result, FS (Factory Stock) classes were instituted.

As is the case with other NHRA classes, the cars are classified by advertised horsepower to weight, with special consideration being given to those vehicles equipped with supercharged engines, which run in a higher class than naturally aspirated (fuel injection only) cars. Watching the FS class cars run harkens back to the early days of Pro/Stock when the cars were entirely production based.

The Cobra Jet returned in 2010 and again in 2012 with changes, including an optional larger Whipple supercharger for Super/Stock class competition and a choice of either a stock class legal C-4 automatic or a C-3 version for Super/Stock. For 2013, the Cobra Jet sported a 5.0 (302-ci) DOHC aluminum-block Coyote engine mounting CNC-ported four-valve cylinder heads with a naturally aspirated (fuel injection) and two supercharger options that allowed the cars to fit into more Stock and Super/Stock classes. A race-prepared C-4 automatic transmission was standard, along with all the previously listed drag-race-specific components. The 2014 model of the Cobra Jet was even further refined, offering the C-3 automatic transmission.

By this point Ford had been basking in the successes brought by the modern-day Cobra Jet racers who had racked up numerous class records, class wins, factory shootout victories, and a Super/Stock Eliminator title at the 2015 NHRA U.S. Nationals.

The 2016 Cobra Jet was the most sophisticated and deadly of them all. The 50 bodies in white were shipped from the assembly plant to Watson racing, where they were fitted with a 10-point roll cage. The cars were then returned to the assembly plant where they were painted and fitted with the electrical harness, carpet, and headliner. The cars were then shipped back to Watson, where two special lines finished the conversion.

The engines, which were assembled at Performance Assembly Solutions, along with the C-3 transmission, headers, lightweight brakes, fuel delivery system, four-link rear suspension, racing seats, gauges, wheels, and slicks were installed, and the end result was a turnkey Mustang capable of 8-second quarter-mile times for $100,000. And if proof was needed that the cars were 8-second capable, John Calvert recently set the NHRA class record in FS/AA at 8.39 seconds at 162 mph.

To save weight, the power window mechanisms were removed and replaced with standard roll-up window regulators.

As expected in a race-only vehicle, the interior appointments on the Mustang Cobra R were spartan and stripped of any unnecessary weight. Radio, heater, and air bags were deleted. The basic seats that were included would usually be replaced with competition versions by the racer when a roll bar and other required bracing was added. The tilt steering wheel option has been retained to assist with driver positioning. This particular Cobra R model had a radio and heater installed by the selling dealer at the owner's request.

Hajek and other Ford racers worked closely with Ford engineers to prepare the cars for their competition debut at the NHRA Winternationals. In honor of the original Cobra Jet, Hajek lettered four of his cars in the livery of Ford factory team cars from 1968, and asked original drivers Hubert Platt, Gas Ronda, Randy Ritchey, and Al Joniec to attend the event.

In a true stroke of fate, the John Calvert–driven car that was sporting Rice Ford, Holman Ford, and Al Joniec livery won the event just as Joniec had at the 1968 Winternationals, providing Ford with a huge advertising opportunity. The Cobra Jets enjoyed additional success at the NHRA U.S. Nationals with yet another victory.

Because this was a race car and not designed to carry passengers, the rear seat was removed and the area was then covered with thin felt. A foam-filled fuel cell, required for competition, replaced the standard Mustang fuel tank and was mounted in the trunk area.

In 2008, Ford decided to go drag racing in a big way once again, and built 50 specially prepared turnkey Mustangs, the Cobra Jet. Prolific collector, Ford historian, and drag racer Brent Hajek bought the first 10 Cobra Jets and produced and prepared several of them for action at the 2009 NHRA Winternationals. Here Ford racing legend Al Joniec poses with the Hajek Motorsports 2008 Cobra Jet painted to match the car, which Al drove to victory at the 1968 Winternationals. (Photo Courtesy Bob Smith)

The Cobra R gets its venom from a 5.8-liter (351-ci), fuel-injected Windsor-based engine hand built by SVT technicians. The most prominent feature that sets this engine apart from other Windsor engines found in Mustangs of the era is the larger intake plenum and throttle body assembly. Power steering is retained, but the ratio and feel have been changed through the use of a special pulley. And since the radio has been deleted, there was no problem adding solid-core racing ignition wires. Extensive shock tower bracing added structural rigidity and enhanced the handling characteristics of the Cobra R.

As a tribute to the 1968 Ford factory team, Hajek Motorsports also had several of its other cars painted in similar fashion to the cars driven by Hubert Platt, Randy Ritchey, and Gas Ronda for competition at the 2009 NHRA Winternationals. (Photo Courtesy Bob Smith)

The 2008 Cobra Jet Mustang was race ready as delivered with all non-essential accessories deleted; a roll bar, race shifter, and full complement of gauges were added to monitor the engine. As race cars go, the Cobra Jet's interior was surprisingly well appointed. (Photo Courtesy Bob Smith)

Once the finish paint has been applied the front subframe/cradle containing engine, transmission, race-prepped front suspension, and brakes are mated with the body. (Photo Courtesy Evan Smith)

John Calvert launches the Hajek Motorsports Al Joniec/Rice and Holman Ford off the starting line on its way to a repeat of Joniec's 1968 Winternationals victory, proving that lightning can strike twice. (Photo Courtesy Bob Smith)

Each Mustang Cobra Jet receives a special vehicle identification number (VIN) tag and an additional disclaimer tag that informs the buyer that the car is for track use only and does not comply with safety or emissions standards required for street use. (Photo Courtesy Evan Smith)

Ford took advantage of lessons learned through decades of racing and advances in modern technology such as multi-cam, multi-valve cylinder heads, variable valve timing, and direct injection to develop its Cobra Jet engines. The exhaust headers fitted to this display engine are a direct adaptation of drag racing technology first developed in the early 1960s. (Photo Courtesy Evan Smith)

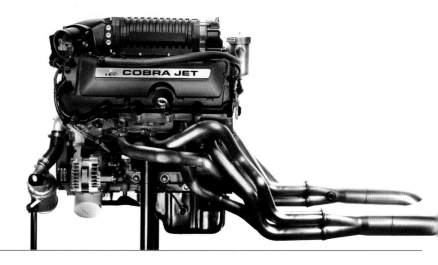

This is a naturally aspirated 5.0 Coyote V-8 that Ford used to power the 2012 and 2013 versions of the Cobra Jet Mustang. The NHRA rates this particular combination at 380 hp. (Photo Courtesy Evan Smith)

The 2016 Cobra Jets get their venom from a Whipple supercharged 5.0 Coyote V-8 that the NHRA rates at 575 hp. With this combination, Cobra Jet Mustangs cover the quarter-mile in the 8-second range when run in the FSS/A class. (Photo Courtesy Evan Smith)

Completed 2012 Cobra Jet Mustangs are covered in plastic to protect them from dust and dirt prior to delivery. The 2012 version of the Cobra Jet was available in red, white, and blue. (Photo Courtesy Evan Smith)

The interior of the latest version of the Cobra Jet Mustang shows advances made since 2008. The custom Eparco racing steering wheel has buttons to control the Line Loc and Launch Control, which are essential parts on any drag car. The roll bar, Hurst shifter, Corbeau race seats, and full instrumentation complete the driver's compartment. (Photo Courtesy Evan Smith)

Because there is no need to carry luggage in this Mustang, the fuel cell, weight box, and battery are mounted in the trunk. Adding weight over the rear wheels for traction is a trick drag racers have been using for decades. (Photo Courtesy Evan Smith)

Automotive journalist and drag racer Evan Smith is suited up and ready to make some test passes in a new Cobra Jet Mustang to evaluate its performance. (Photo Courtesy Evan Smith)

Prior to making a pass down the quarter-mile, the Cobra Jet Mustang's Hoosier slicks are heated up thoroughly with a water burnout. Once the tires are hot and sticky, the car will be staged into the starting beams, and when the Christmas tree is activated, the fun begins. (Photo Courtesy Evan Smith)

Chevrolet

WE STILL CALL THEM COPO AFTER ALL THESE YEARS.

Chevrolet came back to the world of factory-supported drag racing in 2012 with the introduction of its purpose-built COPO Camaro race cars. As a tribute to the 1969 ZL-1 COPO Camaro's production numbers, Chevrolet announced that 69 units would be built. And as with the Mustang Cobra Jet, these special cars were intended for racing use only and not street legal.

In a fashion similar to that used by Ford, the Camaro bodies were shipped to a subcontractor for conversion. Interiors were fitted with racing seats and gauge packages. The engines were assembled at the GM Performance Build Center in Wixom, Michigan, and car owners were offered the unique opportunity of participating in the build of their own engine.

Chevrolet powered the beast with two versions of a supercharged LS-based 5.3-liter (327-ci) V-8 stuffed with specially selected speed parts from many of the same manufacturers used by Ford. Lightweight valves filled the cylinder heads and a Whipple 90-mm throttle body fed fuel into a GM-designed Hi-Ram intake manifold that required a bulge in the car's fiberglass hood. Camshafts were special hydraulic roller tappet grinds. Also available was a naturally aspirated 7.0-liter (427-ci engine). All three engine

After clearing the quarter-mile speed and timing traps, the parachute has been deployed to slow the flying steed. A roof-mounted Go-Pro camera records the run from the perspective of the car. (Photo Courtesy Evan Smith)

offerings were backed by a race-prepared Powerglide 2-speed automatic transmission. The suspension and brakes were drag race ready with light discs at all four wheels, along with adjustable shocks and rear links. A Strange 9-inch Ford rear was available with axle ratios ranging from 4.10 to 4.86.

The COPO Camaro program proved to be so successful that an additional 69 cars were constructed in 2013, with the LS-based 5.7-liter (350-ci) engine replacing the 327, and both 396- and 427-ci engines added, which gave Chevrolet the advantage of competing in more Stock and Super/Stock classes than their rivals. All three engine offerings were naturally aspirated, with a G-Force manual transmission available along with the Powerglide automatic.

In 2014 and 2015, the COPO program was improved upon once again with an LS-based 350-ci engine with 2.9-liter supercharger joining the three naturally aspirated engines. The Powerglide automatic was replaced by a race-prepared ATI TH-400 and the manual transmission was dropped.

General Motors stepped up its game with the 2016 COPO Camaro, making it structurally stiffer while at the same time 133 pounds lighter and calling it "the King of the quarter-mile." Adjustable front suspension was added, along with the adjustable four-link in the rear, and an aluminum center section with spool and gun-drilled axles. Non-power assisted rack-and-pinion steering helped get weight off the front of the car. The trunk was filled with dual batteries, the fuel cell, and a weight box. The body was treated to a new aerodynamics kit and supercharged cars received a carbon-fiber hood in place of the heavier fiberglass unit. Engines and transmissions remained unchanged from the previous year.

The COPO emblem announces that this Camaro is something very special and dangerous to its competition. Attendance at the Roy Hill Drag Racing School is a good idea before attempting to drive a car with the power of a COPO Camaro on a dragstrip. Eight-second drag cars are not for the novice driver.

Weighing the required 3,540 pounds when powered by the supercharged 350-ci engine, the 2016 COPO Camaro falls into the NHRA FS/A class. With little more than a tune-up to the turnkey car's computer by his friend Bryon Durham, Marco DeCesaris promptly set the class record at 8.91 seconds at 153 mph with his 2016 COPO.

In 2012, Chevrolet returned to drag racing with the appropriately named COPO Camaro. And to honor the production number of the original 1969 ZL-1 COPO cars, it was decided to build 69 units of the new car. In a fashion similar to that followed by Ford with the Cobra Jet Mustangs, Chevrolet shipped bare Camaro bodies to a subcontractor, where they were converted into non-street-legal drag cars. Each new version of the COPO Camaro has been improved based upon knowledge gained and the rules for the appropriate classes. This is the 2015 COPO of Marco DeCesaris, a longtime drag racer from Maryland.

While the interior of the COPO may appear show ready with its amenities, have no doubt that these cars are all business and any weight-adding creature comforts have long since been removed. Roll bar, window net, and safety harness are all required for NHRA class competition. The race shifter controls the modified TH-400 automatic transmission.

Engines for all of the COPO cars, in this case the supercharged version of the LS-based 350-ci V-8, are specially assembled at the GM Performance Build Center in Wixom, Michigan, and are race ready when received.

Cooler outside air is ducted into the Whipple supercharger via this intake scoop, which extends through the radiator support and grabs outside air from above the car's grille.

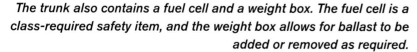

The trunk also contains a fuel cell and a weight box. The fuel cell is a class-required safety item, and the weight box allows for ballast to be added or removed as required.

The Whipple supercharger that force-feeds the 350 engine has its air/fuel charge cooled by this intercooler to provide more horsepower.

The lettering on Marco DeCesaris's COPO Camaro proudly proclaims it to be the NHRA National Record Holder in the FS/A class. This was attained with an 8.91-second run at more than 153 mph.

Marco's COPO is shod with lightweight Weld racing wheels on all four corners, and the COPO logo has even been carried over to the center caps on the front wheels, which is a nice touch.

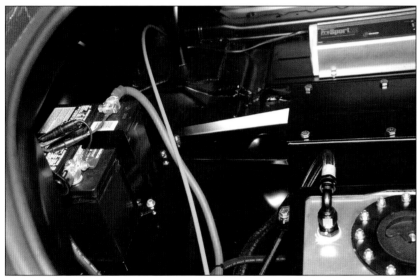

The COPO Camaro's already small trunk space has been rendered useless through the addition of two batteries, which add traction-enhancing weight over the rear wheels.

Chrysler

DRAG PAC IS BACK.

Chrysler had hatched a plan to catch the folks at Ford and General Motors napping by introducing a factory-built race car to the public in 2008. Unfortunately a number of internal setbacks kept the cars from becoming available until late in the 2009 season, well behind the debut of the Mustang Cobra Jet. Dubbed the Drag Pac Challenger, the original runs of these cars, while factory built for racing, were nowhere near turnkey ready.

For an investment of more than $30,000, the prospective racer took delivery of a stripped Dodge Challenger equipped with a 5.7-liter (354-ci) or 6.1-liter (372-ci) fuel-injected, modern-style Chrysler Hemi engine backed with either a 5-speed automatic or 6-speed manual transmission.

Not included were electronics, brakes, or a fuel system. The cars had no rear-axle housing or axles, merely a trailer-style straight beam with generic wheels to move the car on.

The front windshield was spot glued in place to allow for easy removal when installing a roll bar. The side glass was lightweight polycarbonate. A lift-off carbon-fiber hood with a large scoop that sealed to the engine throttle body was included. The cars were devoid of sound deadeners, sealers, safety equipment, carpet, or a back seat. Chrysler advertised that the cars would weigh approximately 1,000 pounds lighter than the production Challenger.

The production run was set at 100 cars, but it is unlikely that anywhere near that number was built. An interesting aside is the fact that the Drag Pac Challenger's wheelbase is 1 inch shorter than the production version.

Having sold out the entire run of 2009 Drag Pac cars, Chrysler continued the program into 2010, with the cars being delivered in approximately the same state as the 2009 version. The SRT8 6.1-liter Hemi, backed by a choice of automatic or manual transmission, was the standard engine for the program. Not only did Mopar offer a turnkey version of the Drag Pac Challenger for the first time, it also raised the bar by fitting it with the 510-ci Viper V-10 engine, backed by a competition 2-speed automatic transmission.

Now delivered with racing goodies similar to those found in the Mustang Cobra Jet and COPO Camaro, including an eight-point roll cage, special front K-member with drop-out crossmember, fuel cell, solid rear axle, lightweight front brakes, manual rack-and-pinion steering, lightweight seats, lightweight instrument panel, racing wheels and tires, the aspiring

As a comparison, the COPO Camaro factory racer (right) is shown here parked alongside a production model of the Camaro. Although the differences are striking, the race version is still based upon the same models that are available from a Chevrolet dealer.

Mopar racer was not required to complete his factory race car any longer.

At the unveiling of the 2015 Drag Pac car, Chrysler revealed that the V-10 was gone and in its place was the naturally aspirated 7.0-liter (426-ci) aluminum-block Hemi. The transmission of choice was a modified version of the 727 TorqueFlite, one of the best automatics ever to roll out of Detroit. Along with all the same deletions and performance upgrades found in the previous model, Chrysler also revealed a 9-inch rear-axle housing with aluminum center section.

And as a teaser, Chrysler engineers gave onlookers a peek at a nearby supercharged Hellcat Hemi that they intimated may be destined for the Drag Pac program in the near future.

With the roll bar and safety harnesses in place, the interior of the Drag Pac Challenger now looks like an NHRA Factory Stock class race car and is legal for competition. (Richard Brady Photo Courtesy Jack Hazelgren/Les Norton)

Unlike its rivals at Ford which sold the Cobra Jet Mustang as a turnkey race car, Chrysler delivered the first series of Drag Pac Challengers as little more than a rolling chassis. The engine was mounted, but there was no rear-axle assembly, rear brakes, transmission, wiring harness, roll bar, fuel system, or other components. The cars had a beam axle with little more than trailer wheels mounted in the back to allow the vehicle to be moved. (Photo Courtesy Les Norton)

The Challenger's trunk is filled with twin batteries, the class-required fuel cell, and extra bracing that reinforces the structure of the car to stop it from flexing under the extreme loads it encounters when racing. (Richard Brady Photo Courtesy Jack Hazelgren/ Les Norton)

Les Norton's completed Drag Pac Challenger painted in patriotic colors and Salt City Dodge logo. Note that the NHRA class designation on the window is A/Stock Automatic. This was prior to the NHRA legislating specific classes for the Drag Pac Challengers, Cobra Jet Mustangs, and COPO Camaros to compete in. (Richard Brady Photo Courtesy Jack Hazelgren/Les Norton)

Les Norton puts the Salt City Dodge Drag Pac Challenger through its paces. He's seen here heating the tires prior to making a run on his way to a class victory. (Richard Brady Photo Courtesy Jack Hazelgren/Les Norton)

The other half of the two-car Salt City Dodge racing team is the potent V-10-powered 2011 Factory Super Stock/E class Drag Pac Challenger of Jack Hazelgren. Painted in a similar fashion to the Factory Stock class team car, this one is also driven by Les Norton. (Photo Courtesy Jack Hazelgren)

EPILOGUE

As a car enthusiast since the age of 12, I feel blessed to have personally witnessed and enjoyed the color and styling of the cars of the 1950s, the muscle cars and factory racers of the 1960s, suffered through the days of poor quality and performance in the 1970s and early 1980s, and come out the other side to see the American performance car make one of the greatest comebacks ever with the currently available models.

Being of the old school, I ordered cars with few creature comforts to maximize performance, so imagine my reaction to a car that makes minimal emissions, has no cold-starting problems, doesn't need to be constantly tuned, makes more horsepower out of less than 300 ci than a 400-plus-inch big-block from the 1960s, runs on regular fuel, and has more amenities and creature comforts than I know how to operate.

I am both baffled and amazed by the technology applied to making all these things possible. I am so happy that American car manufacturers are back in the performance business after all these years and that in the case of certain models, retro-look styling has been embraced.

What I do fear is a generation of young people who aren't waiting for the motor vehicle office to open on the day they become eligible to drive or don't bother to drive at all. I fear a generation of people who will never know the true passion of being a car enthusiast, seeing an automobile as merely a means of conveyance. I can't imagine the day when the sound of a powerful American V-8 engine no longer quickens pulses or turns heads. That would be a sad day indeed.

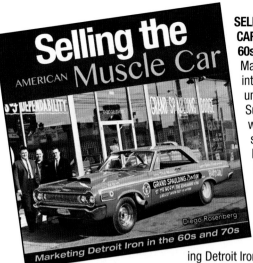
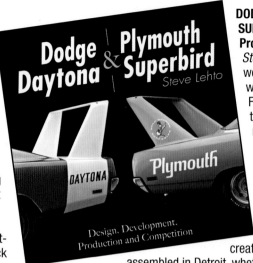
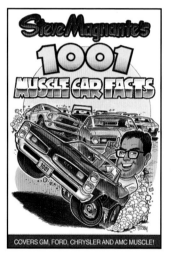
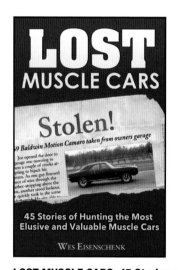